DB2 Universal 1
Application De\
Certification Guide

ISBN 0-13-091367-7

90000

IBM DB2 Certification Guide Series

DB2 Universal Database V7.1 Application Development Certification Guide
  by Sanyal, Martineau, Gashyna, and Kyprianou

DB2 Universal Database V7.1 for UNIX, Linux, Windows, and OS/2 Database Administration Certification Guide, Fourth Edition
  by Baklarz and Wong

DB2 Universal Database in Application Development Environments
  by Shirai, Barber, Saboji, Naick, and Wilkins

DB2 Universal Database V6.1 Certification Guide, Third Edition
  by Cook, Harbus, and Shirai

DB2 Universal Database in the Solaris Operating Environment
  by Shirai, Michel, Wilding, Logan, and Bauch

DB2 Cluster Certification Guide
  by Cook, Janacek, and Snow

DB2 Universal DRDA Certification Guide
  by Brandl, Bullock, Cook, Harbus, Janacek, and Le

DB2 Replication Certification Guide
  by Cook and Harbus

DB2 Universal Database and SAP R/3, Version 4
  by Bullock, Cook, Deedes-Vincke, Harbus, Nardone, and Neuhaus

The Universal Guide to DB2 for Windows NT
  by Cook, Harbus, and Snow

DB2 Universal Database v7.1 Application Development Certification Guide

STEVE SANYAL ■ DAVID MARTINEAU
KEVIN GASHYNA ■ MICHAEL KYPRIANOU

PRENTICE HALL PTR, UPPER SADDLE RIVER, NEW JERSEY 07458
www.phptr.com

© **Copyright International Business Machines Corporation 2001. All rights reserved.**
Note to U.S. Government Users — Documentation related to restricted rights — Use, duplication or disclosure is subject to restrictions set forth in GSA ADP Schedule Contract with IBM Corp.

Editorial/production supervision: *Nicholas Radhuber*
Cover design director: *Jerry Votta*
Cover designer: *Bruce Kenselaar*
Manufacturing manager: *Maura Zaldivar*
Marketing manager: *Debby vanDijk*
Acquisitions editor: *Michael Meehan*
Editorial assistant: *Linda Ramagnano*

IBM Corporation:
Consulting Editor: *Sheila Richardson*
Manager, DB2 UDB Certification Program: *Susan Visser*

PH PTR

Published by Prentice Hall PTR
Prentice-Hall, Inc.
Upper Saddle River, NJ 07458

Prentice Hall books are widely used by corporations and government agencies for training, marketing, and resale. The publisher offers discounts on this book when ordered in bulk quantities.
For more information, contact
    Corporate Sales Department,
    Phone 800-382-3419; FAX: 201-236-7141
    E-mail: corpsales@prenhall.com
Or write: Prentice Hall PTR
    Corporate Sales Department
    One Lake Street
    Upper Saddle River, NJ 07458

All products or services mentioned in this book are the trademarks or service marks of their respective companies or organizations.

All rights reserved. No part of this book may be
reproduced, in any form or by any means,
without permission in writing from the publisher.

Printed in the United States of America
10 9 8 7 6 5 4 3 2

ISBN 0-13-091367-7

Prentice-Hall International (UK) Limited, *London*
Prentice-Hall of Australia Pty. Limited, *Sydney*
Prentice-Hall Canada Inc., *Toronto*
Prentice-Hall Hispanoamericana, S.A., *Mexico*
Prentice-Hall of India Private Limited, *New Delhi*
Prentice-Hall of Japan, Inc., *Tokyo*
Pearson Education Asia Pte. Ltd.
Editora Prentice-Hall do Brasil, Ltda., *Rio de Janeiro*

This book is dedicated to the family and friends of the authors who tolerated our absences, mornings, evenings, and weekends while creating this book:

Sara,
Simone, Brandon, and Naomi,
Mishma,
Andreas, and Georgia

Contents

Foreword		xv
Preface		xvii
Chapter 1	**Introduction to Database Applications for DB2**	1
1.1	Objectives	2
1.2	DB2 UDB Server Instances and Databases	2
1.2.1	DB2 UDB Client Instances	3
1.2.2	DB2 UDB Environment	4
1.2.3	DB2 Node and Database Directory	5
1.2.4	Database Manager Configuration	6
1.2.5	DB2 Profile Registry	7
1.2.6	Environment Variables	7
1.2.7	Local vs. Remote Clients	8
1.3	Database Objects	8
1.3.1	Tables	9
1.3.2	Data Types	9
1.3.3	Indexes	10
1.3.4	Schemas	11
1.3.5	Transactions	11
1.3.6	Locks	12
1.3.7	Packages	12

1.4	SQL Concepts	12
	1.4.1 Querying Data	13
	1.4.2 Modifying Data	13
1.5	DB2 Application Structure	14
	1.5.1 Connecting to a Database	14
	1.5.2 Dynamic and Static Statement Execution	15
	1.5.3 Statement Life Cycle	15
	1.5.4 Committing or Rolling Back Changes	17
	1.5.5 Disconnecting from a Database	18
1.6	Summary	18

Chapter 2 DB2 Programming Roadmap — 19

2.1	Objectives	19
2.2	Administrative API	20
2.3	Embedded SQL	20
	2.3.1 Static Embedded SQL	21
	2.3.2 Dynamic Embedded SQL	21
2.4	Driver-based Application Solutions	22
	2.4.1 Application Software Layers	23
	2.4.2 CLI/ODBC	23
	2.4.3 ADO and OLE DB	23
	2.4.4 JDBC	24
	2.4.5 SQLj	24
	2.4.6 Perl Scripts Using the DBI	24
2.5	Net.Data	25
2.6	DB2 Extenders	25
2.7	Summary	25

Chapter 3 DB2 Programming Features and Strategies — 27

3.1	Objectives	28
3.2	Data Manipulation Strategies	28
	3.2.1 System Catalogs	28
	3.2.2 Summary Tables	29
	3.2.3 User-Defined Types	31
	3.2.4 Common Table Expressions	31
	3.2.5 Compound SQL	32
	3.2.6 Cursor Types and Scope	33
	3.2.7 Prepared Statements	34
	3.2.8 Use of Parameter Markers	34

3.2.9	Deferred Prepare	35
3.2.10	Identity Columns	35
3.2.11	Triggers	36
3.2.12	Stored Procedures	38
3.2.13	DB2 Built-In and User-Defined Functions	38
3.2.14	STAR Schema Table/Index Design	39
3.3	Concurrency and Transaction Management	40
3.3.1	Unit of Work	40
3.3.2	Database Locking Strategies and Isolation Levels	41
3.3.3	Distributed Unit of Work	44
3.3.4	Stored Procedures	44
3.3.5	SQL Stored Procedures	46
3.3.6	DB2 Stored Procedure Builder	48
3.4	Database Packages and Query Performance	54
3.5	Summary	56

Chapter 4 Embedded SQL Programming — 57

4.1	Embedded SQL Overview	58
4.1.1	Creating Packages	58
4.1.2	Binding Applications	62
4.1.3	Binding Utilities	66
4.1.4	Blocking	67
4.2	Static Embedded SQL	68
4.2.1	Host Variables	68
4.2.2	Connecting to Databases	70
4.2.3	Transactions Involving Multiple Databases	71
4.2.4	Connecting from an Application	72
4.2.5	Error Handling—Using and Interpreting the SQLCA	74
4.2.6	Error Handling—Message Retrieval	77
4.2.7	SQLCODE vs. SQLSTATE	78
4.2.8	Program Logic for Error Handling	78
4.2.9	Indicator Variables	78
4.2.10	Data Retrieval Methods	80
4.2.11	Using Cursors	83
4.2.12	Application-Level Locking	89
4.2.13	Searched Updates/Deletes	89
4.3	Dynamic Embedded SQL	90
4.3.1	First Look at Dynamic SQL	91

4.3.2	Dynamic SQL Phases	93
4.3.3	Other Concepts	94
4.3.4	Types of Dynamic SQL Statements	95
4.3.5	SQLDA Data Structure	96
4.3.6	SQLVAR Elements	97
4.3.7	Output SQLDA	98
4.4	Comparing Dynamic SQL with Static SQL	100
4.5	Summary	103

Chapter 5 Administrative APIs — 105

5.1	DB2 APIs	105
5.2	Application Migration Considerations	111
5.2.1	Changed APIs and Data Structures	111
5.3	Context Management APIs	111
5.4	Summary	114

Chapter 6 CLI/ODBC and OLE DB Programming — 115

6.1	Objectives	115
6.2	CLI and ODBC Overview	116
6.2.1	Advantages of CLI	116
6.3	Setting up the CLI Environment	119
6.3.1	DB2 UDB Installation	119
6.3.2	Database Cataloging	120
6.3.3	CLI Bind Files	120
6.3.4	Configuring CLI	121
6.3.5	Accessing a DB2 Database via ODBC	121
6.3.6	ODBC Development Considerations	122
6.4	Basic Program Flow for a CLI Application	122
6.4.1	Initializing Handle Types and Connecting	123
6.4.2	Connecting to One or More Data Sources	124
6.4.3	Disconnecting and Termination	125
6.4.4	Transaction Processing	125
6.4.5	Diagnostics and Error Processing	129
6.5	Advanced Programming Features	131
6.5.1	Supported Cursor Types	131
6.5.2	Catalog Functions	132
6.5.3	Executing Statements	133
6.5.4	Retrieving Results with Scrollable Cursors	138
6.6	DB2 OLE DB Driver	149

6.6.1	DB2 OLE Automation	150
6.6.2	Installing the OLE DB Driver	152
6.7	Summary	152

Chapter 7 Java Programming 155

7.1	Objectives	155
7.2	JDBC Programming	156
7.2.1	DB2 JDBC Driver Versions	157
7.2.2	Changing between DB2 JDBC Driver Versions	158
7.2.3	DB2 JDBC Development Prerequisites	158
7.2.4	DB2 JDBC Applet (or net) Driver	159
7.2.5	DB2 JDBC Application (or app) Driver	160
7.2.6	JDBC Driver Registration	161
7.2.7	Supported Data Types	162
7.2.8	JDBC Interfaces	163
7.2.9	`DriverManager`	163
7.2.10	`Connection`	164
7.2.11	`Statement`	165
7.2.12	`ResultSet`	166
7.2.13	`SQLException`	167
7.2.14	Executing Statements	168
7.2.15	Using Prepared Statements	169
7.2.16	Retrieving Result Sets	170
7.2.17	NULL Values	171
7.2.18	Updating Rows in a Result Set	171
7.2.19	Specifying Result Set Type in JDBC 2.0	172
7.2.20	Using Scrollable Result Sets	173
7.2.21	Calling Stored Procedures	174
7.2.22	Batch Execution	175
7.2.23	Large Objects	176
7.2.24	Meta Data	177
7.2.25	Concurrency and Isolation Levels	178
7.2.26	Using `DataSource` Objects and `Connection` Pooling	179
7.2.27	Java Naming and Directory Interface Support	181
7.2.28	JDBC Static SQL	181
7.3	SQLj Programs	181
7.3.1	Required Packages	184
7.3.2	SQLj Syntax	184

7.3.3	Host Variables	184
7.3.4	Result Set Iterators	185
7.3.5	Positional Iterators	186
7.3.6	Named Iterators	187
7.3.7	Default `ConnectionContext`	188
7.3.8	User-Defined `ConnectionContext` Classes	189
7.3.9	Execution Contexts	190
7.3.10	Properties of User-Defined SQLj Classes	191
7.3.11	SQLj Translator	191
7.3.12	DB2 Profile Customizer	192
7.4	Java Stored Procedures	192
7.4.1	Setting up an Environment for JDBC 2.0 Stored Procedures	194
7.5	Java UDFs	194
7.6	Summary	194

Chapter 8 Net.Data — 197

8.1	Objectives	197
8.2	Advantages	198
8.2.1	Easy to Use	198
8.2.2	Highly Compatible	198
8.2.3	Easily Integrated	199
8.3	Scripting Language	199
8.3.1	Comment Blocks	200
8.3.2	Define Blocks	200
8.3.3	Function Blocks	200
8.3.4	Document Blocks	202
8.4	Language Environments	204
8.4.1	Database Access	205
8.4.2	REXX	209
8.4.3	Perl	210
8.4.4	Java	210
8.5	Performance	212
8.5.1	Live Connection Manager	212
8.5.2	Cache Manager	213
8.6	Summary	213

Chapter 9 Perl Programming　　215

- 9.1　Objectives　　215
- 9.2　Advantages of Perl　　215
- 9.3　Setting up the Perl Environment　　216
  - 9.3.1　DB2 UDB Installation　　216
  - 9.3.2　Database Cataloging　　217
  - 9.3.3　CLI Bind Files　　217
  - 9.3.4　Configuring CLI　　217
  - 9.3.5　Installing Perl　　218
  - 9.3.6　Installing the Perl DBI　　218
  - 9.3.7　Installing the DBD::DB2 Module　　219
- 9.4　Basic Program Flow　　220
  - 9.4.1　Initialization　　220
  - 9.4.2　Transaction Processing　　221
  - 9.4.3　Error Handling　　223
  - 9.4.4　Disconnecting and Termination　　223
- 9.5　Summary　　223

Chapter 10 DB2 Extenders　　225

- 10.1　Objectives　　225
- 10.2　Text Extender　　226
  - 10.2.1　Indexes　　228
  - 10.2.2　Text Extender UDFs　　231
  - 10.2.3　Text Extender APIs　　233
- 10.3　Net Search Extender　　233
  - 10.3.1　Benefits of Net Search Extender　　233
  - 10.3.2　Search Capabilities　　234
  - 10.3.3　Search Functions　　234
- 10.4　AIV Extenders　　234
  - 10.4.1　AIV Extender UDFs　　235
- 10.5　XML Extender　　235
  - 10.5.1　Mapping XML to a Relational Database　　238
  - 10.5.2　XML Columns　　239
  - 10.5.3　XML Collections　　240
- 10.6　Summary　　240

Appendix A DB2 UDB Application Development Test Objectives	**243**
Appendix B DB2 UDB Application Development Sample Exam	**247**
Appendix C DB2MALL Database	**265**
Appendix D Application Troubleshooting	**271**
D.1 Obtaining an SQL Error	272
D.2 Isolating Error Location	272
D.3 Diagnostic Error Files	272
D.3.1 db2diag.log	273
D.3.2 db2alert.log	273
D.3.3 Dump Files	274
D.3.4 Trap Files	274
D.3.5 jdbcerr.log	274
D.4 Tracing Facilities	274
D.4.1 DB2 Trace (db2trc)	274
D.4.2 CLI Trace	275
D.4.3 JDBC Trace	277
Index	**279**

Foreword

One of the biggest challenges that computer professionals face today is finding and taking the time to develop new skills to keep up with the changes in technology. Learning new technologies and developing skills in the use of industry-leading products increase our value as professionals. We're in the fastest paced industry in the world, and the skills shortage has placed a premium on our time. This book provides a fast and easy way to help your career with DB2.

Relational database technology was invented at IBM Research over two decades ago. IBM delivered the first commercially available relational database, DB2, in the early 1980s. The promise of relational technology was the ability to represent data in a simple tabular form, access it through the *expressive yet easy-to-learn* SQL query language, and put *that power* in the hands of business analysts and other decision makers. Over the last 20 years, many businesses have realized the value of this promise. Today, tens of thousands of businesses, large and small, all over the world, rely on DB2 databases to store their key corporate data assets and run their businesses both traditionally and over the Web.

As companies move into an Internet age of broadband communications, databases must be able to store and serve huge multimedia files, manage ever-increasing volumes of data, handle the tremendous growth in the number of users, deliver steadily improved performance, and support the next generation of applications. With its virtually unlimited ability to scale, its multimedia extensibility, its industry-leading performance and reliability, and its platform openness, DB2 Universal Database (UDB) has helped lead this evolution. DB2 UDB is the first multimedia, Web-ready relational database management system strong enough to meet the demands of large corporations and flexible enough to serve medium-sized and small businesses.

Developing this new generation of applications requires highly skilled and trained application developers. From a knowledge of application development tools, interfaces such as ODBC and SQLj to a wide variety of new multimedia and XML datatypes, the application developer in the new millennium needs to be an expert in many fields. DB2 integrates well with all the major development tools and leverages your experience and knowledge.

This certification guide is an excellent way to learn about DB2, to develop new skills, and to provide new opportunities for yourself in the computer industry. The included trial copy of DB2 will let you get started quickly and give you hands-on experience, which is so helpful to learning. You'll find that the self-study design lets you proceed at your own pace, learning the material necessary to complete the formal DB2 UDB certification exams for a DB2 UDB Application Developer. Enjoy the certification guide, enjoy using DB2, and enjoy the benefits of being a certified DB2 professional.

Brett MacIntyre

Director, Database Technology
IBM Data Management Division

PREFACE

Welcome to the *DB2 UDB (Universal Database) V7.1 Application Development Certification Guide* for IBM's popular relational database servers. Whether you intend to become an IBM Certified Professional, or are looking for a hands-on resource for developing applications for DB2, read on. This book is an entirely new publication in the DB2 UDB Certification Series, and replaces the application development chapters in the previous editions of the *DB2 UDB Certification Guide*. Those interested in becoming an IBM Certified Professional will want to review the sample questions at the end of each chapter. We also provide exercises and examples with this book, to develop hands-on skills with database development.

Since the focus of this book is developing database applications, it also serves as a companion to the *DB2 UDB V7.1 Administration Certification Guide*. However, we will also cover the fundamentals of the DB2 client/server environment, database objects, and the Structured Query Language (SQL).

Organization

This book consists of ten chapters and several appendices. Each chapter has a set of objectives that are presented at the beginning. We also provide additional resources for many chapters when applicable. Here is a summary of the contents of this book:

- **Chapter 1 Introduction to Database Applications for DB2**—Introduces you to the DB2 client/server environment, database objects, SQL, and the basic structure of a database application.
- **Chapter 2 DB2 Programming Roadmap**—Discusses the various programming interfaces that you can use to develop applications with DB2.

- **Chapter 3 DB2 Programming Features and Strategies**—Explores features and strategies that you can use to maximize your performance, and how to utilize DB2's advanced features such as triggers and stored procedures.
- **Chapter 4 Embedded SQL Programming**—A guide to embedded SQL programming within DB2.
- **Chapter 5 Administration API**—A discussion of the DB2 administrative and context management APIs that allow you to perform tasks such as back up, restore, and load from within your application code.
- **Chapter 6 CLI/ODBC and OLE DB Programming**—We examine the DB2 CLI/ODBC driver and also discuss programming in OLE DB (Oblect Linking and Embedding Database), using interfaces such as ADO (ActiveX Data Objects).
- **Chapter 7 Java Programming**—A detailed discussion of JDBC and SQLj, and how to use each. We also discuss how to write Java stored procedures and User-Defined Functions (UDFs).
- **Chapter 8 Net.Data**—An introduction to programming with an easy-to-use Web application development environment provided with DB2.
- **Chapter 9 Perl Programming**—Discusses writing Perl scripts to access DB2 databases using the Perl DBI (Database Interface).
- **Chapter 10 DB2 Extenders**—A guide to extending DB2 functionality using DB2 Extenders products. This includes Text Extender, Net Search Extenders, Audio, Image, and Video (AIV) Extenders, and XML Extender.
- **Appendix A Test Objectives**
- **Appendix B Sample Exam**
- **Appendix C DB2MALL Database**
- **Appendix D Troubleshooting Techniques**

Exercises are provided for many of the chapters on the companion CD-ROM. Unfortunately, due to time constraints, we were not able to provide these exercises in the book. Please be sure to examine the CD-ROM for the exercises and samples, which illustrate many DB2 features that we discuss in this book.

Certification Exam

This book can be used as a self-study guide to prepare for the DB2 UDB Certification Exam for Application Development.

Experience with DB2 UDB V7.1 is the best way to prepare for any of these certification exams. The exam for DB2 UDB focuses on general concepts covered in this book. We have included additional detail for your benefit, but this is not needed for the exam.

> **Note**
>
> More information about DB2 UDB certification can be found at http://www.ibm.com/certify.

Contents of CD-ROM

We have included a CD-ROM with DB2 trial software and additional development tools. Please refer to the `readme.txt` file on the CD-ROM for details on each item. Included on the CD-ROM are the following software packages:

- DB2 UDB V7.1 Enterprise Edition Try-and-Buy Version
- DB2 UDB V7.1 Text Extender
- DB2 UDB V7.1 Net-Search Extender
- DB2 UDB V7.1 Audio, Image, and Visual Extenders
- DB2 UDB V7.1 XML Extender
- DB2 Perl DBI Driver, DBD::DB2 Version 0.73
- DB2 OLE DB Driver
- Net.Data V7.1

To fit all of these packages onto a single CD-ROM, we only included the U.S. English versions of each piece of software. In addition, we included chapter-specific samples and exercises under the \Book directory structure.

DB2 Mall Database

We created a database for an online mall to be used with this book. The name of the database is `DB2MALL`, and in Appendix C, we describe how to create this database. We also provide a description of all the tables. All of our samples and exercises reference this database, so please familiarize yourself with it. We simplified many of the tables for simplicity and clarity.

Conventions

There are many SQL statements, DB2 commands, and code samples throughout this book. These are all presented in a mono-spaced font. Code samples and SQL are also offset from the main paragraph text, such as:

```
SELECT * FROM product
```

We also highlight important points, tips, and troubleshooting items in offset boxed text.

The names of DB2 online books, such as the *Administration Guide*, are placed in italics. We will also emphasize certain words in italics as needed.

> **Note**
> A note highlights an important point or summarizes a concept

Using the DB2 Online Books

Throughout this book, we will often refer to the DB2 online books that are installed with every DB2 product. They can also be downloaded in PDF format from the DB2 Product and Service Technical Library at:

    http://www.software.ibm.com/data/db2/library

These books provide a wealth of information about configuring and using DB2. Take advantage of them, since they are provided for free. If you are not sure where to look for an answer to a question, there is also a search feature provided with the online books, which is also available on the above Web site.

We will often refer you to the DB2 online books for further background, to allow us to concentrate on more detailed explanations of other topics and to describe advanced concepts.

DB2 Resources on the Internet

Here are several resources on the Internet that are invaluable for DB2 documentation and product support:

Sites

- Official DB2 site at IBM:
  http://www.software.ibm.com/data/db2
- DB2 Technical Library:
  http://www.software.ibm.com/data/db2/library
- International DB2 Users Group:
  http://www.idug.org
- DB2 Magazine:
  http://www.db2mag.com

FTP

- DB2 Fixpaks:
  ftp://ftp.software.ibm.com/ps/products/db2/fixes
- DB2 Tools:
  ftp://ftp.software.ibm.com/ps/products/db2/tools
- DB2 Extenders Fixpaks:
  ftp://ftp.software.ibm.com/ps/products/db2extenders/fixes/

news.software.ibm.com

- `ibm.software.db2.scholars`
- `ibm.software.db2.udb.eee`
- `ibm.software.db2.udb.windows2000`

Usenet

- `comp.databases.ibm-db2`

How This Book Was Created

The four authors of this book are DB2 service analysts at the IBM Toronto Lab. From our experience with tackling thousands of questions and technical problems from DB2 customers, we strived to put together a publication that will help readers reduce the learning curve of DB2. In addition, using our experience with the DB2 UDB product, we have demonstrated useful techniques and highlighted features that will increase the functionality and performance of your database applications.

Most of the material in this book is newly written; however, some of the contents include updated portions from the DB2 UDB V6.1 Certification Guide.

About the Authors

- **Steve Sanyal** is a software architect for Optus E-Business Solutions (A Division of Symcor Services Inc.). He was previously a software developer for the DB2 UDB Application Development Team at the IBM Toronto Lab. He is a certified IBM Solutions Expert as a DB2 UDB Application Developer. He specializes in JDBC, SQLj, CLI/ODBC, OOD/OOP, relational data modeling and J2EE enterprise software architecture and design on UNIX and Intel platforms.
- **David Martineau** is a staff software developer at the IBM Toronto Lab, providing technical support for the DB2 UDB Application Development Team. David has provided sample code for DB2 UDB using interfaces such as ADO, CLI, and Net.Data. Prior to 1998, David was a developer within the DB2 UDB Connect group for one year, where he primarily worked on projects to enhance the performance of ODBC. Prior to joining IBM, David was developing database engines since 1994. His work includes developing support for stored procedures, user-defined functions, and 64-bit integer support.
- **Kevin Gashyna** has been working with DB2 UDB and its predecessors since 1997. He is a certified DB2 UDB V7.1 Database Administrator, Application Developer, and Advanced Technical Expert in DRDA. Kevin is currently a staff software developer with the DB2 UDB Extended Enterprise Edition (EEE) Support Team in the IBM Toronto Lab. He has been involved in several aspects of DB2 on the UNIX and Intel platforms, including application development, connectivity, and clustered environments. Kevin also participated in the creation of the DB2 UDB V7.1 Application Development Certification Exam.

- **Michael Kyprianou** has been working with DB2 UDB and its predecessors since 1995. He is an IBM Advanced Technical Expert in DB2 DRDA and is certified in DB2 UDB Database Administration and Application Development. Michael is currently a staff programmer analyst with the DB2 UDB Application Development Team, prior to which he was team lead for the DB2 UDB Connectivity Group for two years. In these roles, Michael provided technical marketing, electronic, and on-site support to customers all over the world. Michael has also assisted at IDUG conferences offering the DB2 UDB Certification Exam.

Acknowledgments

Steve, David, Kevin, and Michael would like to thank the following people for reviewing this book and supporting them in their efforts:

- Susan Visser, IBM Toronto Lab
- Michael Hvizdos, IBM Toronto Lab
- John Vasilakos, IBM Toronto Lab
- Jennifer Glover, IBM Toronto Lab
- Robert Indrigo, IBM Toronto Lab
- Kelvin Ho, IBM Toronto Lab
- Viki DiGiovine, IBM Toronto Lab
- Juergen Metter, IBM Boeblingen Lab
- Norbert Runge, IBM Silicon Valley Lab
- Gary Wilmot, IBM Silicon Valley Lab
- Ronald Trueblood, IBM Silicon Valley Lab
- Robert Begg, IBM Toronto Lab

CHAPTER 1

Introduction to Database Applications for DB2

The relational database of choice for modern distributed applications is IBM's widely popular DB2 Universal Database (UDB). DB2 UDB V7.1 provides high-performance data access, reliability, and an abundance of advanced features. Whether your application is an e-commerce site on the Web or a directory service such as a Lightweight Directory Access Protocol (LDAP) server, the overall concepts for all database applications remain the same. Database applications mostly perform two major tasks, and are categorized as such. Applications that modify the contents of databases and perform transaction processing are known as Online Transaction Processing (OLTP) applications. Applications that perform ad hoc queries to analyze the contents of databases are known as Decision Support Systems (DSS), or Online Analytical Processing (OLAP) applications.

All applications communicate with DB2 in a client/server environment using the Structured Query Language (SQL) within the context of one or more programming interfaces such as embedded SQL, JDBC, and the Perl DBI (Database Interface). Different interfaces also provide additional features that you may find useful. This is why it is important to understand the options available to you as an application developer.

In this chapter, we introduce fundamental DB2 concepts and describe how applications connect to DB2 and use SQL statements to access and modify data in a DB2 UDB database. We assume that you already know about database objects such as tables and indexes, and that you are also familiar with SQL from the companion to this guide, *The DB2 V7.1 Administration Certification Guide*. We still cover each of these topics briefly within this chapter to ensure you have an understanding of them for the purposes of the certification exam.

You can find a complete reference for SQL and DB2 database objects in the *SQL Reference*, which is included among the DB2 online books. The *SQL Getting Started* guide is another online book that includes a good tutorial on SQL. If you require information about installing

DB2, please refer to the DB2 *Quick Beginnings* books applicable to your environment, or read Chapter 2 of *The DB2 V7.1 Administration Certification Guide*.

1.1 Objectives

In each chapter, we will begin with a set of goals for the reader. These goals will describe the concepts you should be familiar with after reading the chapter and completing the exercises. After reading the first chapter, you should have a general understanding of:

- The DB2 UDB client server environment.
- Database objects that will be relevant to you as an application developer.
- How SQL is used to interact with DB2 databases.
- The common programming structure of all database applications.

We begin by giving you an understanding of how DB2 UDB V7.1 is organized.

1.2 DB2 UDB Server Instances and Databases

A database is simply an organized collection of related data. High-end Relational Database Management Systems (RDBMS) such as DB2 UDB provide an encapsulated client server environment where a persistent database server process serves requests from external client applications. Every DB2 instance is an RDBMS engine process that is uniquely named on a particular system. A DB2 database is created within the context of a specific DB2 instance. To create a DB2 database, you need to install a DB2 UDB V7.1 server product. The DB2 UDB V7.1 product packages are as follows:

- **Satellite Edition (SE)** – A special RDBMS engine with a small footprint that is intended for occasionally connected systems. It will not accept incoming database requests from remote clients.
- **Personal Edition (PE)** – An RDBMS engine that will not accept incoming remote database requests. Available on Windows NT, Linux, and OS/2 only.
- **Workgroup Edition (WE)** – An RDBMS engine that will accept incoming database requests from remote clients. Available on Windows NT, Linux, and OS/2 only.
- **Enterprise Edition (EE)** – Similar to Workgroup Edition, but also allows remote and local clients to access data on a host database such as DB2/390 or DB2/400.
- **Enterprise Extended Edition (EEE)** – Similar to Enterprise Edition, with additional support for clusters of database servers in a partitioned database environment. Available on AIX, Windows NT, Solaris, and HP-UX.

Using any of these products, you can create one or more DB2 server instances. Every instance has a name unique to the system on which it is installed, and this name is specified when creating the instance. Each DB2 server instance is a separate DBMS (Database Management System) process within whose context you can create and manage one or more DB2 databases. Every instance can also be configured with regard to memory usage and other parameters in the database manager configuration and DB2 profile registry.

If your server instance has remote client functionality, you can also configure one or more network protocol listeners for the instance to accept incoming database requests from remote clients. Each server instance on a system must have a unique protocol listener. For example, if you have two server instances on your Windows NT system and you want them to be accessible to remote TCP/IP clients, you must configure each to listen on a unique TCP/IP service or port.

1.2.1 DB2 UDB Client Instances

Each DB2 UDB V7.1 product package installation also includes three common client components:

- **DB2 Runtime Client** – Includes DB2 runtime libraries that allow applications to access local and remote DB2 databases.
- **DB2 Administration Client** – Similar to the Runtime Client, but also provides graphical DB2 UDB administration tools, as well as additional utilities and DB2 bind files.
- **DB2 Application Development (AD) Client** – Similar to the Administration Client, but provides DB2 developer tools such as the Stored Procedure Builder (SPB), program precompilers, static libraries, and numerous samples.

Figure 1-1 shows the various DB2 client and server components and their hierarchical nature. By viewing this diagram, you should be aware that DB2 client components are also present in each DB2 server instance. Thus, when we use the term "DB2 client," we may be referring to either a client-only install or the client component on a DB2 server. You can determine which we are referring to based on the following definitions. All DB2 clients are freely downloadable from the official DB2 Web site.

If an application connects to a database within the same instance from which it runs, the application is known as a *local client*. In this case, there is no need to install an additional DB2 Runtime Client since this component is also included within the libraries of the DB2 server instance. On the other hand, if the application is installed on a system other than the DB2 UDB server, or run on a different instance on the same system, the application is known as a *remote client*. The DB2 Runtime Client component must be installed on each remote workstation or system executing the application.

In some cases, you may have installed a DB2 server product on one platform and will be running an application on a different platform. For example, you may have DB2 UDB V7.1 EE installed on AIX, but your SQLj applications will run on Windows NT. In this case, you will need to obtain a DB2 UDB AD client for Windows NT. When you install any DB2 UDB client on a Windows 95/98/NT workstation, a client instance called "DB2" will be automatically cre-

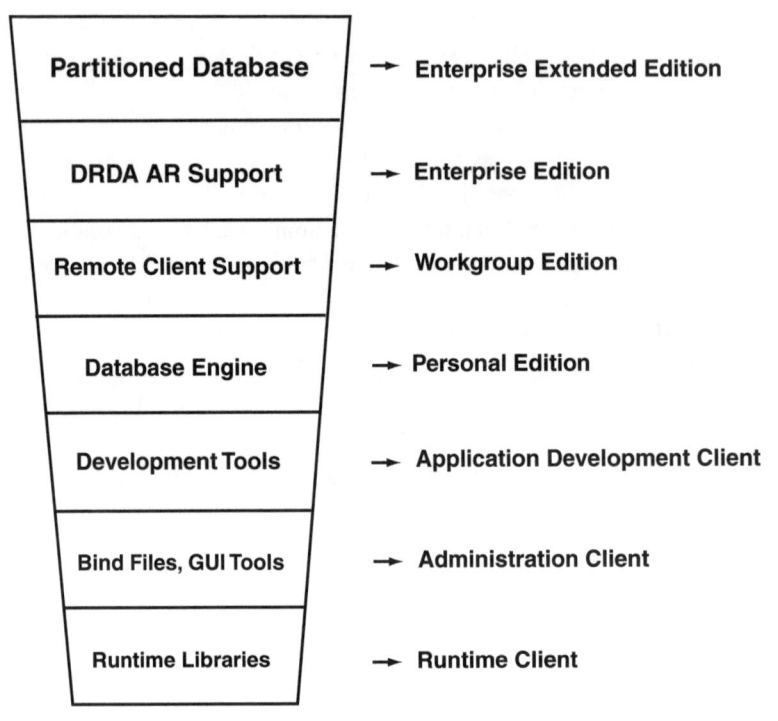

Figure 1-1 DB2 UDB V7.1 software components.

ated. On UNIX platforms, you can create multiple client instances using the `db2icrt` command. Figure 1-2 illustrates how a DB2 UDB Runtime Client connects to a DB2 server instance.

1.2.2 DB2 UDB Environment

It is important to understand the DB2 client/server environment to set up local and remote applications to access DB2. There are a number of instance-specific environment considerations that we will discuss in this section. Every DB2 client and server instance consists of the following components:

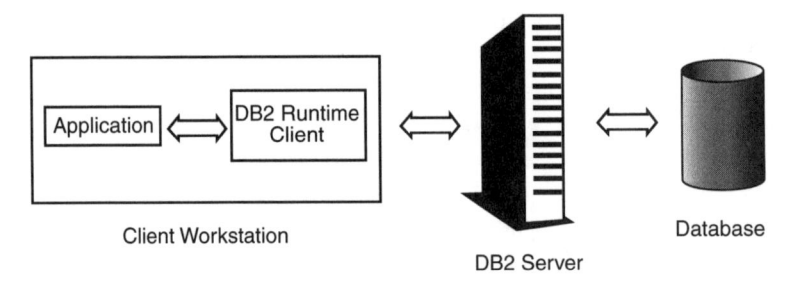

Figure 1-2 DB2 UDB Runtime Client.

- DB2 node directory.
- DB2 database directory.
- DB2 database manager configuration.
- DB2 profile registry entries.
- DB2 environment variables.

We approach these one by one, and then discuss some interesting nuances. In many of the sections below, we will discuss DB2 commands. To run these commands, you will need to use the DB2 Command Line Processor (CLP) or the Command Center. The CLP is a tool included with every DB2 installation. It allows you to administer DB2 databases and instances and run dynamic SQL. We will use this tool throughout the book in many examples. To start the CLP shell on Windows platforms, select **Start->Programs->IBM DB2->Command Line Processor**. On UNIX platforms, simply type db2 at the command line.

The Command Center is a Graphical User Interface (GUI) utility provided with the Administration Client that lets you perform all of the same tasks as the CLP as well as create scripts from the commands you run. You can start the Command Center from the DB2 Control Center, or on Windows platforms, you can open it from the IBM DB2 folder from the Start menu.

> **TIP** You can also enter DB2 commands directly from the operating system prompt by prepending them with "db2". This is useful when you want to pipe the output of various commands to utilities such as more or grep. In Windows environments, you will need to open a DB2 command window from the IBM DB2 folder, or you can issue the "db2cmd" command from a regular MS-DOS command prompt.

> **Troubleshooting**
>
> If you have trouble getting the DB2 command line to work, ensure that the DB2INSTANCE environment variable has been set. See details in the section below on environment variables.

1.2.3 DB2 Node and Database Directory

Each DB2 client has a node directory containing entries for all remote DB2 server instances the client can access. The term "remote instances" in this case also includes other instances on the same machine. Each instance on the same machine is cataloged separately based on a unique network protocol listener. Directory entries are added using the CATALOG <protocol> NODE command. For example, to catalog a node called steve on the system sanyall, which has a TCP/IP listener for the instance on port 50000, we would catalog the instance from a remote client as:

```
CATALOG TCPIP NODE steve REMOTE sanyall SERVER 50000
```

If a server instance is being used as the client, then there is no node cataloged for the local instance. To list all of the nodes in the DB2 node directory, use the following DB2 command:

```
LIST NODE DIRECTORY
```

For each node in the DB2 node directory, you can catalog one or more databases. To catalog the DB2MALL database at the node named steve, use the following command:

```
CATALOG DB DB2MALL AT NODE steve
```

If you are cataloging the database on the local instance, omit the "AT NODE" portion of the command. You may often want to access multiple databases on different instances that have the same name. For example, you may have two online mall databases, both called DB2MALL, one at the node called steve and another at a node called prod. You cannot refer to both of them as DB2MALL since it will be impossible to tell them apart from their names. Instead, you can create a database alias for one of them or for both.

In our example, we assume that our production database is on the node called prod and our development database is on the node called steve. We will catalog the production database using the name prodmall and the development database using the name devmall as follows:

```
CATALOG DB DB2MALL AS prodmall at NODE prod
CATALOG DB DB2MALL AS devmall at NODE steve
```

We can now refer to each of them uniquely in our application as prodmall and devmall, respectively. If no alias is specified when you catalog a database, the database alias is automatically the same as the database name.

> **Note**
>
> When you catalog a database alias, it must refer to a local database name or a remote database alias. You cannot create an alias of a local database alias.

1.2.4 Database Manager Configuration

Each client and server instance has a database manager configuration file. Client instances have fewer parameters than server instances. You can look at the database manager configuration from the CLP using the following command:

```
GET DBM CFG
```

Each parameter name is placed in brackets and is preceded by a text description. All of the parameters are described in detail in the *Administration Guide* online book. To update a database configuration parameter, use the syntax:

```
UPDATE DBM CFG USING <parameter> <value>
```

To learn more about these parameters, refer to the *Administration Guide*.

1.2.5 DB2 Profile Registry

Some of the DB2 UDB environment is controlled by entries stored in the DB2 profile registry. The objective of this registry is to consolidate and manage DB2 environment settings at different level scopes. Registry settings can apply to an entire instance, or globally to all instances on a system. The db2set command is used to set and query entries in the DB2 profile registry. To view a list of all the profile registry entries that can be set, use the following command:

```
db2set -lr
```

To view the entries that are applicable to your current environment, use the command:

```
db2set -all
```

To set a parameter value, use the syntax:

```
db2set parameter=value [-i instance_name | -g ]
```

If neither optional clause is used, the parameter is set for the current instance. The -i option indicates that the parameter will be set for a particular instance (including all physical nodes in a DB2 UDB EEE environment), while the -g option sets the parameter globally for the physical system. Further usage of this command is described in the *Command Reference*, and all of the environment and registry variables that can be set are described in Appendix D of the *Administration Guide*.

1.2.6 Environment Variables

The most important environment variable that must be set is the DB2INSTANCE variable. This variable must be set to the name of the instance that is being accessed by the common set of DB2 client libraries. For example, on an AIX system, there may be two DB2 server instances, db2inst1 and db2inst2, and two DB2 client instances, db2cli1, and db2cli2. Each of these instances will have their own DB2 database and node directories, along with database manager configuration and instance-level DB2 profile registry variables. The DB2INSTANCE variable must be set to distinguish which set of instance-specific settings to use.

If a user named joe also wanted to run applications that accessed the DB2 Runtime Client, he must also include the DB2 libraries in his environment settings. On UNIX, this means including the sqllib/lib directory in his LIBPATH. On Windows and OS/2, this involves adding sqllib\bin to the PATH variable.

1.2.7 Local vs. Remote Clients

The major difference between local clients and remote clients is the manner in which the DB2 client libraries communicate with the DB2 database engine. As we discussed above, all client applications access the DB2 libraries by referencing them in their environment and setting the `DB2INSTANCE` variable. When a database is accessed from a local client, the DB2 shared libraries communicate with a DB2 server agent process using shared memory segments for Inter-Process Communication (IPC). Remote clients use network protocol-specific buffers to communicate with a remote DB2 server agent. Generally speaking, IPC over a shared memory segment is faster than over a network connection.

It is possible for applications running on the same local instance to behave like remote clients by cataloging a TCP/IP loopback connection. In some cases, this may be a necessity, while in others it may provide a useful way to test an application that is developed locally but may run on a variety of remote clients.

The most applicable example is on AIX systems, which by default can have a maximum of 11 shared memory segment attachments per process. Since each database connection requires one shared memory segment attachment, an application can have at most 10 concurrent local connections (the eleventh segment is reserved). To get around this limitation, you can configure a TCP/IP loopback connection to the local instance.

Let's assume that the local instance has a TCP/IP listener corresponding to the service named `db2tcp`, and we want to access the `DB2MALL` database. TCP/IP loopback can be configured as follows:

```
UNCATALOG DB DB2MALL
CATALOG DB DB2MALL AS mall
CATALOG TCPIP NODE local AT 127.0.0.1 SERVER db2tcp
CATALOG DB2 mall AS DB2MALL AT NODE local
```

As we mentioned earlier, this can be a useful way to test your applications by eliminating network transfer lag since a local TCP/IP connection should be almost as fast as IPC. It is useful to test remote applications this way if possible, since applications may follow a slightly different code path within the DB2 libraries depending on whether a database is local or remote.

1.3 Database Objects

Before we explore how to access DB2 databases using SQL, we begin by describing application-related database objects. Even if you are already familiar with relational databases, you may find the following sections useful, because different vendors often vary in their terminology even though the overall concepts remain the same. This section discusses how to structure your understanding of fundamental relational database concepts toward the DB2 family of products. In general, database objects are created using the syntax:

```
CREATE <object-type> <object-name> ...
```

Similarly, you can delete a database object using the syntax:

```
DROP <object-type> <object-name> ...
```

Some database objects can also be modified after they are created using the syntax:

```
ALTER <object-type> <object-name> ...
```

Each DB2 database contains a set of system catalog tables that contain information about all database objects within the database, as well as statistics associated with those objects. By default, all object names are created in uppercase, even if you specify the name in lowercase. For case-sensitive names, you should put double quotes (") around the name of each object.

> **TIP** Database statistics are key for obtaining better query performance. Statistics should be maintained and updated using the `RUNSTATS` command. See the *Administration Guide* and *Command Reference* for details.

1.3.1 Tables

A table is an unordered set of data records consisting of rows and columns. Each row is known as a record, and each column within a row is a field within that record. Permanent (base) tables are created using the `CREATE TABLE` statement, which defines a logical view of how the data is stored on disk. DB2 also has derived temporary tables, which we discuss in Chapter 3.

1.3.2 Data Types

Each column within a table is based on a data type. The data type of a column indicates the length of the values in it and the kind of data that is valid for it. There are two major categories of data types in DB2 UDB V7.1:

- Built-in data types.
- User-Defined Types (UDTs).

Built-in data types are defined by DB2 UDB. UDTs are categorized as follows:

- User-defined distinct type – Enables you to create a new data type that has its own semantics based on existing built-in types.
- User-defined structured type – Lets you create a structure that contains a sequence of named attributes, each of which has a data type.
- User-defined reference type – Is used to reference a row in another table that uses a user-defined structured type.

The latter two types are part of DB2's object relational features, and we will not delve into them in this book. We will discuss how to make use of UDTs in general in Chapter 3.

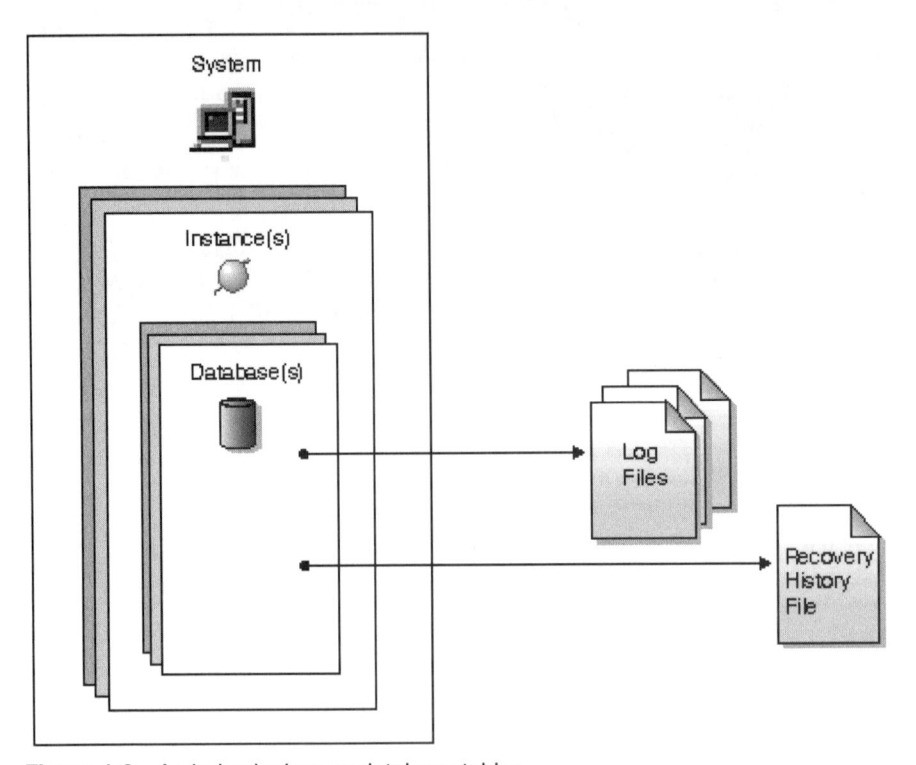

Figure 1-3 An index lookup on database tables.

1.3.3 Indexes

Indexes are physical objects that are associated with a single permanent table (see Figure 1-3). You can define multiple indexes on the same table. Indexes are used to ensure uniqueness of data values and/or improve SQL query performance. Using indexes allows data to be sorted and accessed more quickly and avoids the time-consuming task of sorting data in temporary storage. DB2 UDB updates indexes automatically when data is inserted, updated, and deleted from a table.

> **Note**
>
> The maintenance overhead of indexes will negatively impact the performance of INSERT, UPDATE, and DELETE statements.

Indexes can be defined in ascending or descending order (dependent on the database code page), they can be unique or nonunique, and they can involve a single column's data values or be compound indexes defined on multiple columns. They can also be defined to support both forward and reverse scans.

> **TIP** The DB2 Explain facility can be used to provide index usage information for every explainable SQL statement. Refer to the *Administration Guide* for instructions.

1.3.4 Schemas

Schemas are database objects used in DB2 UDB to logically group a set of database objects. Most database objects are named using a two-part naming convention (schema_name.object_name). The first part of the name is referred to as the schema, and the second part is the name of the object. When the schema is not specified, objects are referenced in SQL statements using an implicit schema, which by default is your authorization ID. The CURRENT SCHEMA special register within DB2 contains this qualifier and can be modified by your application at bind time, or by issuing the SET CURRENT SCHEMA command at runtime.

> **Note**
> When accessing DB2/390, the CURRENT SCHEMA is referred to as the CURRENT SQLID.

1.3.5 Transactions

A transaction is a set of one or more SQL statements that execute as a single atomic operation. The term "unit of work (UOW)" is synonymous with the term "transaction." A transaction either succeeds or fails, and is started implicitly with the first executable SQL statement in a program. A transaction is completed when either an explicit COMMIT or ROLLBACK is encountered. An implicit COMMIT or ROLLBACK can occur when a DB2 UDB application terminates.

> **Note**
> It is best to COMMIT or ROLLBACK any outstanding transactions explicitly before terminating your application, because the nature of an implicit rollback varies in different operating environments.

1.3.6 Locks

DB2 UDB is a multiuser database product designed for concurrent access. As users request data, DB2 UDB uses locking strategies to avoid resource conflicts and maintain data integrity. For example, as SQL statements are processed in a transaction, an application connection may obtain locks. Locks are released when the resource is no longer required at the end of the transaction. The locks are stored in memory on the database server in a structure known as a *locklist*. DB2 UDB supports two types of locks, table locks and row locks.

The locking strategy used by DB2 UDB during transaction processing is specified using an isolation level. The isolation level is defined when binding an application. In addition, for JDBC and CLI (Call Level Interface) applications, the isolation level can be set as a connection property or attribute, respectively.

1.3.7 Packages

Packages are database objects that contain executable forms of SQL statements. Each statement is contained within a *section* of a package and references a specific statement within a single program source module. Packages are not referred to directly in an SQL query and remain largely transparent to the application developer.

> **Note**
>
> Only the corresponding program source module can invoke the contents of a package. Otherwise, an SQL0818 timestamp conflict error will occur.

Packages are stored in the database system catalog tables and contain the DB2 UDB access plan that was selected by the DB2 optimizer during BIND or PREP. This is known as static binding since it is performed prior to statement execution.

1.4 SQL Concepts

SQL is the industry-standard language for defining and querying relational databases. It is largely based on the relational algebraic operators select, project, and join. SQL also includes additional operators for inserting, updating, and deleting data, as well as creating database objects and administering access to them. These qualities separate SQL into three categories:

- **Data Manipulation Language (DML)**—Allows you to query and modify data within database tables.
- **Data Definition Language (DDL)**—Allows you to create database objects.
- **Data Control Language (DCL)**—Allows you to administer access rights to database objects.

For most of this book, we will be focusing on DML, since this is the main focus of OLAP and OLTP applications. In this section, we will describe the basic forms of DML queries. We will describe more advanced features in Chapter 3. Every RDBMS vendor has a slightly different brand of SQL; however, if you are already familiar with SQL from using another vendor's product, you should have no problem picking up SQL in DB2 UDB.

1.4.1 Querying Data

Data is queried from one or more tables using a SELECT statement. The data returned is known as a result set. A SELECT statement only specifies the criteria the result set must match, not how DB2 should return it. The DB2 optimizer makes this decision by constructing an access plan based on current database statistics from the system catalog tables and the types of plans it has been instructed to consider (using a setting called the query optimization level). The structure of a SELECT statement is explained using the following example, which returns all new inventory requests sorted by store in the past 10 days:

```
SELECT s.store_name, p.product_name, r.unit_cost,
r.order_date
FROM product p, store_purchase r, store s
WHERE s.store_id=p.store_id AND
p.product_id=r.product_id AND
r.order_date > CURRENT DATE - 10 DAYS
ORDER BY s.store_name
```

The column list directly follows the SELECT keyword, and the corresponding table names are specified after the FROM keyword. Finally, restrictions on which rows to retrieve are placed after the WHERE clause using SQL-standard Boolean syntax. In addition, each column is referred to using a correlation name, which has been chosen as p for the product table, r for the store_purchase table, and s for the store table. Correlation names are mandatory whenever there is ambiguity, such as for the product_id column, which is in both the product and store_purchase tables. Finally, we use an ORDER BY to sort the rows in the result set. Sorting takes additional time and can considerably slow down query performance, so you should consider using unsorted queries if possible.

There are also more complex forms of the SELECT statement. We cover some of them in Chapter 3, as well as in the advanced SQL sections of *The DB2 UDB V7.1 Administration Certification Guide*.

1.4.2 Modifying Data

You can modify data in DB2 tables using INSERT, UPDATE, and DELETE statements. An INSERT statement allows you to add one or more rows to a table. There are two ways to perform an insert. First, you can specify the values for the columns in each row to be inserted using the VALUES clause:

```
INSERT INTO TABLE1 (COL1, COL2) VALUES(1, 2)
```

Here, we specify the names of all the columns we will include values for, prior to the VALUES clause. This is often useful if the order of columns is different from the table definition or if you are inserting the default value or a NULL value into columns that are not specified. If you are going to insert a value into every column, you do not need to include a column list. We recommend always using the column list, however, for style and clarity.

You can also insert rows into a table by selecting rows from another table as the second method. Here is an example:

```
INSERT INTO TABLE1(COL1, COL2) SELECT (C1, C2) FROM T1
```

In many cases, rows will already exist in the database, and we need to update them. For example, we may wish to update the amount of an item in stock after a purchase is made in our online mall database. We do this using an UPDATE statement:

```
UPDATE product SET units_in_stock=units_in_stock-10
WHERE product_id=123123
```

Our statement decreases the quantity on hand for product 123123. As you can see, an UPDATE statement allows you to specify a WHERE clause. Without specifying a WHERE clause in this statement, you would update every row in the table! This is the same for a DELETE statement. For example, if we wanted to delete the row we just updated, we would issue the statement:

```
DELETE FROM product WHERE productid=123123
```

You can make your WHERE clause as complicated as you like. You can use Boolean operators such as AND and OR, equality operators such as =, >, <, <>, and other comparison operators such as LIKE and BETWEEN. These are fully documented in the *SQL Reference*.

1.5 DB2 Application Structure

Database applications issue SQL queries within the context of a programming interface such as embedded SQL, CLI/ODBC, JDBC, or SQLJ. All of these APIs follow the same series of steps when executing an SQL query, also known as a statement. We will try to describe the common structure of database applications in this section.

1.5.1 Connecting to a Database

Before an application can make requests to a DB2 database using SQL, it must connect to it. The general syntax for doing this in DB2 is demonstrated using a connection for the DB2MALL database:

```
CONNECT TO DB2MALL USER ssanyal USING mypass
```

The user's ID follows the USER clause and the password follows the USING clause in the CONNECT statement. For implicit connections, both of these clauses can be omitted. Your application can use an implicit connection when CLIENT authentication is used or when it is connecting to a local database. For details on CLIENT authentication, consult the *Administration Guide*.

DB2 Application Structure

In many Application Programming Interfaces (APIs), you won't need to specify a CONNECT statement using this syntax. Instead, you will use an API call, which will do this for you.

1.5.2 Dynamic and Static Statement Execution

Once connected, applications can execute SQL statements in two ways, dynamically and statically. To execute an SQL statement statically, the statement must be statically prepared and bound to the database. When a query is statically bound, the compiled instructions about how to execute it are stored in a database package. You can also generate an SQL statement at runtime and run it dynamically, in which case DB2 will have to prepare an access plan. A dynamic query's access plan is never permanently stored in the database, so it may need to be generated each time it is executed. DB2 does have a package cache that stores the access plans for dynamic queries to improve performance, but this is not permanent storage. Beginning in the next chapter, we will continue this discussion so that you will gain better awareness about when to use static and when to use dynamic SQL.

1.5.3 Statement Life Cycle

Every SQL statement has a life cycle. The nature of a statement's life cycle depends on whether it seeks to query the database or modify its contents, and whether it is dynamic or static. A dynamic statement must first be prepared. Here is a pseudocode example of a PREPARE for a SELECT statement issued against the product table of the DB2MALL database:

```
STMT = "SELECT * FROM product"
PREPARE S1 FROM :STMT
```

The statement is initially stored in the variable STMT. This variable is then referenced as a *host variable* in the PREPARE statement, S1, by preceding it with a colon (:). We will discuss host variables in detail in Chapter 4.

The PREPARE operation performs two tasks; first it checks the statement for syntax errors, and then it creates an access plan. The access plan contains a compiled set of instructions the database manager must perform to execute the query. A single query can have many access plans. The DB2 optimizer estimates the cost for a subset of possible plans and chooses the one with the lowest cost.

> **TIP** To accurately estimate the cost of an access plan, the database statistics must be up-to-date. The Database Administrator (DBA) should regularly ensure that the statistics are current by issuing the RUNSTATS command.

> **Troubleshooting**
>
> You can view the access plan your application is using with the DB2 Explain facility. You can also measure query performance using the `db2batch` tool. This can help you when investigating performance problems. See the *DB2 Administration Guide* and the *Command Reference* for details.

Once a statement has been prepared, it can be executed. Upon execution of a `SELECT` statement, the database manager retrieves all rows that match the criteria specified and places them into a temporary table, which is read using a cursor. This retrieved data is known as the result set for that statement. Statements that modify the database are not immediately written to disk. Instead, they are written to the database transaction logs and written to disk after the application issues an implicit or explicit `COMMIT`.

While there is an actual `EXECUTE` command for `INSERT`, `UPDATE`, and `DELETE` statements, a `SELECT` statement is executed by opening a database object known as a cursor. A cursor is used to navigate through the result set that was generated when the query was executed. The most basic type of cursor is used to scroll forward through a result set one row at a time. Some forms of cursors also allow you to update or delete data as it is being viewed, scroll backwards, or jump instantly to any row you desire in the result set. Updatable cursors also allow you to modify or delete the row where the cursor is currently positioned. A cursor is initially created for a prepared statement using a `DECLARE` operation, which associates it with a statement as the following example shows:

```
DECLARE C1 CURSOR FOR S1
```

Here, we have created a cursor called `C1` for the statement we previously prepared, which we referred to as `S1`. If this had been a statically executed statement, we would have declared it as follows:

```
DECLARE C1 CURSOR FOR SELECT * FROM product
```

As you can see, here we have specified the SQL query directly in the cursor declaration rather than referencing it with a variable element as we do in dynamic SQL. This is important, because the variable `STMT` that we used earlier could have been assigned at runtime, and thus the same piece of code could have been used to prepare *any* SQL query. This is the true power of dynamic SQL, whereas in static SQL, a query must be hard-coded.

In both cases, after having declared the cursor, we then execute the statement and open the cursor by simply issuing:

```
OPEN C1
```

When the statement is executed, a result set is built and stored inside a temporary table. Each row of data is then retrieved using a `FETCH` operation as follows:

```
FETCH C1
```

After all of the rows from the result set have been fetched in this manner, the database manager returns a +100 return code to indicate that no more data is available. At this point, the application should close the cursor using the CLOSE command on the cursor:

    CLOSE C1

> **Note**
>
> Cursor names must be unique within a program source module. You should never declare another cursor with the same name in a source module.

Once the cursor is closed, the result set is discarded, but this is not necessarily the end of this statement. Once it has been prepared, we can execute it more than once. This saves the overhead of generating the access plan multiple times. This is possible because DB2 stores the prepared form of the statement in its package cache, thereby allowing you to reuse it.

You may never have to actually declare cursor names and fetch on them using the syntax noted above. Most interfaces such as CLI or JDBC will shield you from requiring this. However, you should be aware that no matter which programming interface you are using, the base operations described above are actually occurring.

1.5.4 Committing or Rolling Back Changes

Earlier, we discussed database objects known as transactions. An application run can have many transactions. Each ROLLBACK cancels changes made during the current atomic unit of work, whereas issuing a COMMIT applies these changes. For example, when purchasing something from the mall database, several tables need to be updated:

- The product table needs to have the quantity purchased subtracted from the quantity on-hand for each item purchased. This involves one or more UPDATE operations.
- The invoice table needs to have a record inserted.
- The customer_order table needs to have one or more rows inserted.

What if the application were to crash before all of these operations were complete? Or even worse, what if the database manager itself crashed due to a system outage or other reason? The database may end up in an inconsistent state since the entire unit of work was not completed.

To prevent this from occurring, the application needs to COMMIT or ROLLBACK each unit of work. This allows the database manager to permanently apply or cancel the changes made by the application, respectively. In the customer purchase example, a COMMIT would only be issued if all three of the steps were completed.

> **TIP** Issuing a `COMMIT` and `ROLLBACK` also frees up resources such as database locks. This allows other concurrent connections to gain access to resources. Your application should try to isolate its database operations from the rest of its processing and issue a `COMMIT` or `ROLLBACK` as frequently as possible.

1.5.5 Disconnecting from a Database

After completing database operations, the application should disconnect from the database. This is done using the `CONNECT RESET` command. It is good design for your applications to explicitly clean up their connections and it is also wise to disconnect from the database if the application will not be performing database operations in the near future. This can also free up resources such as locks, which was discussed in the previous section.

1.6 Summary

In this chapter, we began by introducing you to the DB2 client server environment. We learned that each DB2 server instance is a separate database manager, and that DB2 client instances are remote clients that access databases managed by a DB2 server instance. DB2 commands and SQL can be run outside of an application using the CLP or Command Center.

Persistent data within a database is stored in base tables, and we learned about various database objects such as schemas, indexes, and packages. We also provided a quick overview of SQL and the four types of DML statements: `SELECT`, `INSERT`, `UPDATE`, and `DELETE`. Statements can be executed statically or dynamically. In the former case, an access plan is persistently stored in a database package. In the latter case, the access plan is generated at runtime.

Data can be retrieved using a `SELECT` statement, which produces a result set. The result set is a temporary table that is traversed using a cursor. Multiple SQL statements can comprise an atomic operation known as a transaction. The changes made during a transaction are either committed or rolled back at the end of the transaction.

Based on these concepts, application-database interaction can be summarized in a series of steps. First, the application must connect to the DB2 database it wishes to access. It can then perform as many queries as it likes, using as many transactions as required. Finally, it must disconnect from the database.

CHAPTER 2

DB2 Programming Roadmap

There are a variety of flexible alternatives for programming with DB2. Over the past decade, a number of standardized programming interfaces for database access have been developed, including Open Database Connectivity (ODBC), Java Database Connectivity (JDBC), SQLj, and Object Linking and Embedding Database (OLE DB). These interfaces provide functions and methods that perform many of the DB2 and SQL commands discussed in the previous chapter. For example, to PREPARE a statement using the DB2 CLI driver, you would call the SQLPrepare() function.

This type of abstraction is a key to the driver-based approach of these interfaces. It allows the interface to define operational details, but vendor-specific syntax and native API calls are hidden in the driver code. Third parties are also able to develop their own drivers for commercial databases, although they often may not have access to certain native API calls that the DBMS vendor does.

DB2 also provides support for embedded SQL programming as an alternative to using software drivers. The drawback to software drivers is often that there are many layers of code involved when performing any operation, which can be slower than the more direct approach of using embedded SQL.

2.1 Objectives

After reading this chapter, you should have an understanding of:

- The programming interfaces that can be used to access DB2 databases.
- The differences and key advantages of each interface.
- How to choose a suitable programming interface as your solution.

2.2 Administrative API

We begin by briefly describing the DB2 UDB Administrative API, which differs from all of the other interfaces we will discuss in that it is used for issuing DB2 administrative commands rather than for running SQL queries. The Administrative API allows you to develop applications that can administer and monitor DB2 instances and databases as well as import and export data. All of these commands can also be issued using the DB2 Command Line Processor (CLP), using syntax that is described in the *Command Reference*. After the CLP parses the syntax of the command that was issued, however, it in turn calls the same Administrative API functions that are also available to you as an application developer. You can find this API documented in the *Administrative API Reference*.

In general, for many automated tasks, it is easier to write a DB2 script that is processed by the CLP, but you can also create powerful applications that surpass the capabilities of any script by using the Administrative API yourself. For example, you can create your own set of tools for regularly monitoring your DB2 instances for free space, and by analyzing the usage pattern, you can project when you will run out of space and thereby issue a warning to the Database Administrator (DBA).

The Administrative API also contains a subset of functions known as the Context Management API. This API can be used to explicitly manage contexts for creating database connections and instance attachments. By default, all processes have a single context, and thus can only have a single database connection or instance attachment at any time. However, you may wish to write applications using the Administrative API that monitor several instances simultaneously, using a separate thread for each. In this scenario, you can create a multicontext environment using the Context Management API for maintaining several instance attachments at the same time.

You can also incorporate this approach into embedded SQL applications, where you may want to have several transactionally independent connections open simultaneously. For example, the DB2 CLI/ODBC driver makes extensive use of the Context Management API to accomplish this task.

2.3 Embedded SQL

Applications can be written with SQL statements embedded within a host language. The SQL statements provide the database interface, while the host language provides the remaining support needed for the application to execute. The supported host languages are:

- C/C++
- FORTRAN
- COBOL
- Java (SQLJ)

SQL statements placed in an application are not specific to the host language. The database manager provides a way to convert the SQL syntax for processing by the host language.

For the C, C++, COBOL, or FORTRAN languages, this conversion is handled by the DB2 precompiler. The DB2 precompiler is invoked using the `PREP` command. The precompiler converts embedded SQL statements directly into DB2 runtime services API calls.

For the Java language, the SQLJ translator converts SQLJ clauses into JDBC statements. The SQLJ translator is invoked with the `SQLJ` command.

When the precompiler processes a source file, it specifically looks for SQL statements and avoids the non-SQL host language. It can find SQL statements because they are surrounded by special delimiters. For the syntax information necessary to embed SQL statements in the language you are using, see the *Application Development Guide*.

Chapter 4 in this book describes this topic in more detail.

2.3.1 Static Embedded SQL

When the syntax of embedded SQL statements is fully known at precompile time, the statements are referred to as static SQL. This is in contrast to dynamic SQL statements whose syntax is not known until runtime.

> **Note**
> Static SQL is not supported in interpreted languages such as REXX.

The structure of an SQL statement must be completely specified for a statement to be considered static. For example, the names for the columns and tables referenced in a statement must be fully known at precompile time. The only information that can be specified at runtime are values for any host variables referenced by the statement. However, host variable information, such as data types, must still be precompiled.

When a static SQL statement is prepared, an executable form of the statement is created and stored in the package in the database. The executable form can be constructed either at precompile time or at a later bind time. In either case, preparation occurs before runtime. The authorization of the person binding the application is used, and optimization is based upon database statistics and configuration parameters that may not be current when the application runs.

2.3.2 Dynamic Embedded SQL

Dynamic SQL support statements accept a character-string host variable and a statement name as arguments. The host variable contains the SQL statement to be processed dynamically in text form. The statement text is not processed when an application is precompiled. In fact, the statement text does not have to exist at the time the application is precompiled. Instead, the SQL statement is treated as a host variable for precompilation purposes and the variable is referenced during application execution. These SQL statements are referred to as dynamic SQL.

Dynamic SQL support statements are required to transform the host variable containing SQL text into an executable form and operate on it by referencing the statement name. These statements are described in the *Application Development Guide*.

> **Note**
>
> The content of dynamic SQL statements follows the same syntax as static SQL statements, but with the following exceptions:
> Comments are not allowed.
> The statement cannot begin with `EXEC SQL`.
> The statement cannot end with the statement terminator. An exception to this is the `CREATE TRIGGER` statement, which can contain a semicolon (;).

You may want to use dynamic SQL when:

- You need all or part of the SQL statement to be generated during application execution.
- The objects referenced by the SQL statement do not exist at precompile time.
- You want the statement to always use the most optimal access path based on current database statistics.

2.4 Driver-based Application Solutions

Embedded SQL applications require that a vendor's precompiler first precompile the application and then the resultant source code be compiled and linked directly with a vendor's library. In most cases, the application will also have to be bound to the database that it is accessing so that the database can generate an access plan based on static queries made within the application. If a developer wishes for their application to work against another vendor's database, then they need to repeat these steps for the alternate database. A lot of work, but at least the source code should not need to be modified.

An alternative approach to accessing databases is to use a driver-based solution. This solution involves a driver manager with which the application interfaces. The driver manager provides a set of industry-standard interfaces (APIs) to access a data source. An application is written to call these APIs and then compiled and linked with the manager's libraries. During the execution of the application, the manager loads the correct vendor-supplied driver to access the appropriate data source. If a developer wishes to access a different vendor's data source, then all they need to do is ensure that the client has the appropriate driver correctly installed. Listed below are a number of driver-based solutions for DB2.

2.4.1 Application Software Layers

In DB2, the common client interface for all higher-level drivers is the DB2 Call Level Interface (CLI). For example, the JDBC driver translates its calls into CLI, as does the Perl DBI and Net.Data's DTW_SQL language environment. This was done since CLI was already a highly functional driver that was designed to meet several open standards, primarily ODBC. Since ODBC is being phased out, however, the next release of DB2 UDB will use a proprietary common client interface.

2.4.2 CLI/ODBC

Both DB2's CLI standard and Microsoft's ODBC standard were originally based on the X/Open CLI standard. The ODBC standard provides a set of CLIs or APIs for accessing a vendor's database. The ODBC standard requires that a vendor supply their own driver and provide a set of function calls for accessing that database. How complete a vendor's set of APIs is compared to the set listed by the ODBC standard determines what level of compliance the driver is at.

IBM's DB2 CLI driver can be used on its own to access a DB2 database or as an ODBC driver. DB2 conforms to most of the Level 3 compliance for ODBC. The CLI driver contains additional functions that cannot be used through an ODBC interface. To make use of these functions, the CLI driver must be linked to the application program directly, rather than be used as an ODBC driver.

To develop CLI applications, you will need the IBM DB2 UDB Developer's Software Kit. This kit includes all of the necessary header files and libraries for compiling and linking CLI applications. To develop ODBC applications, you will need an ODBC Developer's Software Kit. IBM does not provide this kit, except for its OS/2 platform. Microsoft supplies this kit for Windows platforms, and for UNIX platforms, a number of vendors can be found. Details for developing ODBC/CLI applications can be found in Chapter 6.

2.4.3 ADO and OLE DB

ADO is Microsoft's ActiveX Data Objects set of classes. These classes provide a set of methods for accessing data from a multitude of sources. Not only can these sources be from relational databases, they can also be from nonrelational databases such as Hypertext Markup Language (HTML), mail, video, text, or just about anything else. The data access is handled under the hood of ADO, and access can be provided by different services such as Remote Data Services (RDS), ODBC, or OLE DB.

RDS is an old service that we will not be discussing in this book. ODBC is a very popular service that has very widespread use within the data access industry and is discussed in Chapter 6. OLE DB is the new data access service of the future. OLE DB is designed to provide access to several relational and nonrelational data sources. We introduce this driver to you at the end of Chapter 6. It has been placed at the end of the chapter that discusses ODBC because OLE DB will likely replace ODBC in the near future.

2.4.4 JDBC

The universal database programming interface for Java is JDBC. JDBC programs are run using dynamic SQL. DB2 V7.1 provides support for JDBC 1.22 and JDBC 2.0 on the Intel and UNIX platforms. DB2 also provides a Type II JDBC driver for Java applications and servlets. This is known as the app driver. For Java applets, DB2 provides the net driver, which is a Type III driver. Both types of drivers are available for each JDBC version supported. In addition, DB2 provides support for many JDBC 2.0 advanced features. These features are part of the JDBC 2.0 Standard Extensions API. Among the features supported by DB2's JDBC 2.0 drivers are connection pooling using data source objects, Java Naming and Directory Interface (JNDI) support, and the Java Transaction API (JTA) support for XA transactions.

To develop JDBC applications, you will need the Java Development Kit (JDK). JDK 1.1.8 is provided with the Application Development Client. To develop JDBC 2.0 applications, you will need to download the Java 2 SDK Standard Edition for Core API support. To use the JDBC 2.0 Standard Extensions API, you will need to download the Java 2 SDK Enterprise Edition. You can obtain these by following the links listed in the "Additional References" section of Chapter 7.

There are several key advantages if you decide to develop your database applications in Java. First and foremost, your Java bytecode can run on any platform, so it is easily portable. Second, you can save the cost of expensive compilers and other development tools if you have a small business. Java is also still a relatively new technology, so there are many ongoing efforts to extend its functionality and performance. SQLj is discussed in detail in Chapter 7.

2.4.5 SQLj

SQLj allows you to embed SQL statements into your Java programs and statically bind them to DB2 databases. As we have mentioned, static SQL generally provides better performance than dynamic SQL since the query access plan is stored in a database package. You still enjoy Java's code portability and its rich API using this approach. SQLj is discussed in detail in Chapter 7.

2.4.6 Perl Scripts Using the DBI

Perl has become a very popular scripting language for various UNIX platforms and can also be found for the Windows platform. Its source code is available as part of the Open Source Standard and many binaries can be downloaded from the Perl Web site. Perl is especially popular for use with Web servers through the Common Gateway Interface (CGI). It is primarily because of this that Perl has developed and provided an interface for accessing relational databases. The interface for this is the Database Interface (DBI).

DBI provides a set of standard class methods for which database vendors can supply an interface to their databases. These drivers are known as Database Drivers (DBD). Vendors usually supply these drivers for free, and they can usually be found at the Perl Web site. To develop Perl applications that access DB2, you will need Perl, the DBI module, and the DBD::DB2 driver. Chapter 9 discusses this in detail.

2.5 Net.Data

Intranet and Internet Web solutions that use more than one programming language can both benefit greatly from the features built into the Net.Data product. Net.Data is a Web page generation application that runs on the Web server used to integrate dynamic content from various data sources. It provides a macro scripting language that can be used to tie together new code, such as Java servlets, with legacy applications written in languages such as Perl or REXX. It also provides methods to access some databases through native database interfaces. Additional databases can be accessed as ODBC data sources.

The scripting language is easy to use and is useful for quick deployment of Web solutions. Net.Data can generate documents formatted using HTML or Extensible Markup Language (XML) with style sheets. It is supported on many platforms, including NT, OS/2, AIX, Solaris, HP-UX, Sequent, Red Hat Linux, Caldera Linux, OS/390, and OS/400. Net.Data is a simple but powerful application that is suitable for quick deployment of Web solutions or as a tool to integrate legacy applications.

2.6 DB2 Extenders

DB2 Extenders is a collection of User-Defined Functions (UDFs) and API libraries used to extend the functionality of SQL when working with different media types. This includes documents, audio clips, images, and video clips. Any application, regardless of the programming language, can take advantage of DB2 Extenders by referencing these UDFs in their SQL statements.

The DB2 Extenders Family is composed of several products, including Text Extender, Net Search Extender, Audio, Image, and Video (AIV) Extenders, XML Extender, and Spatial Extender. The platform availability varies for each DB2 Extender product. All products are available on most UNIX and Intel platforms. Some DB2 Extender products are also available on OS/390. Using products from the DB2 Extenders Family is a great way for getting additional media functionality from your applications with very little change to user code.

2.7 Summary

There are many programming interfaces that can be used to access DB2 databases. Each method has a set of key advantages. Depending on the task, a suitable programming interface should be selected. This chapter has reviewed the key advantages of several programming interfaces.

Administrative APIs are useful for performing DB2 administrative tasks from an application. Embedded SQL is best suited for applications where the best possible performance is critical. ODBC, ADO, and OLE DB programming interfaces are best suited for applications that need to be independent of the data source. They provide greater application portability. CLI provides a native interface for DB2 databases that is compatible with ODBC. JDBC and SQLj programming interfaces are the only programming interfaces available for applications coded in Java. Net.Data is suitable for quick deployment of Web solutions or as a tool to integrate legacy applications. Perl scripts are useful for generating dynamic Web pages. DB2 Extenders are useful for getting lots of additional media data functionality from your applications by referencing UDFs inside SQL statements.

CHAPTER 3

DB2 Programming Features and Strategies

Database applications provide programmers with the challenge of utilizing DBMS resources efficiently. DB2 provides rich features such as User-Defined Functions (UDFs), stored procedures, concurrency, and transaction management. Using these features properly make the difference between well-tuned applications and headaches such as deadlocks and poor performance.

For example, a remote application that makes dozens of needless queries will suffer a bottleneck in terms of network traffic and DBMS processing time. In contrast, an application that effectively uses DB2 to perform business logic and function-related tasks saves tremendous client-side overhead, and will see significant performance benefits. One of the keys to success is to experiment and find the right balance that suits your environment.

With the explosion of the Internet and e-business, there are thousands of businesses that run Web applications and use DB2 as a backend to manage their data. These applications are generally designed with a three-tier strategy in mind. The client Web browser is the first tier, the Web application running on the Web server is the middle tier, and a DB2 server (usually on a separate system) is the backend. It makes sense in this case to download business functions involving database operations to the DB2 server as much as possible to reduce processing in your Web applications. Computation and data processing are two examples of business functions that can be downloaded in this manner.

In this chapter, we offer strategies to structure your database applications better by utilizing DB2 server-side features. If you are new to database programming or to DB2, you may wish to revisit this chapter again after you have read the remainder of the book and gained a thorough understanding about the steps involved in developing a database application, which we described in Chapter 1. We will also teach you general techniques to use in your applications, which are applicable to all programming interfaces such as using UDFs and casting User-Defined Types (UDTs).

3.1 Objectives

Effective use of DBMS resources can avoid potential application problems. The first section of this chapter will discuss important programming considerations and data manipulation strategies such as referencing system catalogs, creating complex database objects, creating UDTs, creating common table expressions, and using compound SQL statements. It will also look at the various cursor types, the advantages of prepared statements, the usage of identity columns, the usage of table triggers, and the usage of the STAR schema. The second section will review concurrency and transaction management issues such as unit of work, locking strategies, isolation levels, and distributed unit of work. The next section will discuss writing SQL stored procedures and using the DB2 Stored Procedure Builder. The last section will discuss database packages and query performance. The goal of this chapter is to provide an awareness of the following issues:

- Data manipulation strategies.
- Concurrency and transaction management issues.
- SQL stored procedures and DB2 Stored Procedure Builder.
- Database packages and query performance.

3.2 Data Manipulation Strategies

Proficiency in SQL and understanding database objects should be one of your main objectives as a database programmer. For example, if you are performing a query on a large table repeatedly, your Database Administrator (DBA) may wish to create summary tables instead. In addition, your applications can use temporary tables to store their data instead of caching it in memory.

You can also download considerable business functions in terms of computation and data processing to a DB2 server by taking advantage of features such as User-Defined Functions (UDFs) and stored procedures. You should try to do this whenever possible to consolidate your database programming code as much as possible. This makes for easier code maintenance, and extends code reuse by making it available to clients of any type. For example, if you create a UDF written in Java, you can call that UDF from a database application written in any supported language. This is possible because the language in which the UDF is written is transparent to the application.

3.2.1 System Catalogs

A description of the logical and physical structure of the data in each DB2 database is stored in the system catalog tables. The system catalog tables are defined in the SYSIBM schema, and a set of views for these tables are defined in the SYSCAT schema. You can query these tables yourself to extract useful information. For example, to determine the base tables that were used to construct a specific view, you could query the SYSIBM.SYSVIEWDEP table to find out the dependencies for the view. This might be useful if the base tables had primary keys and you could improve query performance by rewriting the query to use the base tables instead of the views.

Still, unless you are writing a data access interface, or applications such as monitoring tools or a data model extraction tool, as an application developer you may not need to concern yourself with the system catalogs. You should be aware of their existence, however, and their role in DB2. For example, the DB2 CLI driver will often query the system catalog tables to obtain information such as the parameters for a stored procedure. This may lead to additional queries being issued by the driver that are transparent to the application, and which are not needed if you know all of the stored procedure parameters.

As a developer, you should familiarize yourself with troubleshooting tools such as the CLI trace, which will let you see if additional queries are being issued. You can then set configuration keywords or write your application to avoid these queries. We describe how to use trace facilities within DB2 in Appendix C.

3.2.2 Summary Tables

A summary table is a table whose definition is based on the result of a query. As such, the summary table typically contains precomputed results based on the data existing in the table or tables that its definition is based on. If the SQL compiler determines that a dynamic query will run more efficiently against a summary table than the base table, the query executes against the summary table and you obtain the result faster than you otherwise would.

To create a summary table, you use the `CREATE SUMMARY TABLE` statement with the `AS fullselect` clause and the `IMMEDIATE` or `REFRESH DEFERRED` options.

You have the option of uniquely identifying the names of the columns of a summary table. The list of column names must contain as many names as there are columns in the result table of the full select. A list of column names must be given if the result table of the full select has duplicate column names or has an unnamed column. An unnamed column is derived from a constant, function, expression, or set operation that is not named using the `AS` clause of the select list. If a list of column names is not specified, the columns of the table inherit the names of the columns of the result set of the full select.

When you create a summary table, you have the option of specifying whether the summary table is refreshed automatically when the base table is changed, or whether it is refreshed by using the `REFRESH TABLE` statement. To have the summary table refreshed automatically when changes are made to the base table or tables, specify the `REFRESH IMMEDIATE` keyword. An immediate refresh is useful when:

- You have queries that take a long time to complete when run against a base table.
- The base table or tables are infrequently changed.
- The refresh is not expensive.

The summary table, in this situation, can provide precomputed results. If you want the refresh of the summary table to be deferred, specify the REFRESH DEFERRED keyword. Summary tables specified with REFRESH DEFERRED will not reflect changes to the underlying base tables. You should use summary tables where this is not a requirement.

A summary table defined with REFRESH DEFERRED may be used in place of a query when it conforms to the restrictions for a full select of a REFRESH IMMEDIATE summary table, except:

- The SELECT list is not required to include COUNT(*) or COUNT_BIG(*).
- The SELECT list can include MAX and MIN column functions.
- A HAVING clause is allowed.

The CURRENT REFRESH AGE special register specifies the timestamp duration value with a data type of DECIMAL(20,6). This duration is the maximum duration since a REFRESH TABLE statement has been processed on a deferred refresh summary table. It determines if a summary table can be used to optimize the processing of a query. The SET CURRENT REFRESH AGE statement enables you to change the value of the CURRENT REFRESH AGE special register. The value must be 0 or 99999999999999 (9999 years, 99 months, 99 days, 99 hours, 99 minutes, and 99 seconds).

- Zero (0) means that the only summary tables defined with REFRESH IMMEDIATE may be used to optimize the processing query.
- 99999999999999 means that any summary tables defined with REFRESH DEFERRED or REFRESH IMMEDIATE may be used to optimize the processing of a query. Note the keyword ANY is shorthand for 99999999999999.

Summary tables defined with REFRESH IMMEDIATE are applicable to both static and dynamic queries and do not need to use the CURRENT REFRESH AGE special register. Setting the CURRENT REFRESH AGE special register to a value other than zero should be done with caution. By allowing a summary table that may not represent the values of the underlying base table to be used to optimize the processing of the query, the result of the query may not accurately represent the data in the underlying table. This may be reasonable when you know the underlying data has not changed, or you are willing to accept the degree of error in the results based on your knowledge of the data.

With activity affecting the source data, a summary table over time will no longer contain accurate data. You will need to use the REFRESH TABLE statement.

Here are some of the key restrictions regarding summary tables:

1. You cannot alter a summary table.
2. You cannot alter the length of a column for a base table if that table has a summary table.
3. You cannot import data into a summary table.

4. You cannot create a unique index on a summary table.
5. You cannot create a summary table based on the result of a query that references one or more nicknames.

Refer to the *DB2 UDB SQL Reference* for a complete statement of summary table restrictions.

3.2.3 User-Defined Types

While DB2 provides base data types, you can create your own User-Defined Types (UDTs). Each UDT is based on a base data type. The use of UDTs adds additional integrity to the implementation of your data model. For example, imagine that you have two different tables with a column that measures weight. One uses kilograms, and the other uses pounds. If both columns were defined as the INTEGER data type, it would be easy to forget that they represent different units of measure. One might even perform arithmetic computations that would produce meaningless results. To guard against this, your DBA may implement the data model with UDTs called POUND and KILOGRAM. This would be done as follows:

```
CREATE DISTINCT TYPE pound AS INTEGER WITH COMPARISONS
CREATE DISTINCT TYPE kilogram AS INTEGER WITH COMPARISONS
```

For your application to query tables that have POUND or KILOGRAM columns, you must cast the UDT back to its base type. For example, if you have a table called T1 with column C1 whose type is POUND, you would query this column for all the rows of the table with the following query:

```
SELECT INTEGER(c1) FROM t1
```

Conversely, to update or insert a value for column C1, you must use the base data type and cast it to the UDT. An example of a dynamic query to do this is as follows:

```
INSERT INTO T1 (c1) VALUES ( POUND(?) )
```

As long as you appropriately cast your UDTs, you can access them in your application. Simply be aware that your application can only use the DB2 base data types, whereas UDTs are used to enforce integrity and add structure.

3.2.4 Common Table Expressions

A common table expression is a local temporary table that can be referenced many times in an SQL statement. This temporary table only exists for the duration of the SQL statements that define it. Every time that a common table expression is referenced, the results will be the same. This means that the SQL statement that generates the table will not be reproduced each time the common table expression is referenced. A temporary table is defined during an SQL statement by using the WITH clause. For example:

```
WITH <Common name1> AS (<SELECT Expression>), <Common
name2> AS (<SELECT Expression>), … SELECT <column>, … FROM
<table_name> <where_clause>

<table_name> is either a table in the database or a <Common
name> defined by the WITH statement.
```

After the definition of a common table expression, you can use it in an SQL statement as you would any other table. You can use a common table expression as many times as you wish. You can even create a common table expression based on a previously created common table expression.

As a construed example, consider the following SQL:

```
WITH prod_quantity AS
(    SELECT product_id, SUM(quantity) AS quantity
     FROM customer_order_item
     GROUP BY product_id
),
PROD_totals AS
(    SELECT -1 as product_id, SUM(quantity) AS total
)
(SELECT product_id, quantity
FROM prod_quantity
UNION
SELECT product_id, totals
FROM totals
)ORDER BY 1 DESC
```

3.2.5 Compound SQL

Compound SQL can be used to perform a number of SQL statements in a single block. There are no special coding techniques required because compound SQL is composed of combined SQL statements. The SQL statements that make up a compound SQL statement are called sub-statements. Compound SQL reduces both overhead at the server and network traffic. Compound SQL can be atomic or not atomic. When DB2 UDB executes *atomic* compound SQL statements and any one of the substatements fail, then any changes made by the other substatements are rolled back. When DB2 UDB executes *not atomic* compound SQL statements and a substatement fails, none of the changes made by the other substatements are rolled back. An example of compound SQL could be in a banking environment:

```
EXEC SQL BEGIN COMPOUND ATOMIC STATIC
     UPDATE SAVINGS SET
        BALANCE = BALANCE - :transfer
WHERE ATMCARD = :atmcard;
```

```
            UPDATE CHECKING SET
              BALANCE = BALANCE + :transfer
    WHERE ATMCARD = :atmcard;

            INSERT INTO ATMTRANS (TTSTMP,CODE,AMOUNT)
              VALUES(CURRENT TIMESTAMP, :code, :transfer);

    COMMIT;

END COMPOUND;
```

In this scenario, atomic compound SQL is used to ensure that all or none of the bank transactions are committed to the database. If the `INSERT` substatement had failed and `BEGIN COMPOUND NOT ATOMIC STATIC` had been specified in the above statement, then the bank would have had changes made to checking and saving accounts, but no record of the ATM transaction would have been made. The `STATIC` clause in compound SQL means that for each substatement, any input host variables will have the value they had when the compound SQL statement was called. For example, if the above example began with a substatement like `SELECT AMOUNT ... INTO :transfer`, due to the `STATIC` clause, the following update and insert statements would *not* use the new value of the `transfer` host variable.

3.2.6 Cursor Types and Scope

Cursors are used to process result sets. All cursors have two main characteristics, type and scope. There are three types of cursors, which are listed below, in terms of increasing overhead:

- Read-only cursors, used by default or specified with a `FOR FETCH ONLY` clause.
- Updatable cursors, specified using the `FOR UPDATE` clause.
- Scrollable cursors, which allow you to move back and forth in a result set.

The latter type is only available in DB2 CLI, and dynamic interfaces such as JDBC, which use the CLI driver. There are also scrollable-updatable cursors, which are only available through keyset cursors in CLI. You should only use updatable cursors when necessary, because they will require greater lock exclusivity and reduce application concurrency.

By the scope of a cursor, we refer to whether the cursor can persist beyond a single unit of work. We discuss the concept of a unit of work in greater detail in the transaction management section of this chapter. By default, a cursor is defined as being `WITHOUT HOLD`, meaning that if you `COMMIT` your transaction, the cursor will be closed. Any subsequent attempts to `FETCH` on the cursor will return `SQLCode SQL0501E`, indicating that the cursor is no longer open.

If you define your cursor `WITH HOLD`, then the cursor will remain open even if you commit a change to the database. This is often useful if you are scrolling through a result set and updating records, committing after each record updated, or a certain number of updates. A

ROLLBACK will close all open cursors on a connection, whether they are defined WITH HOLD or not.

The convention for specifying the type and scope of a cursor is different for each type of programming interface. In embedded SQL, you actually define your cursor type and scope when you declare it. Most other drivers issue calls to the DB2 CLI driver, and will either have their own methods or functions to set cursor properties with CLI calls, or offer you the alternative of specifying these properties as configuration keywords in the db2cli.ini file.

When using features such as autocommit, using a WITH HOLD cursor is often a necessity, especially in multithreaded applications. You should be aware that WITH HOLD cursors will retain their locks across transactions since they remain open. To release the locks on a cursor WITH HOLD, you should close the cursor and subsequently COMMIT changes to the database if the cursor was updatable.

3.2.7 Prepared Statements

One of the keys to application performance is to avoid additional computation and processing. Since SQL specifies the database operation to perform, but not how to execute the operation, DB2 must generate an access plan. Avoiding this cost whenever possible will greatly increase your application performance. When you use static SQL, your application queries are statically bound to a DB2 database and the access plan is stored in a compiled form in the system catalog tables at bind time.

Dynamic SQL has the cost overhead of generating the access plan at runtime. If you are going to execute the same query over and over again in your application, you can avoid having to repeatedly generate the access plan if you PREPARE your statement once and then execute it when needed. If there are variables in your query, then you can specify them as parameter markers and bind these parameters each time before you execute your query. While the steps to accomplish this are the same for every programming interface, the actual methodology differs. Refer to the individual chapters on each programming interface to learn how to prepare, execute, and rebind parameters for statements.

3.2.8 Use of Parameter Markers

Parameter markers allow you to rebind a statement with different input values; however, you should be aware that the DB2 optimizer may generate a faster access plan if literal values are specified in the statement. This is because DB2 can maintain *distribution statistics* for indexed columns. Whether these statistics are maintained is specified at index creation time.

Thus, for queries where literal values are specified in the WHERE clause, these distribution statistics can be used when generating the access plan. If parameter markers are used instead, distribution statistics are not useful, since the parameter values are not known to the optimizer.

3.2.9 Deferred Prepare

There is also a feature in DB2 dynamic SQL programs known as *deferred prepare*. This sends a prepare request in the same network flow as the execute request, and thus improves performance by not requiring a separate flow for each. Deferred prepare is enabled by default in DB2 CLI applications, and can be specified as a `BIND` option in embedded SQL.

3.2.10 Identity Columns

In DB2 V7.1, you no longer have to worry about generating sequential unique values for rows. In previous versions of DB2, a common approach to generating sequential unique values was to `SELECT` the current maximum value for a column in the table using the `MAX` function, and then incrementing this value by one. You can define an identity column in a table as follows:

```
CREATE TABLE IDENTITY ( c1 INT GENERATED ALWAYS AS IDENTITY
(START WITH 1000000, INCREMENT BY 1) PRIMARY KEY, c2 INT)
```

In this table definition, we create a table with an identity column that serves as the primary key for the table. There is also a `CACHE` option that can be included in the identity column definition (`NOT CACHED` by default). This causes DB2 to cache a specified number of values in advance, and improves performance since DB2 won't have to determine the next value in the sequence. However, there is a side effect of caching that may not be desirable. When a database is deactivated, the cached values in an identity column are discarded and can never be used again. This can create sequence gaps.

Notice also that we have a second column called C2 in our `CREATE TABLE` statement. While DB2 will let you create a single-column table in which the column is an identity column that is always generated, there is no valid syntax for inserting data into this table. Thus, a table with an identity column whose values are always generated must always have at least one additional column.

It is always necessary to indicate the column list (excluding the identity column) when inserting one or more rows into an table with an identity column. Otherwise DB2 will return an `SQL0104N` error complaining that the number of columns in the `INSERT` statement does not match the table definition. For example, to insert a row into `IDENTITY`, we would use the syntax:

```
INSERT INTO IDENTITY (c2) VALUES ( ? )
```

There is another small hurdle to deal with when using an identity column. You may often want to use the identity column as a foreign key in another table. Let us say that you want to insert a new record in a table called `CUSTOMER_PURCHASE` when someone makes a purchase for the first time. The `CUSTOMER_PURCHASE` table has an identity column that corresponds to the customer number. Each item purchase is stored in a table called `PURCHASE`, and each record in the `CUSTOMER_PURCHASE` table has a foreign key that references the customer number who purchased the item.

You are then faced with the dilemma of determining the identity of a new customer. One way to solve this problem is to query it back somehow, using another unique key in the CUSTOMER table. But what if there isn't one? Besides, this defeats the purpose of removing the SELECT MAX that was required in previous versions of DB2.

DB2 V7.1 provides a solution, however, by including a function that returns the last uniquely generated value for a connection. To obtain the last value generated, you must use the SYSIBM.IDENTITY_VAL_LOCAL function as follows:

    VALUES(identity_val_local())

This function returns a DECIMAL(31,0) value, no matter what the SQL data type of the identity column is. Thus, you may wish to cast it, using syntax such as:

    VALUES(INT(identity_val_local()))

Be careful when using this function in a multithreaded application, however, because you may have multiple threads performing inserts on the same connection at the same time. You will need to build thread safety around the use of this call into your application. One way to do this is to use a resource allocator such as a semaphore for each connection. Using this strategy, every statement would need to get a resource lock before proceeding. Multiple statements could get a lock, but insert statements that intend to use IDENTITY_VAL_LOCAL would need to obtain an exclusive lock on the resource, thus blocking all other statements from executing while the lock is held.

In general, the IDENTITY_VAL_LOCAL function will return a NULL value under the following circumstances:

- A commit was performed after the insert.
- Other queries were performed after the insert. This function would return a NULL value even if no identity column was involved in the other queries.

This function is fully documented in the *DB2 UDB V7.1 Release Notes*.

3.2.11 Triggers

A trigger defines a set of actions that are executed at, or triggered by, a DELETE, INSERT, or UPDATE operation on a specified table. When such an SQL operation is executed, the trigger is said to be activated.

Triggers can be used along with referential constraints and check constraints to enforce data integrity rules. Triggers can also be used to cause updates to other tables, automatically generate or transform values for inserted or updated rows, or invoke functions to perform tasks such as issuing alerts.

Triggers are useful mechanisms to define and enforce transitional business rules, which are rules that involve different states of the data (for example, salary cannot be increased by more than 10 percent). For rules that do not involve more than one state of the data, check and referential integrity constraints should be considered.

Using triggers places the logic to enforce the business rules in the database and relieves the applications using the tables from having to enforce it. Centralized logic enforced on all the tables means easier maintenance, since no application program changes are required when the logic changes.

Triggers are optional and are defined using the `CREATE TRIGGER` statement.

There are a number of criteria that are defined when creating a trigger which are used to determine when a trigger should be activated:

- The *subject table* defines the table for which the trigger is defined.
- The *trigger event* defines a specific SQL operation that modifies the subject table. The operation could be delete, insert, or update.
- The *trigger activation time* defines whether the trigger should be activated before or after the trigger event is performed on the subject table.

The statement that causes a trigger to be activated will include a set of affected rows. These are the rows of the subject table that are being deleted, inserted, or updated. The trigger granularity defines whether the actions of the trigger will be performed once for the statement or once for each of the rows in the set of affected rows.

The triggered action consists of an optional search condition and a set of SQL statements that are executed whenever the trigger is activated. The SQL statements are only executed if the search condition evaluates to true. When the trigger activation time is before the trigger event, triggered actions can include statements that select, set transition variables, and signal SQL-STATEs. When the trigger activation time is after the trigger event, triggered actions can include statements that select, update, insert, delete, and signal SQLSTATEs.

The triggered action may refer to the values in the set of affected rows. This is supported through the use of transition variables. Transition variables use the names of the columns in the subject table qualified by a specified name that identifies whether the reference is to the old value (prior to the update) or the new value (after the update). The new value can also be changed using the `SET` transition variable statement in before update or insert triggers. Another means of referring to the values in the set of affected rows is using transition tables. Transition tables also use the names of the columns of the subject table, but have a name specified that allows the complete set of affected rows to be treated as a table. Transition tables can only be used in after triggers, and separate transition tables can be defined for old and new values.

Multiple triggers can be specified for a combination of table, event, or activation time. The order in which the triggers are activated is the same as the order in which they were created. Thus, the most recently created trigger will be the last trigger activated.

The activation of a trigger may cause trigger cascading. This is the result of the activation of one trigger that executes SQL statements that cause the activation of other triggers or even the same trigger again. The triggered actions may also cause updates as a result of the original modification, or as a result of referential integrity delete rules that may result in the activation of additional triggers. With trigger cascading, a significant chain of triggers and referential integrity delete rules may be activated, causing significant change to the database as a result of a single delete, insert, or update statement.

3.2.12 Stored Procedures

Stored procedures are another server-side feature of DB2 that you should consider using to consolidate database programming code and increase performance. Since this is a large topic, we have included a separate section later in this chapter to discuss stored procedures in detail.

3.2.13 DB2 Built-In and User-Defined Functions

Built-in and User-Defined Functions (UDFs) can be used to download business functions to DB2 instead of having to implement them within your applications. For example, you may store all of the prices for your `DB2MALL` database in American dollars, but you may wish to quote customers prices in their native currency. Here is an example of a prepared statement you might use to do this:

```
SELECT unit_price, currency('CAD', unit_price)
FROM product WHERE product_id = ?
```

This query would return the price in U.S. dollars, but also return a second column with a price in Canadian dollars. Our UDF called `currency` is called to accomplish this task. The first argument for the UDF is the currency you wish to convert to (in this case, "CAD" for Canadian dollars), and the second argument is the price to convert. By writing a UDF to do this, any application can take advantage of the code you have written.

You can define a UDF using an existing function, or create an external UDF in C, Java, or OLE. The latter is only supported on Windows 32 systems. We cover each of these in their language and interface-specific chapter. Chapter 4 discusses UDFs written in C, Chapter 6 discusses OLE UDFs, and Chapter 7 covers Java UDFs.

An external UDF can run in either FENCED mode or NOT FENCED mode. We recommend you thoroughly test your UDFs in FENCED mode before considering using them in NOT FENCED mode. The latter provides better performance by running within the DB2 agent memory space, but can be dangerous if they terminate abnormally. In contrast, a FENCED UDF runs inside a `db2udf` process, outside of DB2 memory space, and won't harm the agent. The tradeoff is that a FENCED UDF uses shared memory to communicate with the calling agent, which is slower than a UDF that is NOT FENCED.

External UDFs exist as shared libraries on each instance. You should place fenced UDFs in `sqllib/function`, and NOT FENCED UDFs in `sqllib/function/unfenced`, and ensure that these directories are included in your library path configuration.

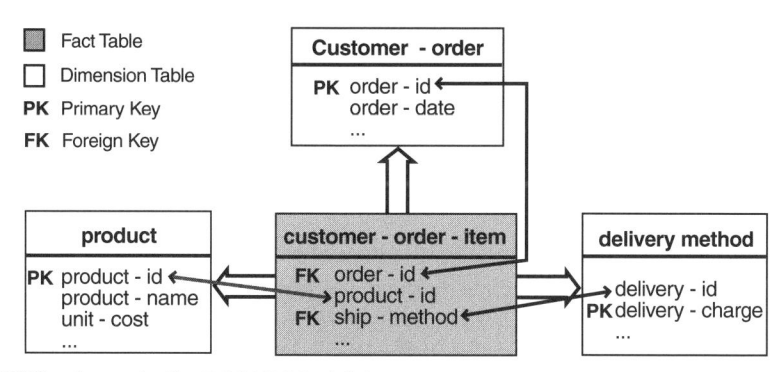

Figure 3-1 STAR schema in the `DB2MALL` database.

3.2.14 STAR Schema Table/Index Design

Databases normally hold large amounts of data that can be updated, deleted, queried, and inserted on a daily basis. Databases in which data is constantly updated, deleted, and inserted are known as Online Transaction Processing (OLTP) systems. Databases that hold large amounts of data and do not have a heavy transaction workload, but do have a large number of concurrent queries executing all the time, are known as Decision Support Systems (DSSs). Certain DSSs have fewer queries, but each query can be very complex. These allow users to examine the data from different perspectives by performing Online Analytical Processing (OLAP).

The functionality of the database is required to provide multidimensional views of relational data, without significant performance effect. DB2 UDB provides this capability using a number of joining methods, SQL statements, and other database features. The next few paragraphs explain the database technology found in DB2 UDB that enhances the performance of OLAP queries.

The concept of a STAR schema is illustrated in Figure 3-1. A business view of a highly normalized database often requires a number of attributes associated with one primary object. Each of these attributes is contained in a separate table.

The following points are characteristic of a STAR schema design:

- There is a large fact table that contains data relating to the dimension tables. In Figure 3-1, the fact table is the `customer_order_item` table. It contains detailed information on each item ordered, including which item was ordered, for which order form, and how it will be shipped.
- There are a number of dimension tables that typically hold descriptive information about an entity that has a small number of rows. In Figure 3-1, the dimension tables are `customer_order`, `product`, and `delivery_method`.
- The primary keys of the dimension tables involved in the STAR schema supply foreign key entries in the fact table. The concatenation of foreign keys from the dimension tables usually forms a small subset of the fact table. In Figure 3-1, the foreign keys are `order_id`, `product_id`, and `ship_method`.

This approach allows as few attributes as possible to be stored in the fact table. The benefit of this is that the fact table is usually very large and therefore any data duplication in this table would be very costly in terms of storage and access times.

OLAP schemas, such as STAR schemas, are frequently used for large databases. These schemas make it very important to access the data in these databases in the optimal manner. Otherwise, the joins involved in the schemas may result in poor performance.

A typical STAR schema includes a large number of indexes. This is due to the ad hoc nature of queries in an OLAP environment. Such as environment is typically not subjected to constant insert or update activity, and therefore does not have to suffer from significant performance degradation as a result of index maintenance.

The prime consideration of indexes in an OLAP environment is to facilitate the joining of tables and the ordering of output. This is particularly important for the fact table where multiple indexes are defined, especially on foreign key columns relating to the dimension tables. The benefit of multiple indexes in this environment is improved query performance against the fact table. The indexes defined on the tables could either be single-column or multi-column indexes.

There are also certain issues to be considered when using multiple indexes in the OLAP environment. The first is that multiple indexes will require a certain amount of space, depending on the number of columns in each index and the size of the tables. The second is that there will be a significant one-time cost when building indexes, perhaps during a bulk load.

3.3 Concurrency and Transaction Management

Although concurrency and transaction management are in fact two separate topics, they go hand-in-hand when considered in terms of database programming strategies. DB2 must ensure the integrity of your data and query results by restricting access to table data by applying row and table locks. We will explain how this is done using isolation levels, as well as how transactions actually define when locks will be held.

Most times, when applications must wait for a lock before a query can be executed, this is known as lock-wait. Lock-wait occurs to guarantee accuracy of results, and to maintain the integrity of the underlying data. Thus, in many cases, applications may experience valid periods of lock-wait.

Almost all of the time, applications encounter problems with lock timeouts or deadlock situations. This is either due to inherent problems with how a transaction is defined or misunderstandings about when locks will be acquired and released. Concurrency is managed by DB2 on a connection level, so if you have multiple connections to the same database within an application, they will be considered concurrent applications and compete for database locks.

3.3.1 Unit Of Work

The term "Unit Of Work (UOW)" is synonymous with the concept of a transaction. It is defined as zero or more SQL queries that execute as a single atomic operation. For example, when a customer makes a purchase in the online mall, there are three steps that must be carried out:

- The inventory of the mall must be updated.
- The customer must be charged for the items purchased.
- Each item purchased must be shipped.

What would happen if the inventory was updated and the customer was charged, but a shipping order entry was never created? Not only would you have an angry customer who never received his or her purchase, you would also wreak havoc with your inventory. Thus, all of the SQL queries for the purchase must be defined as an atomic operation. This is done by issuing a COMMIT only after all of the queries have successfully executed, or issuing a ROLLBACK if any of them failed to do so.

Many programming interfaces will also have two types of connections, transactional and nontransactional. Although DB2 supports these concepts, you should be aware that there is really only one type of connection to a DB2 database, and that is a transactional one. Thus, every SQL query will be a part of a transaction. When you are running in a nontransactional mode, however, the programming interface you are using has enabled a feature called autocommit, which issues a COMMIT implicitly after every SQL query. You must ensure that if your UOW has multiple queries, then you do not have autocommit enabled.

3.3.2 Database Locking Strategies and Isolation Levels

DB2 employs locking strategies to ensure that the data in your result set is accurate, and that the integrity of data is not damaged. Locks can be applied to individual rows in a table or to an entire table. How DB2 manages locks depends on the locking-specific settings for each database (set in the database configuration file), and the isolation level used by the application. In general, you should be aware of two basic types of locks that DB2 will apply:

- Share locks.
- Exclusive locks.

In DB2 there are different kinds of share locks and exclusive locks, but as an application developer, being familiar with these two general types should suffice. As implied, a share lock allows other concurrent applications to read the data that has been locked. Multiple concurrent applications can obtain share locks on a table or a row. A share lock is obtained when reading data, except when the cursor being used is updatable. In contrast, an exclusive lock is obtained on rows that have been inserted, updated, or deleted. Row locks can also get escalated to exclusive table locks, depending on lock resource usage.

Be aware that only a single concurrent application can obtain an exclusive lock on a row or table, and this can only occur if there are no existing share locks or an exclusive lock already present. Of course, if an application has an exclusive lock on an entire table, then no one will be able to obtain any locks on that table as the name "exclusive" implies. The same reasoning applies to an exclusive lock obtained on a row. Both share and exclusive locks are released when a `COMMIT` or `ROLLBACK` is issued. The only exception is a `WITH HOLD` cursor, which retains share locks, but releases exclusive locks.

The way locks are obtained when data is read depends on the isolation level of the current transaction. There are four isolation levels employed by DB2, which are summarized in Table 3-1. All of the isolation levels, except for uncommitted read, will only allow you to read data that has been committed. Since uncommitted data will have exclusive locks placed on it, this prevents you from obtaining a share lock to read it. The way uncommitted read gets around this is by not placing any lock on the row being read. Conceptually speaking, you also don't want to read uncommitted data because it is unreliable. For example, it may be rolled back by the application holding the lock, in which case, the changes will be reversed.

Table 3-1   DB2 Isolation Levels

Isolation Level	Description
Uncommitted Read	No locks are acquired when reading data. Data that has not been committed can be read (dirty read), and the result set can change with each execution (nonrepeatable read).
Cursor Stability	Only committed data can be read, and a share lock is obtained for the current cursor position. The result set is not guaranteed to be the same if the query is executed again (unrepeatable read).
Read Stability	A share lock is obtained for all of the rows in a result set and only committed data is read. If the query is executed again, new rows can appear (phantom read), but all of the rows in the previous result set will also be present since the share locks on these rows are not relinquished.
Repeatable Read	A share lock is obtained for all of the rows processed to obtain the result set. Every time the query is executed, you will get the same results just as with the Read Stability isolation level.

Although the Cursor Stability isolation level only places a share lock on the current cursor position, you should be aware that to compile the result set, every row in the result set must have share lock capability. If not, then the query will wait until the exclusive lock is released, or until a lock timeout occurs. A lock timeout is among several common types of problems that can occur if the correct isolation level for a transaction is not used, or if concurrency conflicts result in your UOW. We have described each of these in Table 3-2, and discuss the isolation levels where these problems commonly occur.

One of the most common problems application developers have is waiting for locks. If you have set the `LOCKTIMEOUT` value in the Database Configuration (DB CFG) file, then an application will time out its query after having to wait for the number of seconds that was set. The consequence of this is that the transaction is rolled back, since the statement failed to execute. Here are the best ways to avoid lock timeouts from occurring:

Table 3-2   Common Concurrency Problems

Problem	Description
Lost Update	Commonly occurs with an isolation level of Cursor Stability or lower. Typically, two queries are executed at the same time in two concurrent applications. Each result set has at least one row that was in the result set from the query in the other application. If the first application updates data and commits changes, the second application will not be aware of these changes, and may unknowingly update the same row when it should not. Thus, the update from the first application is lost.
Nonrepeatable Read	This type of problem also occurs with an isolation level of Cursor Stability or lower. If the same query is issued twice in succession, the results may vary since there are no locks on the whole result set to prevent the rows in it from being deleted or updated.
Phantom Read	A phantom read occurs with all isolation levels except Repeatable Read. When a phantom read occurs, additional rows may be present in the result set if the same query is executed multiple times. This occurs because either new rows were inserted that match the query's condition, or rows that previously did not meet its conditions now do so.
Lock Timeout	Lock timeouts can occur on any isolation level above Uncommitted Read. Each database can specify if the application will wait forever for a lock it needs, or if it will time out and return an error after a certain number of seconds of being blocked from obtaining that lock. A common example is when one application has inserted a row into a table but has not committed it, and a second application tries to select that row as part of a result set. The second application must wait until the insert is committed or rolled back by the first application.
Deadlock	A deadlock only occurs if two concurrent applications prevent each other from obtaining required locks. For example, if application 1 has an exclusive lock on row 1, and is waiting for a share lock on row 2, while application 2 has an exclusive lock on row 2 and is waiting for a share lock on row 1, a deadlock has occurred. If DB2 detects a deadlock, one of the transactions is rolled back and an error is returned.

- Define your UOW to be as short as possible.
- Avoid nondatabase processing within a UOW.
- Architect your applications to avoid competing for resources whenever possible.

The first rule follows the principle of committing as often as possible. This is the best way to avoid lock contention. An easy way to accomplish this is to use autocommit whenever you don't need to manage a UOW over multiple statements. Sometimes programmers may also include additional code that will considerably lengthen transaction time. For example, we once tackled a problem where the developer insisted that the transaction only had three statements, and thus should not cause the kind of long-term lock contention that was being observed. We finally determined that the source of the problem was that they were needlessly parsing text documents in between statements, which considerably lengthened their transaction time!

Our third point is something you should always strive for when you develop your applications. Although it may not always be possible to avoid lock contention, you should always seek to minimize it using the first two methods described.

> **TIP** Lock contention can often result when table scans are required to identify the qualifying rows in a query. If there are exclusive locks on any rows, then lock contention can occur. This can be avoided by ensuring that your queries favor the use of indexes in their access plan. This is done by specifying the members of a `WHERE` clause that favor index-only lookup.

3.3.3 Distributed Unit of Work

A transaction can involve more than a single database, in which case, it is considered a Distributed Unit of Work (DUOW). For example, your online mall may consist of multiple databases, where you have your customer and billing data in a separate database from your product inventory. In this case, a purchase would require you to distribute your transaction over both databases.

Most commonly, a Transaction Manager (TM) such as IBM CICS or Microsoft Transaction Server (MTS) coordinates a DUOW. DB2 supports XA-compliant TMs. In the X/Open standard model, DB2 is classified as a Resource Manager (RM). Applications execute queries against DB2 as normal, but database connections and `COMMIT` and `ROLLBACK` requests are handled by a TM. The Application (AP) communicates with the TM using a TM interface such as Syncpoint (SP) or TX, and the TM correspondingly communicates with an RM using the XA interface (see Figure 3-2).

3.4 Stored Procedures

Stored procedures allow you to download your database operations into libraries that are called locally by a DB2 server instance (see Figure 3-3). Thus, there are two pieces to application code that uses a stored procedure. You must write the stored procedure itself, in a supported language (C or Java) or as an SQL stored procedure. In addition, you must write client-side code that will call the stored procedure. Writing a database application that issues a `CALL` statement to run the stored procedure does this. There are several features in DB2 stored procedures that you can benefit from:

- Network transmissions are not required to execute the SQL in a stored procedure, since the stored procedure runs locally on the DB2 server.
- Database processing will occur on the system that houses your DB2 server and alleviates the processing load from client systems.

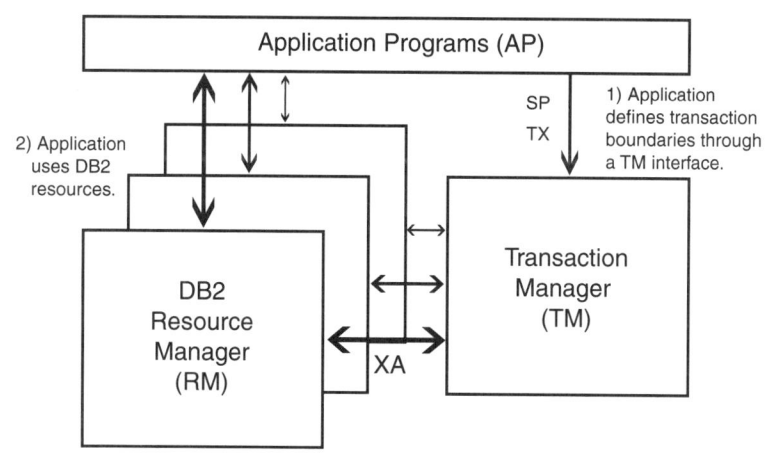

Stored Procedures

Figure 3-2 The TM and RMs exchange transaction information using the X/Open model.

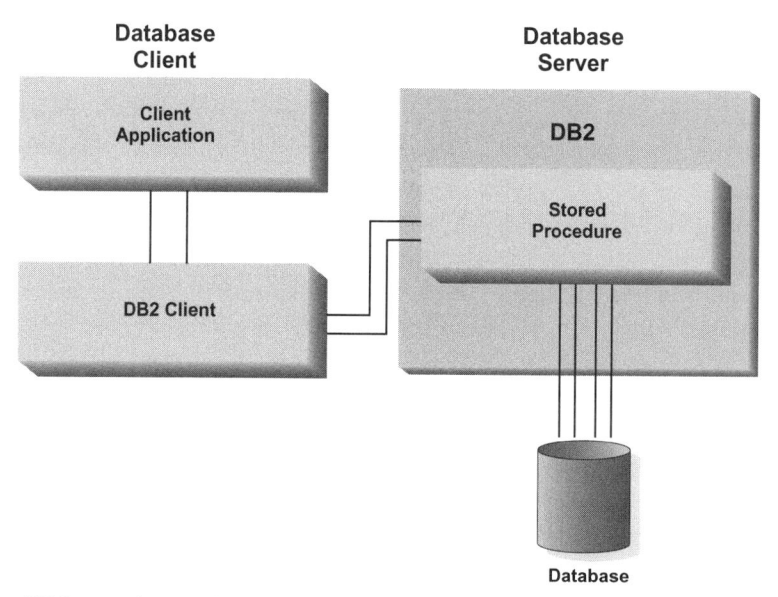

Figure 3-3 DB2 stored procedure.

- Zero or more input and output parameters can be passed into and returned by the stored procedure.
- Zero or more result sets can be returned by a stored procedure to the calling application.

- A calling application from any platform, written in any supported language or interface supported by DB2, can call the stored procedure.
- Database-specific code maintenance is simplified by consolidating it on the DB2 server.
- External stored procedures written in languages such as Java, C, or COBOL can perform other processing (such as reading a file) that you would perform in nondatabase application code.

These are only some of the benefits that you can gain by using stored procedures. DB2 V7.1 now allows you to issue a COMMIT or ROLLBACK from within a stored procedure, which was not previously possible. In addition, as with earlier versions, each DB2 UDB 7.1 instance has a stored procedure cache. Updating the database manager configuration with the setting KEEPDARI ON enables the cache.

As a rule, you should keep this setting off in your development environment when you are making a lot of changes to your code. Once your procedure is stable and you are ready to benchmark it, you should enable KEEPDARI. The reason for this is that once a stored procedure is cached, changes to the stored procedure will not be reflected unless you restart your DB2 instance.

Stored procedures also have certain limitations that you should be aware of:

- Stored procedures cannot create any database connections; they use the connection of the calling program.
- Embedded SQL calling programs cannot retrieve result sets from stored procedures.
- A DUOW cannot be committed or rolled back from within a stored procedure.
- Stored procedures cannot call other stored procedures, except in the case of SQL stored procedures, which can be nested up to 16 levels.

Just as with UDFs, stored procedures can be in FENCED or NOT FENCED mode. A FENCED stored procedure runs within a separate db2dari process. In the case of stored procedures, this is a db2dari process, whereas NOT FENCED ones run within a DB2 agent memory space. Also like FENCED UDFs, stored procedures are normally placed in the sqllib/function directory if they are FENCED, and sqllib/function/unfenced if they are NOT FENCED.

3.4.1 SQL Stored Procedures

You can write stored procedures using SQL; they are called SQL procedures. You can also write stored procedures using languages such as C or Java. You do not have to write client applications in the same language as the stored procedure. When the language of the client application and the stored procedure differ, DB2 transparently passes the values between the client and the stored procedure.

Stored Procedures 47

You can use the DB2 Stored Procedure Builder (SPB) to help develop Java or SQL stored procedures. You can integrate SPB with popular application development tools, including Microsoft Visual Studio and IBM Visual Age for Java, or you can use it as a stand alone utility. To help create your stored procedures, SPB provides design assistants that guide you through basic design patterns, help you create SQL queries, and estimate the performance cost of invoking a stored procedure.

For more information on the DB2 SPB, see the section titled "Stored Procedure Builder" below.

3.4.1.1 Writing SQL Procedures

Like external stored procedure definitions, SQL procedure definitions provide the following information:

- Procedure name.
- Parameter attributes.
- The language in which the procedure is written. For an SQL procedure, the language is SQL.
- Other information about the procedure, such as the specific name of the procedure and the number of result sets returned by the procedure.

Unlike a `CREATE PROCEDURE` statement for an external stored procedure, the `CREATE PROCEDURE` statement for an SQL procedure does not specify the `EXTERNAL` clause. Instead, an SQL procedure has a procedure body, which contains the source statements for the stored procedure.

The following example shows a `CREATE PROCEDURE` statement for a simple stored procedure. The procedure name, list of parameters that are passed to or from the procedure, and the `LANGUAGE` parameter are common to all stored procedures. However, the `LANGUAGE` value of SQL and the `BEGIN...END` block, which forms the procedure body, are particular to an SQL procedure.

```
CREATE PROCEDURE UPDATE_PRODUCT            (1)
(IN PRODUCT_NUMBER INTEGER,                (2)
 IN PRODUCTS_RECEIVED INTEGER)             (2)
LANGUAGE SQL                                       (3)
BEGIN
   UPDATE product                                  (4)
    SET UNITS_IN_STOCK = UNITS_IN_STOCK + PRODUCTS_RECEIVED)
    WHERE PRODUCT_ID = PRODUCT_NUMBER;
END
```

Notes for the previous example:

1. The stored procedure name is UPDATE_PRODUCT.
2. The two parameters have data types of INTEGER. Both are input parameters.
3. LANGUAGE SQL indicates that this is an SQL procedure, so a procedure body follows the other parameters.
4. The procedure body consists of a single SQL UPDATE statement, which updates rows in the product table.

Within the SQL procedure body, you cannot use OUT parameters as values in any expression. You can only assign values to OUT parameters using the assignment statement, or as the target variable in the INTO clause of SELECT, VALUES, and FETCH statements. You cannot use IN parameters as the target of assignment, or INTO clauses.

For a more detailed explanation of SQL stored procedures, see the *DB2 UDB Application Development Guide*.

3.4.2 DB2 Stored Procedure Builder

The DB2 SPB is a Java-based Graphical User Interface (GUI) application used to assist developers in writing, building, and testing stored procedures. It supports rapid development by providing creation wizards and an SQL Assistant, and automating frequently performed tasks. It is installed as an optional component of the DB2 Application Development Client on AIX, Solaris, and Windows.

Both local and remote DB2 databases can be used with the DB2 SPB. It can be used to build stored procedures for the entire DB2 product family, including OS/390, OS/400, AIX, HP-UX, Linux, Solaris, and Windows. Table 3-3 outlines the supported stored procedure types that can be built from the DB2 SPB for each platform.

Note
The DB2 SPB can run stored procedures written in any language. However, you cannot view the source code or modify these procedures unless they are written in Java or the SQL procedure language.

Table 3-3 DB2 SPB Supported Procedure Types

Stored Procedure Type	Supported Platforms
SQL Stored Procedures	OS/2, OS/390, OS/400, AIX, HP-UX, Linux, Solaris, and Windows
SQLj Stored Procedures	OS/2, OS/390, AIX, Linux, Solaris, and Windows
JDBC Stored Procedures	OS/2, OS/390, AIX, Linux, Solaris, and Windows

Stored Procedures

Some stored procedure types require additional software to be installed. For SQL procedures, a C compiler must be installed on the server. In addition, the Application Development Kit must be installed on the server so that SQL-related include files can be located during C compilation. DB2 SPB requires the JDK to be installed on the client to run, as well as to build Java stored procedures. The JDK must be 1.1.7 or higher for Java stored procedures in Version 7.

3.4.2.1 Launching Stored Procedure Builder

On all supported platforms, the DB2 SPB can be started using either the `db2spb` command or from the DB2 Control Center. On Windows platforms, the DB2 SPB can also be started using the Windows' Start menu or from any of the following application development environments:

- Microsoft Visual C++ 5.0 and 6.0
- Microsoft Visual Basic 5.0 and 6.0
- IBM VisualAge for Java 3.x

3.4.2.2 Creating a Project

The first step when starting the DB2 SPB is to create a project. Figure 3-4 shows the DB2 SPB project dialog. You can either create a new project or open an existing project. If you are creating a new project, you must supply a project name, path, and database alias. Additional databases can be added to the project after the project is created. A user ID and password are required to connect to the database. If the database is local, or you are using client authentication, you can click the check box to use your current user ID and password.

3.4.2.3 Development Environment Interface

The DB2 SPB development environment interface uses a three-pane layout. Figure 3-5 shows the DB2 SPB development environment window. The top left pane displays a tree view containing the project name, database aliases, and stored procedures. The top right pane is the main window. It displays information on the object you are currently selecting in the tree view. The bottom pane is used to display output. There is a tab button to toggle between the stored procedure results and informational messages generated when building and registering the stored procedure.

3.4.2.4 Creating Java Stored Procedures

New stored procedures can be added to a project by right-clicking on the stored procedure folder or by clicking on the appropriate icon in the toolbar. JDBC and SQLj stored procedures share the same Java stored procedures creation wizard. When creating a Java stored procedure, you will have the option of creating new code or using existing code from a Java class. The wizard prompts the user through the creation steps. Given the user input, the wizard will generate starter code that can be later edited and customized.

The first screen when starting the Java stored procedure creation wizard outlines the five steps to creating a Java stored procedure. (Figure 3-6 shows the first Java stored procedure creation wizard dialog window.) The five steps are:

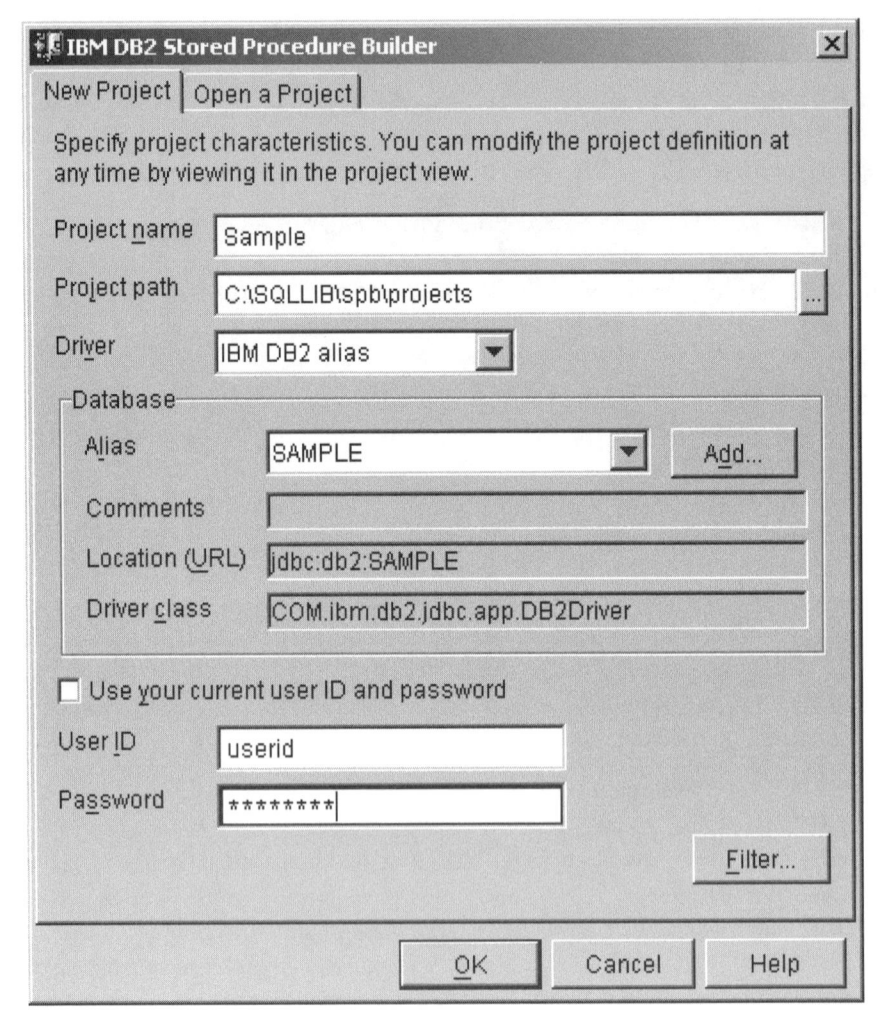

Figure 3-4 Creating a DB2 SPB project dialog.

1. Selecting a stored procedure name.
2. Selecting a pattern for generating starter code.
3. Creating an SQL statement.
4. Selecting input and output parameters.
5. Selecting build and packaging options.

The second step is to choose a stored procedure pattern. The pattern selected determines the style of the starter code generated by the Java stored procedure creation wizard. Figure 3-7 shows Step 2 of the Java stored procedure creation wizard. There are three patterns for SQL statements. The options include one SQL statement, more than one SQL statement, or no SQL

Stored Procedures

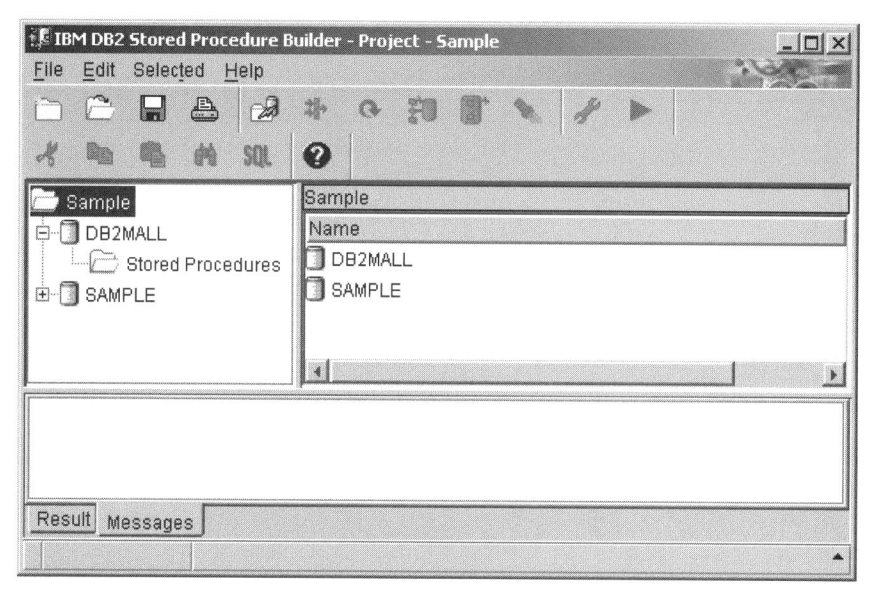

Figure 3-5 DB2 SPB development environment.

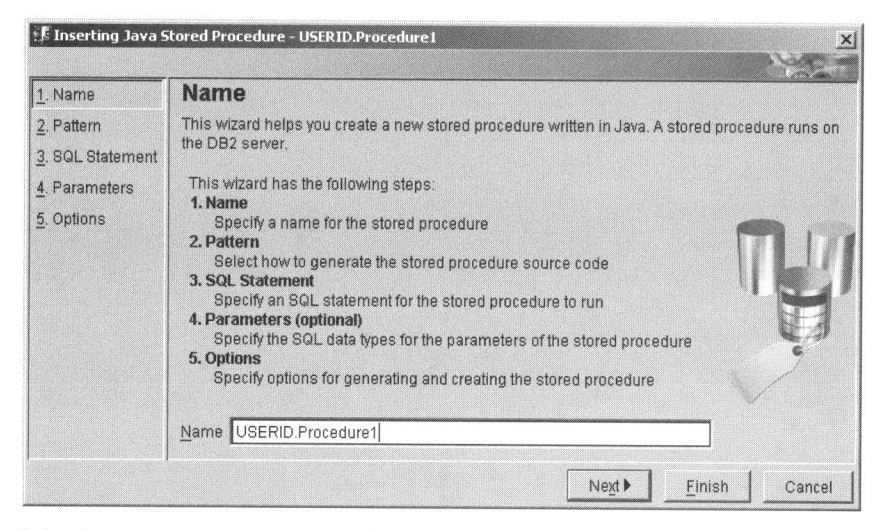

Figure 3-6 Java stored procedure creation wizard—Step 1.

statements. The stored procedure has the option of returning a query result set or output parameters. Error messages can either be handled as Java exceptions or returned through output parameters.

The next step is to create an SQL statement. This can be done manually by entering the query into the text area box or by clicking the *SQL Assist...* button. This button launches a Java

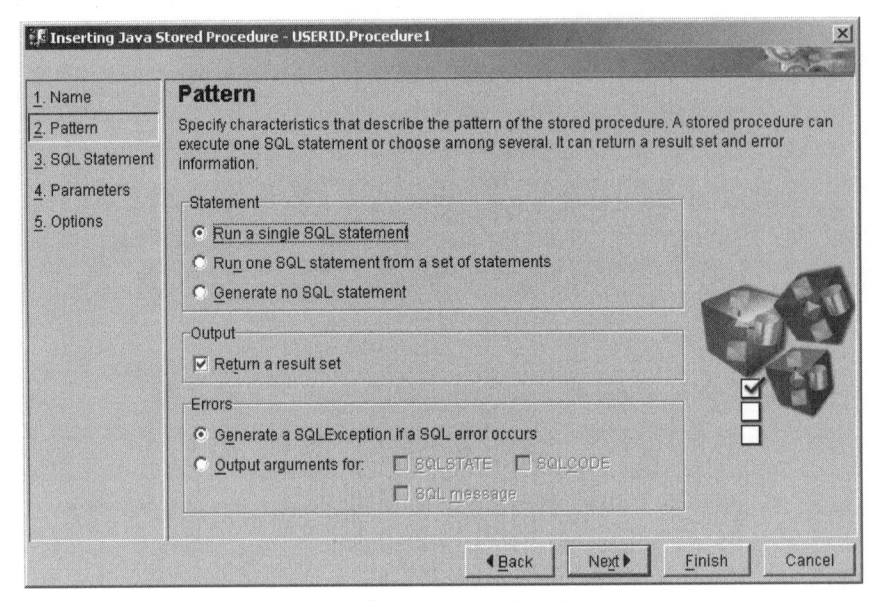

Figure 3-7 Java stored procedure creation wizard—Step 2.

application called SQL Assistant. The SQL Assistant is useful for people who are not familiar with SQL. It can be used to generate simple SQL statements by selecting options from a wizard. When complete, the SQL statement will automatically be copied back into the Java stored procedure creation wizard. Figure 3-8 shows the Java stored procedure creation wizard SQL statement dialog window.

The fourth step is to select the input and output parameters accepted by the stored procedure. These parameters can be used as host variables or parameter marker values for SQL statements. Parameters are added by clicking the *Add...* button. The parameter mode can be defined as IN, OUT, or INOUT. The parameter must also be given a name, Java data type, and SQL data

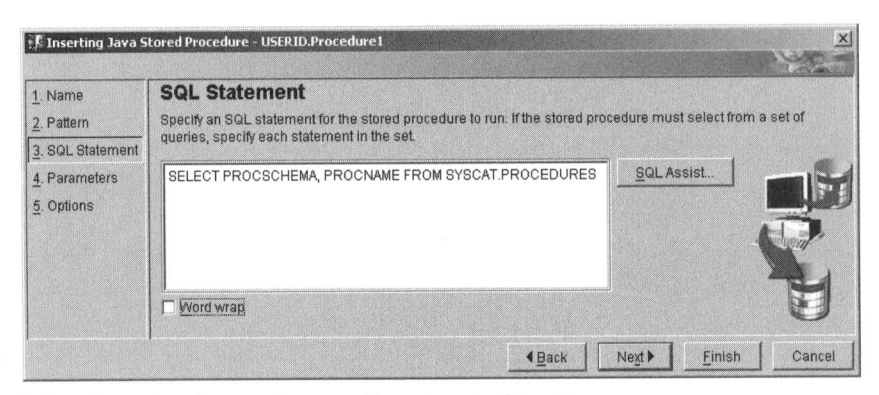

Figure 3-8 Java stored procedure creation wizard—Step 3.

Stored Procedures

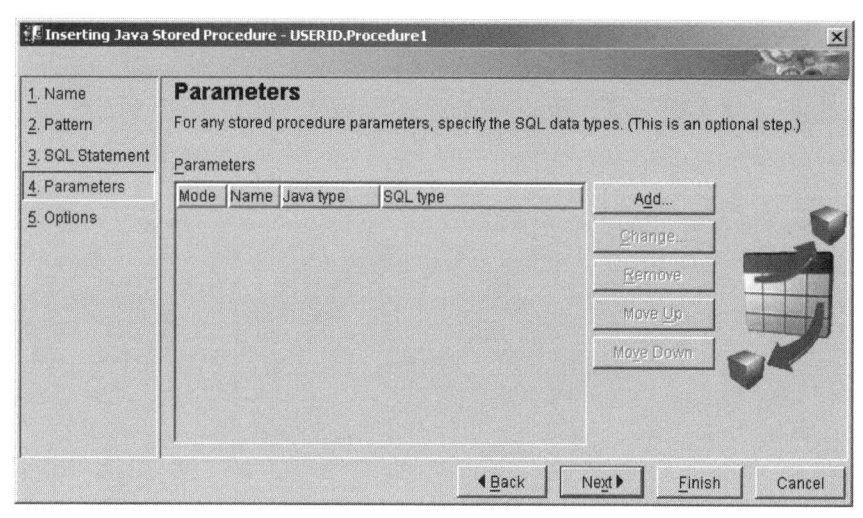

Figure 3-9 Java stored procedure creation wizard—Step 4.

type. Figure 3-9 shows the parameter dialog windows for the Java stored procedure creation wizard.

The final step is to select packaging and building options. Java stored procedures created by the DB2 SPB are packaged in Jar files. The DB2 SPB allows modification of a unique Jar file ID. The stored procedure class can also be given a Java package name. The starter code can either be generated in SQLj or JDBC. By default, on completion of the wizard, the starter code will be built by the appropriate compiler. If you do not want the code to be built, click the "*Generate only*" radio button to disable this feature. Figure 3-10 shows the options dialog window for the Java stored procedure creation wizard.

3.4.2.5 Creating SQL Stored Procedures

Similar to Java stored procedures, SQL stored procedures can be added to a project by right-clicking on the stored procedure folder or by clicking on the appropriate icon in the toolbar. When creating an SQL stored procedure, you will have the option of creating an SQL stored procedure manually, from a file, or using the SQL stored procedure wizard. The wizard prompts the user through the creation steps.

The SQL stored procedure creation wizard dialog windows are very similar to the ones used by the Java stored procedure creation wizard. Most steps are identical except for Step 4, selecting input and output parameters, and Step 5, selecting build and packing options. Since SQL stored procedures do not use Java, the Java type and SQL type fields are replaced with a new field called *Type* inside the parameter dialog. In addition, the Jar ID and Java package name, previously seen in the options dialog, are no longer applicable.

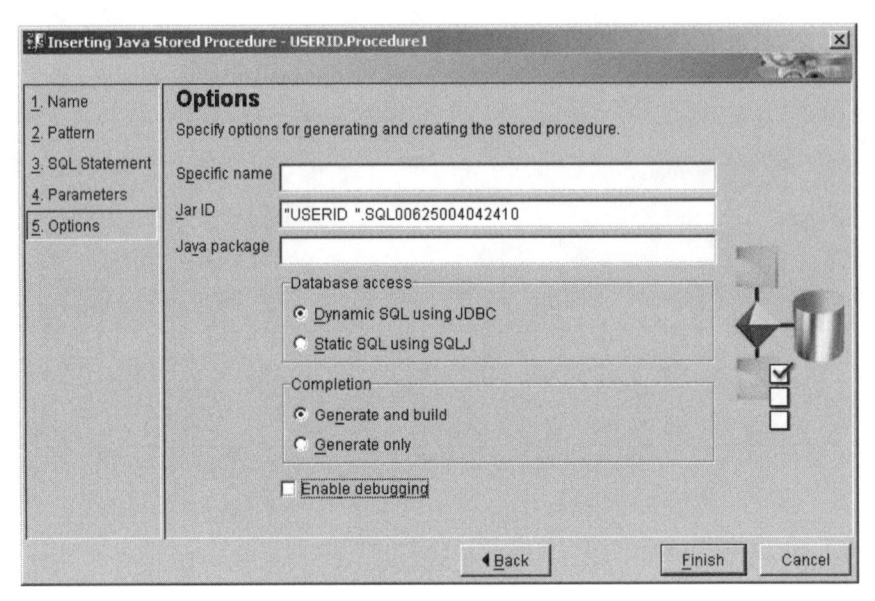

Figure 3-10 Java stored procedure creation wizard—Final Step.

3.4.2.6 Calling Stored Procedures

Stored procedures can be executed from the DB2 SPB by clicking the *Play* button icon or by right-clicking the stored procedure name in the tree view and selecting *Run*. If the stored procedure is expecting input parameters, the DB2 SPB will prompt you for the required input data. Once the input parameters have been supplied values, the stored procedure will execute and display the results in the output pane under the *Result* tab. Figure 3-11 shows a sample of a stored procedure being called from the DB2 SPB.

3.5 Database Packages and Query Performance

We would like to impart upon you a fundamental understanding about how all applications communicate with DB2, and this involves a short discussion of how packages are bound in embedded SQL. The popularity of embedded SQL on the Intel and UNIX platforms has decreased with the emergence of more portable programming interfaces. However, embedded SQL in COBOL is the prevalent database programming method for host systems such as DB2/390, and there are still many legacy applications on common server platforms as well. In addition, embedded SQL forms the foundation for DB2 UDB programming, since even driver-based interfaces use embedded SQL source modules at the base level.

The reason for this is best understood by returning to our discussion about the database objects known as packages, which were introduced in the first chapter. We explained that packages store the compiled set of instructions that constitute the access plan chosen by the DB2 optimizer. However, this is not the complete picture. Only *statically bound* statements in source modules contain an access plan. By the term *"statically bound,"* we mean that the SQL state-

Database Packages and Query Performance 55

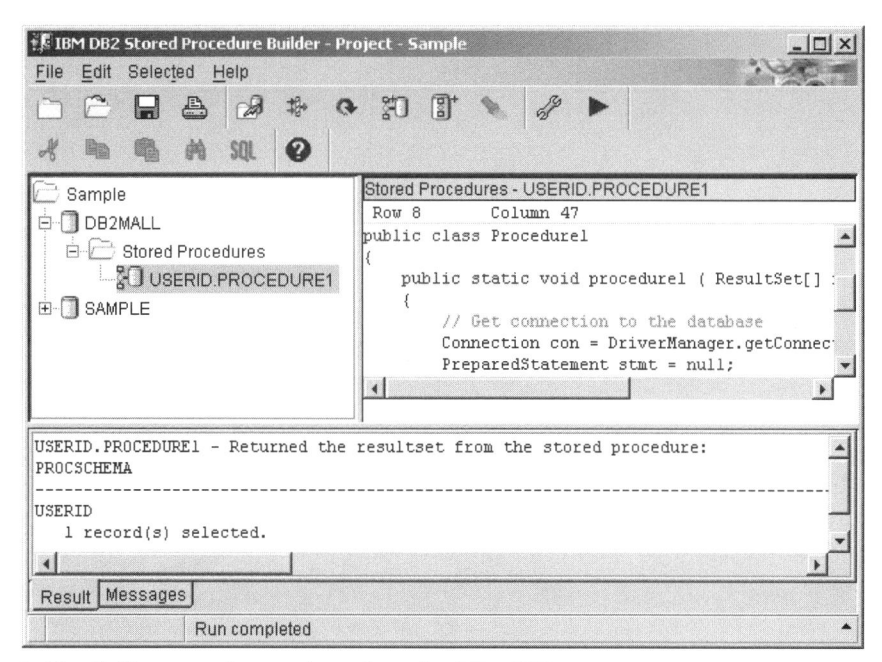

Figure 3-11 Calling stored procedures from the DB2 SPB.

ment is known prior to runtime and is directly embedded into the application. Furthermore, this embedded statement has a one-to-one correspondence with a package section containing an access plan in the system catalog tables.

This is different from the dynamically bound statement life cycle that we explored. Dynamically bound statements first undergo a PREPARE operation to generate the query access plan. Each PREPARE operation references a package section within the system catalog tables, just like statically bound statements. However, these package sections are empty, since the statement's access plan is dynamically generated at runtime and is never stored on disk. This is why a dynamic (runtime) SQL interface such as the DB2 CLI/ODBC driver has packages that must be bound against each database being accessed. The developers who wrote the DB2 CLI/ODBC driver integrated their own dynamic SQL source modules into the DB2 CLI driver library. These modules are referenced every time an application executes a statement using the driver.

One might ask then, why do dynamically bound statements have a package at all? The reason for this is because of how DB2 caches statements to improve performance. Each database within an instance has a *package cache*, which is referenced using the package and section ID. This requires a source module for every dynamic SQL application since only source modules can be used to produce a bound package. This is not necessarily the easiest method to handle dynamic statements; however, this design predates DB2 UDB and goes back to the earliest versions of the DB2 product, when interfaces such as ODBC were in their infancy.

If you are developing your applications with a dynamic SQL interface, consider adding static SQL to your code as well. For many programming languages, you have the option of mixing your dynamic SQL code with static SQL for specific queries. Although this may seem like an additional maintenance headache, you will see major performance improvements using this strategy.

3.6 Summary

This chapter overviewed many features about DB2 that an application programmer should be aware of. When designing an application to access a database, the more a programmer understands about the environment that they are using, the better off they will be in designing an application that executes efficiently and with the best possible performance. To this end, DB2 offers many advanced features such as stored procedures, summary tables, and common tables. The programmer must also be aware of how they affect the database. So, understanding compound SQL and how transactions and locking work are crucial to avoid unnecessary resource conflicts or even deadlocks within the database system.

This chapter also covered some programming tools and techniques available to the developer, such as the SPB and SQL stored procedures. Unfortunately, it is out of the scope of this book to cover these in more detail, but take some time to explore their usefulness. The SPB primarily uses Java, and is used to write stored procedures. Java is covered in detail in Chapter 7.

CHAPTER 4

Embedded SQL Programming

Embedded SQL programming was introduced in a previous chapter in this book. While many of the alternatives to embedded SQL programming offer faster and easier ways to develop applications, it is nevertheless useful to understand and know how to program using embedded SQL. Static statements offer great performance benefits, and are only possible through embedded SQL. If you are migrating applications from mainframes like S/390 or using COBOL, you may prefer embedded SQL. Although this chapter deals mainly with embedded SQL programming, it introduces some fundamental concepts like cursors, Type 2 connects, and so on, which you may need to incorporate in your application even if you are not using embedded SQL.

In a static embedded SQL application, data is exchanged between DB2 UDB and the application using host variables. These variables are defined in the native programming language such as C, COBOL, FORTRAN, and Java. You will become familiar with the proper declaration and usage of host variables in this chapter.

A precompiler for each of these programming languages is provided with the DB2 Application Development Client. The precompiler is used to convert embedded SQL statements into a series of API (Application Programming Interface) requests (as was discussed in the previous chapter).

Data is stored in DB2 UDB databases as tables, or sets of records. An unordered set is retrieved from the database using the `SELECT` statement. The output of the `SELECT` statement is known as the result set, or result table. The result set is examined using cursors. You will learn how to declare cursors and use them to read, update, and delete a single record at a time in this chapter.

When the SQL statement or the database objects it accesses are not known until runtime, applications are developed using dynamic SQL. In this chapter, you will find out what is involved in coding dynamic statements using embedded SQL.

4.1 Embedded SQL Overview

Figure 4-1 illustrates the steps involved in building an embedded SQL application. These are as follows:

1. Create source files that contain programs with embedded SQL statements.
2. Connect to a database, then precompile each source file.
3. The precompiler converts the SQL statements in each source file into DB2 UDB runtime API calls to the database manager. The precompiler also produces an access package in the database, and optionally a bind file, if you specify that you want one created. We will discuss packages and bind files in the following sections.
4. Compile the modified source files (and other files without SQL statements) using the host language compiler.
5. Link the object files with the DB2 UDB and host language libraries to produce an executable program.
6. Bind the bind file to create the access package if this was not already done at precompile time, or if a different database is going to be accessed.
7. Run the application. The application accesses the database using the access plan in the package.

4.1.1 Creating Packages

A *package* is a database object that contains optimized SQL statements. A package corresponds to a single-source programming module, and *sections* correspond to the SQL statements contained in the source program module.

A programming module that contains embedded static SQL statements requires precompiling, during which time the precompiler generates a package (by default). This package contains sections that correspond to embedded SQL statements. A section is the compiled form of an SQL statement. While every section corresponds to one statement, every statement does not necessarily have a section. An optimized *access plan* will be stored in the section. The package can be stored directly in the database, or the data needed to create the package can be stored in a bind file. Creating a bind file and binding it in a separate step is known as *deferred binding*.

A program module that contains embedded dynamic SQL statements has an associated package and sections, but in this case, the sections are used as placeholders for the SQL statement that will be dynamically prepared. There are no access plans stored in the sections because they are in embedded static SQL modules.

Like views and tables, packages have an associated schema name. The fully qualified name of a package is SCHEMA-NAME.PACKAGE-NAME.

In most cases, application developers use deferred binding. Deferred binding requires a two-step process:

Embedded SQL Overview

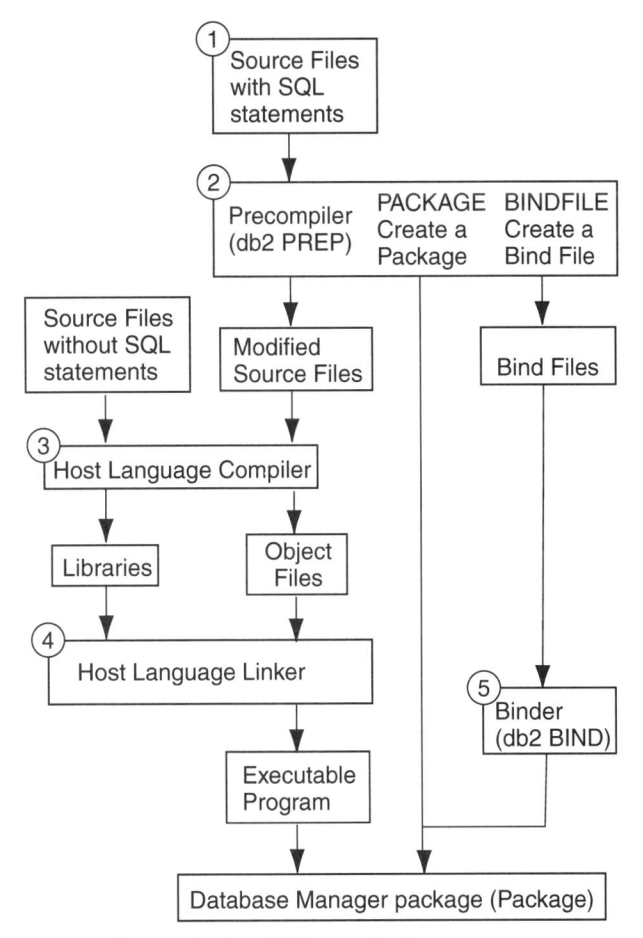

Figure 4-1 Process for creating embedded SQL applications.

- Creating a bind file (which contains information to create a package).
- Binding the package bind file to the database.

Let's examine these steps. First, we need to create a bind file. The bind file is generated by the precompiler when the appropriate option is specified. The precompiler can be invoked with the PREP or PRECOMPILE command using the Command Center or Command Line Processor (CLP).

The precompiler input is always a source programming module with embedded SQL statements. Each DB2 UDB supported programming language has its own precompiler provided with the DB2 Software Developer's Kit. The file extension of the source program module is used to determine which precompiler (for example, C, C++, COBOL, or FORTRAN) will be invoked.

In Table 4-1, the input host language source file extensions and modified source file output extensions are provided. The examples in this book are written in C. Therefore, the embedded SQL program files are named `program-name.sqc` and the precompiler output files are named `program-name.c`. The name of the source module is important because the precompiler will use this as the name of the package unless otherwise specified.

Table 4-1 Precompile File Extensions

Host Language	File Extension (input - source)	File Extension (output - modified source)
C	.sqc	.c
C++ (case-sensitive - AIX)	.sqc	.C
C++ (case-insensitive - OS/2, Windows)	.sqx	.cxx
COBOL -use TARGET and/or OUTPUT options to use other extensions	.sqb	.cbl
FORTRAN (UNIX)	.sqf	.f
FORTRAN (OS/2, Windows)	.sqf	.for

If you issue the following DB2 UDB commands/statements, then you would create an application package called `USERID.SAMPLE1` in the `DB2MALL` database. This package would contain a lot of information about the embedded SQL statements, apart from the host variable values required to execute the embedded SQL statements that are contained in the file `sample1.sqc`.

```
CONNECT TO DB2MALL USER USERID USING PASSWORD
PRECOMPILE sample1.sqc
CONNECT RESET
```

There are additional steps required before you have an executable application. All database objects specifically referenced (tables, views, and so on) must exist during the precompile phase because in this example, deferred binding is not being used. The other inconvenient aspect of not creating a separate bind file is that the entire database would need to be provided, along with the application to the end-user, since the package only exists in the database. The data needed to create the package is not contained in a separate bind file in this example.

Let's look at an example of deferred binding with the DB2 UDB commands/statements:

```
CONNECT TO DB2MALL USER USERID USING PASSWORD
PRECOMPILE sample1.sqc BINDFILE
CONNECT RESET
```

This example demonstrates the use of the precompiler option `BINDFILE`. This option is used to generate an output file, which contains all of the data needed to create the package for the source module. By using this option, this data is stored in a file called `sample1.bnd`. You

Embedded SQL Overview

can change the name of the output bind file, but in this example, we did not rename the bind file. To avoid confusion between source program modules, bind files, and package names, try to avoid renaming any of these objects. To create the package using a different name, use the option `PACKAGE USING <PACKAGE-NAME>`. To create the package using a different schema name, use the option `COLLECTION <SCHEMA-NAME>`.

The name of the package is determined when the `sample1.bnd` file is bound to the database. If the same user were to bind this package, the name of the package would be `DB2MALL.SAMPLE`. If the database objects do not exist during precompile, only warnings will be generated, and the bind file will be created. (Object existence and authentication SQL codes are treated as warnings instead of errors.) The `BIND` command verifies the existence and access privileges of database objects and will only be successful once the required objects are present.

> **Note**
>
> Database objects referenced in embedded static SQL programs must exist in the database during package creation (PRECOMPILE without BINDFILE option or BIND).

For each source program module containing embedded static SQL statements, a corresponding package must exist in the database. Let's assume that we are creating an application which accesses two different DB2 UDB databases. The objects referenced in the application must exist in the database for the package to be created successfully. Therefore, we will develop the application using two different program modules. Each program module or source file represents a database package. If we keep the SQL statements for each database in separate packages, the bind will be successful. We can then compile and link the program modules together into a single executable.

Any `PRECOMPILE` error messages will be reported to the display or to a message file. The error message file can be specified using the `MESSAGES` option when issuing the `PRECOMPILE` command. It is recommended to send the messages to an output file so you can examine the file to determine the cause of the errors. Errors during precompile could include invalid host variable definitions and incorrect SQL statements.

When precompiling, you can also determine whether the SQL embedded in the program conforms to different syntaxes and standards. For example, you can check to see if the application works against DB2 for OS/390, or is ISO/ANS SQL92-compliant. This is done using the `LANGLEVEL`, `SQLFLAG`, and `SQLRULES` options when precompiling the program.

It is important to remember that an embedded dynamic SQL programming module does have associated packages, but it does not contain access plans or executable sections. For example, suppose an SQL program contains four static SQL statements and two dynamic SQL statements in a single source module. There would be four SQL sections (each with an access plan) created and stored in the database within a single package.

4.1.2 Binding Applications

The most common method of binding in application development is deferred binding. When deferred binding is used, the information about the SQL statements is stored in the bind file created by the precompile process. This bind file must be bound against the database to create a package. Once the package exists in the database, there is no longer any need to bind the application.

The SQL statements from the bind file are examined during the bind process, and the current database statistics are used to determine the best method of data access. At this point, an access plan is chosen by the DB2 UDB optimizer. This access plan is then stored in the database system catalog tables. An access plan is only created for static embedded SQL statements. Embedded dynamic SQL statements have a package and a section number assigned, but there is no access plan created until the statement is executed.

The bind process needs to be performed following each successful precompile of the application source modules. When the bind file is created, a timestamp is stored in the package. The timestamp is sometimes referred to as a *consistency token*. This same timestamp is also stored in the database when the bind is completed and is used to ensure that the resulting application executes the proper SQL statement.

The modified source module (output from the precompile) will attempt to execute SQL statements by package name and section number. If the required package and section are not found, the following message will be returned:

```
SQL0805N Package "pkgschema.pkgname" was not found.
SQLSTATE=51002
```

If the required package and section exist in the database system catalogs, the timestamp is then checked. If the timestamp in the application executable does not match the timestamp stored in the system catalog tables in the database, the following message is returned:

```
SQL0818N A timestamp conflict occurred.
SQLSTATE=51003
```

4.1.2.1   Authorization Considerations for Static SQL

If the package does not yet exist in the database, the user who issues the BIND must have BINDADD authority for the database or be a member of a group which has this authority. The user must also have one of these privileges: IMPLICIT_SCHEMA on the database (if the schema name of the package does not exist) or CREATEIN on the schema (if the schema name already exists). The person who binds the package by default becomes the package owner, unless the OWNER keyword is specified during the BIND. In addition, since static statements execute with privileges of the package owner authorization ID, that userid must also have the proper privileges for all of the referenced objects in the SQL statements referenced in the bind file information. These privileges must be explicitly granted to the user binding the packages, or to PUBLIC. If the privileges are granted to a group of which the user is a member, but not granted explicitly to the user, the bind will fail.

Embedded SQL Overview 63

Unqualified database objects in embedded static SQL programs are by default qualified with the userid of the package owner. Alternatively, you may specify the QUALIFER keyword during the BIND to indicate the qualifier name for unqualified objects in static SQL statements. Table 4-2 summarizes the behavioral characteristics of static SQL with respect to the authorization ID used for statements and the qualifier for unqualified database objects, depending on whether or not the OWNER and QUALIFIER options are used during the BIND.

Table 4-2 Static SQL—Authorization and Qualifier Summary

BIND keyword	Authorization ID	Qualification Value for Unqualified Objects
OWNER and QUALIFIER NOT specified	ID of the user binding the package	ID of the user binding the package
OWNER specified	ID of the user specified in OWNER bind option	ID of the user specified in OWNER bind option
QUALIFIER specified	ID of the user binding the package	ID of the user specified in the QUALIFIER bind option
OWNER and QUALIFIER specified	ID of the user specified in OWNER bind option	ID of the user specified in the QUALIFIER bind option

Once the package exists in the database, any person with EXECUTE privilege on the package can issue any of the SQL statements contained in the package, even if the individual does not have explicit privilege on the database object. This is a feature of embedded static SQL program modules. It allows end-users access to a portion of data contained in a table without defining a view or column-level privileges.

4.1.2.2 Authorization Considerations for Dynamic SQL

Unlike static SQL, dynamically prepared statements can be made to execute under the authorization ID of either the user that binds the package (the package owner) or the user who executes the application, depending on which option is used for the DYNAMICRULES keyword during the bind.

Under DYNAMICRULES RUN (the default), the person who runs a dynamic SQL application must have the privileges necessary to issue each SQL statement (it specifies that the authorization ID of the user executing the package is to be used), as well as the EXECUTE privilege on the package. The privileges may be granted to the user's authorization ID, to any group of which the user is a member, or to PUBLIC. With DYNAMICRULES RUN, the person binding the application only needs BINDADD authority on the database, if the program contains no static SQL.

When using the DYNAMICRULES BIND option, the authorizations and privileges required are similar to static SQL. That is, the user that binds a dynamic SQL application (the authorization ID of the package owner) must have BINDADD authority as well as the privileges necessary to perform all the dynamic and static SQL statements in the application. The user that runs the application inherits the privileges associated with the package owner authorization ID, and therefore only needs the EXECUTE privilege on the package.

> **Note**
>
> If you bind packages with DYNAMICRULES BIND, and have SYSADM or DBADM authority or any authorities that the user of the package should not receive, consider explicitly specifying OWNER to designate a different authorization ID. This prevents the package from automatically inheriting SYSADM, DBADM, or other unnecessary privileges on dynamic SQL statements from the userid that binds the application.

The authorization ID privileges and qualifier values used for the DYNAMICRULES RUN and BIND options are summarized in Table 4-3.

Table 4-3 Dynamic SQL—Authorization and Qualifier Summary

DYNAMICRULES option	Authorization ID	Qualification Value for Unqualified Objects
RUN (default)	ID of user executing package	Owner's authorization ID, whether or not the owner is explicitly specified. It can be superseded by the CURRENT SCHEMA special register.
BIND	Implicit or explicit value of OWNER bind option	Implicit or explicit value of the QUALIFIER bind option.

4.1.2.3 Examining Packages and Timestamps

We have briefly discussed packages and timestamps. Let's examine how we can verify that the bind file and packages in the database match. When the BIND command is successful, a single entry in the system catalog view, SYSCAT.PACKAGES, is created. There are a number of columns defined for this table. We will not go into a complete explanation here, but let's look at the timestamp column. The timestamp associated with a package is actually stored in the column named UNIQUE_ID. If you were to successfully issue the command:

    BIND db2look.bnd MESSAGES msg1.out

then the SYSCAT.PACKAGES view would have a new entry for this bind file with the package name DB2LOOK and the package schema as your authorization user ID. Any error or warning messages would be written to the file called msg1.out. To examine the timestamp contained in the db2look.bnd file, there is a utility provided with DB2 UDB called db2bfd.

To display the contents of a bind file, issue the following from the CLP:

    db2bfd -b BIND c:\programs files\sqllib\bnd\db2look.bnd

Here is the output of the above command:

Embedded SQL Overview

```
c:\progra~1\sqllib\bnd\db2look.bnd:  Header Contents

Element name       Description                Value
------------       -------------------------  ------------------
bind_id            Bind file identifier       :BINDV710:
headerl            Bind file header length    :4032:
relno              Bind file release number   :0x700:
application        Access package name        :DB2LOOK :
timestamp          Access package timestamp   :eBBsBdEQ: 2000/04/29 01:44:01:92
creator            Bind file creator          :NULLID  :
endian             Bit representation         :L: Little Endian (Intel)
sqlda_doubled      Indicates if SQLDA doubled :1:
insert             DB2/PE buffered inserts    :0:
max_sect           Highest section number used :62:
num_hostvars       Number of host variables   :296:
num_stmt           Number of SQL statements   :310:
statements         Offset of SQL statements   :4032:
declarel           Size of data declarations  :10370:
declare            Offset of data declarations :69548:
prep_id            Userid that created bindfile:NULLID  :
date_value         Date/Time format           :0: Default (Default)
stds_value         Standards Compliance Level :0: SAA (Default)
isol_value         Isolation option           :2: Uncommitted Read (Defined)
blck_value         Record blocking option     :1: Block All (Defined)
sqler_value        SQLERROR option            :0: (Defined)
level_value        Level option               : : (Defined)
colid_value        Collection ID option       : : (Defined)
vrsn_value         Version option             : : (Default)
owner_value        Package owner option       : : (Default)
qual_value         Default Qualifier option   : : (Default)
text_value         Text option                : : (Default)
vldte_value        Validate option            :1: (Default)
expln_value        Explain option             :0: (Default)
actn_value         Action option              :1: (Default)
rver_value         REPLVER option             : : (Default)
retn_value         Retain option              :1: (Default)
rlse_value         Release option             :0: (Default)
dgr_value          Degree of I/O parallelism  :1: (Default)
str_value          String delimiter option    :0: (Default)
decd_value         Decimal delimiter option   :0: (Default)
csub_value         Character subtype option   :0: (Default)
ccsids_value       Single byte CCSID option   :0: (Default)
ccsidm_value       Mixed byte CCSID option    :0: (Default)
ccsidg_value       Double byte CCSID option   :0: (Default)
decprc_value       Decimal precision option   :0: (Default)
dynrul_value       Dynamic rules option       :0: (Default)
insert_value       DB2/PE buffered inserts    :0: (Default)
explsnap_value     Explain snapshot           :0: (Default)
funcpath_value     UDF function path          : : (Default)
sqlwarn_value      SQL warnings               :1: (Default)
queryopt_value     Query optimization         :5: (Default)
cnulreqd_value     C Null required option     :1: (Default)
generic_value      Generic option             : : (Default)
```

```
defprep_value     Deferred prepare option    :2: (Default)
trfgrp_value      Transform group option     : : (Default)
federated_value   Federated server option    :0: (Default)
```

Note that the timestamp is encoded as `eBBsBdEQ` and the decoded timestamp is also shown. This timestamp is the exact time when the `PRECOMPILE` command was used to generate the bind file.

To confirm that this bind file (`db2look.bnd`) has been bound to the database, issue this SQL statement once connected to the database:

```
SELECT PKGSCHEMA, PKGNAME, UNIQUE_ID
    FROM SYSCAT.PACKAGES
    WHERE PKGNAME = 'DB2LOOK'
```

The output of this SQL statement should contain a single-row result with a `UNIQUE_ID` matching the bind file, as shown here:

```
PKGSCHEMA         PKGNAME         UNIQUE_ID
--------          -------         ---------
nullid            dB2LOOK         eBBsBdEQ
```

The `UNIQUE_ID` contained in the bind file matches this value. Therefore, you know that this bind file has been successfully bound to the database.

4.1.3 Binding Utilities

The CLP is a dynamic SQL application that is provided with DB2 UDB. The packages associated with the utilities, like the DB2 CLP, are included in the `sqllib` directory, in the `bnd` subdirectory.

The bind files associated with the DB2 CLP and utilities are found in a list file called `db2ubind.lst`. Specifically, the bind files associated with the DB2 CLP are: `db2clpcs.bnd`, `db2clprr.bnd`, `db2clpur.bnd`, `db2clprs.bnd`, and `db2clpnc.bnd`.

> **Note**
>
> Each CLP bind file is created with different isolation levels. This allows a user the ability to change the isolation level when using the CLP utility, using the `CHANGE ISOLATION LEVEL` command.

These bind files must have been bound to the database you wish to access using the DB2 Command Center, the DB2 CLP, or the Client Configuration Assistant (CCA).

> **Note**
>
> To bind the DB2 UDB utilities (for example, CLP, IMPORT, EXPORT), issue the command: `BIND @db2ubind.lst BLOCKING ALL SQLERROR CONTINUE`.

To bind a number of packages using a single `BIND` command, add the `@` character in front of the source file. When this character is encountered, DB2 UDB will assume that the file contains a list of bind files and not a bind file itself.

4.1.4 Blocking

Record blocking is a feature of DB2 UDB which reduces data access time across networks when an application is retrieving a large amount of data. Record blocking is based on cursor type and the amount of storage allocated on the DB2 UDB server to perform record blocking. Cursors are used in applications to manipulate multirow result sets from a DB2 UDB server.

The DBM configuration parameter known as `ASLHEAPSZ` specifies the amount of memory used to buffer data on the server for applications requesting multiple data records. For applications executing on remote clients, the buffer is specified by the DBM configuration parameter `RQRIOBLK`.

You can think of record blocking as data retrieval caching. Record blocking options are described in Table 4-4. Usually, you would specify `BLOCKING ALL` for applications that perform many queries. An *ambiguous cursor* is a cursor that has been defined without any reference to its intended usage in an SQL statement. As we will see, all cursors are defined using a `SELECT` statement. They are used in a `SELECT`, `DELETE`, or `UPDATE` statement.

The default blocking option for static embedded applications is `BLOCKING UNAMBIG`. The default blocking option for CLI applications and the CLP is `BLOCKING ALL`.

Table 4-4 Record Blocking Options

BLOCKING <option>	Record Blocking Behavior
UNAMBIG	All cursors except those specified as `FOR UPDATE` are blocked.
ALL	Ambiguous cursors are blocked.
NO	No cursors are blocked.

Record blocking affects the way you, as an application developer, declare your cursors within your application. The more specific you are with your cursor declarations, the more likely DB2 UDB will use record blocking appropriately. If record blocking is enabled, the cache is allocated when the cursor is opened. It is deallocated when the cursor is closed. Therefore, to avoid wasting memory resources on the server, avoid keeping cursors open if they are no longer required.

> **Note**
>
> All cursors used for dynamic SQL statements are assumed to be ambiguous.

> **New**
>
> Starting with V7.1 of DB2 UDB for the Intel and UNIX platforms, two new bind options are supported, `SQLERROR CONTINUE` and `VALIDATE RUN`. In previous releases, these options were available with only DB2 UDB for OS/390.
>
> This allows the programmer to port the DB2 UDB for OS/390 applications that make use of these options to the rest of the DB2 UDB family.
>
> See the *Application Development Guide* for more information.

4.2 Static Embedded SQL

In this section, we will cover the main components of static SQL applications, including how to connect to databases, how to retrieve data, and how to handle errors.

4.2.1 Host Variables

Host variables are used to pass data between an application and the database manager. These variables are declared in a special manner in the host language program module. During precompilation, the host variables are converted to corresponding host language variables (for example, C variables or COBOL data items). One of the major output files generated during precompilation is the modified source module. Within this module, precompile runtime function calls are used to actually manipulate the host variables.

When you use host variables in SQL statements, you must prefix the host variable name with a colon (:).

Remember that the host variable is used in two ways in a program:

- Within SQL statements (always precede the variable with a colon).
- Outside of SQL statements (treat host variables like any other variables).

Host variables can only be used within static SQL statements. Dynamic embedded SQL statements use parameter markers instead of host variables. Each programming language has slightly different rules for declaring host variables, but there are many similarities; for instance, every host variable must be declared in a `DECLARE` section.

> **Note**
>
> REXX does not support host variables. REXX is not considered a static SQL application development environment.

There are two types of host variables:

- Input host variables—These specify values to be passed to the database manager from the application during statement execution. For example, an input host variable is used in the following SQL statement:

    SELECT customer_name from customer where customer_name =
    <input host variable>

- Output host variables—These specify values to be returned from the database manager to the application during statement execution. For example, an output host variable is used in the following SQL statement:

    SELECT INTO <output host variable> FROM CUSTOMER
    WHERE CUSTOMER_NAME = 'Mike Kyprianou'

Host variables must be defined within the BEGIN DECLARE SECTION and the END DECLARE SECTION. You may decide to have multiple DECLARE sections in a single source module. This really depends on your coding preference. Be sure that all of the host variables used in your SQL statements have been defined within a DECLARE section. During precompile, the programming language scope of data variables is not taken into account. This means that all host variables must be unique within a single source module being precompiled, even if they are locally scoped, as in the C programming language. Small program modules may be better suited to your programming style. This will help avoid incorrect host variable declarations. A host variable cannot be redefined within the same programming module. Its definition must be compatible with the DB2 UDB data type to which it corresponds in the SQL statement.

> **Note**
>
> Using the bind file dump tool (db2bfd), you can display host variable declarations within a bind file (for example, db2bfd -v db2look.bnd).

Figure 4-2 demonstrates an example of declaring host variables in the C programming language. The host variable product_name corresponds to the DB2 UDB data type of CHARACTER. The host variable store_id corresponds to the DB2 UDB data type SMALLINT. From the figure, we see that the actual declaration of the variable product_name follows C language variable definition rules. Note that the programmer should not declare any other C variable as product_name. The EXEC SQL clause lets the precompiler know that this data is to be interpreted and replaced with a C API call to the DB2 UDB engine. The ending semicolon (;) lets the precompiler know that the SQL statement is complete

When developing C applications, host variables for CHARACTER column types should be defined one character more than the column definition. The extra character will store the null-

```
EXEC SQL BEGIN DECLARE SECTION;
/* place all host variables here */
varchar          product_name[20];
smallint         store_id;
EXEC SQL END DECLARE SECTION;
```

Figure 4-2 Host variables using C.

terminator character. If you do not provide for the null-terminator character, the resulting value may be truncated.

Figure 4-3 is an example of declaring host variables in a COBOL application. As in the C example, do not declare a variable outside of the `BEGIN DECLARE` and `END DECLARE` sections. This example defines a host variable `product_name` that would correspond to the DB2 UDB `CHARACTER` data type.

```
EXEC SQL BEGIN DECLARE SECTION END-EXEC.
* place all host variables here
01 product_name  PIC X(20).
EXEC SQL END DECLARE SECTION END-EXEC.
```

Figure 4-3 Host variables using COBOL.

DB2 UDB comes with `db2dclgn`, a declaration generator tool that makes the task of declaring host variables for database objects to be referenced in an application a little easier. Given a database and table name, it generates an output file containing the host variable declarations for the specified table. For example, Figure 4-4 shows the output from `db2dclgn` in the C language format for the `PRODUCT` table in the `DB2MALL` database.

As you can see from Figure 4-4, the output from the command allows you to have the declarations for host variables without needing to look up the declarations in the documentation. You can modify the generated declarations as needed.

For more information on the `db2dclgn` command, you can issue the command `db2dclgn -h` or review the DB2 UDB V7 *Command Reference*.

4.2.2 Connecting to Databases

The SQL statement used for connecting to a database is:

```
CONNECT TO <dbname> USER <userid> USING <password>
```

If another database server is to be used, then the SQL statement to release the current connection is:

```
CONNECT RESET
```

The `CONNECT RESET` statement causes an implicit `COMMIT` to be performed. If the application needs to perform a single transaction (Unit of Work, or UOW) involving more than one database, then the application must use a Type 2 connect. The behavior of the CONNECT

Static Embedded SQL

The command:

```
db2dclgn -d DB2MALL -t PRODUCT -l c
```

generates a `product.h` file which contains:

```c
struct
{
  sqlint32 product_id;
  struct
  {
    short length;
    char  data[20];
  } product_name;
  short store_id;
  double unit_cost;
  double unit_price;
  double sale_price;
  struct
  {
    short length;
    char  data[10];
  } supplier_id;
  sqlint32 units_in_stock;
  sqlint32 units_on_order;
  sqlint32 reorder_level;
  sqlint32 reorder_quantity;
  char status[1];
  SQL TYPE IS BLOB(102400) picture;
} product;
```

Figure 4-4 Using the DB2 UDB declaration generator, `db2dclgn`.

statement is dependent on the PRECOMPILE parameter setting CONNECT when it was precompiled or the SET CLIENT API call.

4.2.3 Transactions Involving Multiple Databases

If a transaction requires access to more than one database, then it is considered a Distributed Unit of Work (DUOW) transaction. A DUOW application must use a special type of database connection known as a Type 2 connection. The default CONNECT behavior is known as a Type 1 connection. Since the syntax of SQL statements is verified during the precompile phase of application development, the connection options can be set using precompile options. They can also be set using the SET CLIENT API call. Here we look at the PREP options that are used for Type 2 connections. They include:

- `CONNECT (1|2)`—The `CONNECT 2` option will allow a connection to multiple databases within a UOW.
- `DISCONNECT ( EXPLICIT | AUTOMATIC | CONDITIONAL )`—This option is used to determine how and when connections are to be released. `AUTOMATIC` indicates that all connections are to be disconnected at a `COMMIT`. The `CONDITIONAL` keyword indicates that database connections that have been marked `RELEASE` or have no open `WITH HOLD` cursors, are to be disconnected at `COMMIT`. Finally, `EXPLICIT` indicates that only those database connections that have explicitly been marked for `RELEASE` with the `RELEASE` statement are to be disconnected at `COMMIT`.
- `SQLRULES ( DB2 | STD )`—Specifies whether or not Type 2 connections are to be processed according to DB2 UDB rules (DB2) or the standard rules (STD) based on ISO/ANS SQL92. The DB2 option permits the SQL `CONNECT` statement to switch the current connection to another established (dormant) connection. The `STD` option permits the SQL `CONNECT` statement to establish a new connection only.
- `SYNCPOINT ( NONE | ONEPHASE | TWOPHASE )`—This option is used to specify how commits or rollbacks are to be coordinated among multiple database connections. The `NONE` keyword is used to specify that the transaction will not be coordinated using a Transaction Manager (TM). The `ONEPHASE` parameter is used to specify that no TM will be used for transaction control, and a commit will be sent to each of the participating databases. The `TWOPHASE` parameter is used to specify that the TM will perform two-phase commit transactions.

4.2.4 Connecting from an Application

Figure 4-5 is an example of establishing a connection to a DB2 UDB database using host variables. The example is a C program module that takes two arguments as its input, `szUserid` and `szPassword`. Since the userid and password will be supplied by the end-user, the programmer must use host variables.

Also note that the input arguments are copied to the local variables containing the userid and password. The variables containing the userid and password are local to this function, but remember that to the DB2 UDB precompiler, they are valid DB2 UDB host variables and must be unique in the entire source module.

In Figure 4-5, a connection to a database called `DB2MALL` is established. This connection should be explicitly performed by your application. The connection will establish the authorization ID for this session. In this example, the authorization ID is passed into the module as the variable `szUserid`. Usually, your application will only use the resources of a single database at a time. This is known as a Type 1 connection application. If more than one database is used, then other items must be considered. A special user variable called `CURRENT SERVER` is assigned by DB2 UDB following a successful connection.

You can establish a database connection implicitly using a default database. The default database is defined using the registry profile variable `DB2DBDFT`. When the application is ini-

```
/***************************************************************
** Source File Name = connect.sqc
**
** PURPOSE: This program will establish a database
** connection as defined by the dbname host variable.
** STATEMENTS Used:
**         - CONNECT TO ....
** Concepts:
**         - Establishing a database connection
***************************************************************/
#include <stdio.h>
#include <stdlib.h>
#include <string.h>
#include "MALL.h"
int Establish_Connection ( char *szUserid, char *szPassword
)
{
   EXEC SQL BEGIN DECLARE SECTION;
      char userid[9];
      char passwd[19];
      char dbname[19];
   EXEC SQL END DECLARE SECTION;

   strcpy (userid,szUserid);
   strcpy (passwd,szPassword);
   strcpy (dbname,"DB2MALL");

   EXEC SQL CONNECT TO :dbname USER :userid USING :passwd;
   return SQLCODE;
```

Figure 4-5 Establishing a database connection using host variables.

tialized and the first SQL statement is executed, an implicit connect will occur if an explicit connection has not been made.

Implicitly establishing a database connection is not the recommended approach because it is based on a DB2 UDB registry profile setting. Therefore, always code an explicit database connection in your application. You should also include the userid and password as shown in Figure 4-5.

Once the database connection has been established in your application, it will remain until:

- CONNECT RESET is issued to terminate the database connection.
- CONNECT TO is issued to another database.
- DISCONNECT is issued (generally used for Type 2 connection situations).

When your application terminates, always issue a CONNECT RESET before termination to release your connection to the database and explicitly complete any active transactions.

> **Note**
>
> The DB2 CLP or DB2 UDB Command Center utility will perform a CONNECT RESET when the TERMINATE command is issued.

The return code of the module in Figure 4-5 is an SQLCODE. If the database connection is unsuccessful, the SQLCODE will be a negative number. If the database connection is successful, the SQLCODE will be a value of zero. A positive value for SQLCODE indicates a warning condition. We will examine more about error handling in the following sections.

4.2.5 Error Handling—Using and Interpreting the SQLCA

As with most application development environments, proper error handling is essential for creating and maintaining a quality program. Every SQL statement issued from an application can result in either a successful or error condition. The primary means of determining the result of an SQL statement is for the application developer to examine the contents of the SQL Communications Area (SQLCA). The SQLCA is a host language data structure defined by DB2 UDB. It contains data elements that are populated by DB2 UDB during SQL processing.

Your application must declare an SQLCA prior to the issuing of any SQL statements. There are two methods of defining the SQLCA in your program:

- Using an EXEC SQL INCLUDE SQLCA statement.
- Declaring a structure called sqlca as defined in the DB2 UDB header files.

Table 4-5 details the SQLCA structure.

> **Note**
>
> The SQLCA is automatically provided in the DB2 UDB REXX environment.

The SQLCA data structure shown in Table 4-5 is used as the primary means of error handling between the application and DB2 UDB. It is critical that your application checks the contents of the SQLCA following the processing of each SQL statement. Failure to examine the SQLCA contents can cause unexpected errors to occur. For many errors that occur, a corresponding action is usually suggested (and can be coded into your application).

Static Embedded SQL

Table 4-5 SQLCA Data Structure

Element Name	Data Type	Description
sqlcaid	CHAR(8)	An eye-catcher to help visually identify the data structure. It should contain the string 'SQLCA'.
sqlcabc	INTEGER	Contains the length of the SQLCA. This should always contain the value 136.
sqlcode	INTEGER	Probably the most important element of the SQLCA structure. Contains the SQL return code. If the SQL statement was processed successfully, then this value is zero. If the value is positive, then a warning was returned and the SQL statement was successfully processed. If the value is negative, then an error occurred and the SQL statement was not successfully processed.
sqlerrml	SMALLINT	Contains the length of the character string in the element sqlerrmc. The value can be from 0 to 70. If the value is 0, then the contents of sqlerrmc can be deemed irrelevant.
sqlerrmc	VARCHAR(70)	Contains one or more message tokens separated by the value xFF. These tokens are substituted for variables in the error/warning descriptions. The separator is used to pass multiple arguments/tokens. Usually, this element contains the product signature, but it can also be used when a successful connection is made.
sqlerrp	CHAR(8)	The product signature is a character string that represents the type of DB2 database server currently being used. For example, SQL07010 states that the current server is DB2 UDB V7.1.0. In this case, it indicates version 7, release 1, and modification level 0. In addition, the three letters identify the server product, in this case DB2 UDB. If sqlcode is not zero, then this element usually contains an 8-character representation of the program module that reported he error.
sqlerrd	Integer Array	This array of six integer values can contain extra diagnostic information when error conditions occur. This will generally be empty if there are no errors, except for the sqlerrd[6] field from a partitioned database. sqlerrd[1] - Code page conversion information. sqlerrd[[2] - Code page conversion information. Compound SQL - If this is associated with compound SQL, it will indicate the number of statements that failed. sqlerrd[3] If a PREPARE - # of returned rows (estimate). If UPDATE/DELETE/INSERT - # of affected rows. If Compound SQL - Accumulation of all substatement rows. If CONNECT - 1 if database is updatable, 2 if it is not.

Table 4-5 SQLCA Data Structure (Continued)

Element Name	Data Type	Description

`sqlerrd`	Integer Array	`sqlerrd[4]`
		If a PREPARE - Relative cost estimate of required resources
		If Compound SQL - # of successful substatements if a CONNECT.
		0 - One-phase commit from down-level client.
		1 - One-phase commit.
		2 - One-phase commit read-only.
		3 - Two-phase commit.
		`sqlerrd(5)`
		DELETE/INSERT/UPDATE - # of rows affected (due to constraints or triggers).
		Compound SQL - # of rows affected (due to constraints or triggers).
		CONNECT - Authentication type value:
		0 - Server.
		1 - Client.
		2 - DB2 connect used.
		3 - DCE security used.
		255 - Unspecified authentication.
		`sqlerrd(6)` - For a partitioned database, the partition number that reported the error or warning. If no errors, the partition number of the coordinator partition.

`sqlwarn`	Character Array	A set of indicators corresponding to various warning conditions, each blank or W. SQLWARN0 - Global indicator; blank if no warnings, `W' otherwise. SQLWARN1 - `W' if string column was truncated, `N' if null terminator was truncated. SQLWARN2 - `W' if null values were not used in function. SQLWARN3 - `W' if # of host variables does not match number select list columns. SQLWARN4 - `W' if prepared DELETE/UPDATE doesn't contain WHERE clause. SQLWARN5 - Reserved. SQLWARN6 - `W' if the result of a date was adjusted. SQLWARN7 - Reserved. SQLWARN8 - `W' if character that couldn't be. converted was substituted with another.

Table 4-5 SQLCA Data Structure (Continued)

Element Name	Data Type	Description
`sqlwarn`	Character Array	SQLWARN9 - `` `W' `` if errors in arithmetic expressions ignored. SQLWARN10 - `` `W' `` if conversion error assigning data into SQLCA.
`sqlstate`	CHAR(5)	A return code that indicates the outcome of the most recently executed SQL statement. This is DB2 platform-independent.

4.2.6 Error Handling—Message Retrieval

The SQLCA data structure is useful in determining if errors have been encountered in your application. How do you get this information? DB2 UDB provides translated message files that can be referenced using a specific DB2 UDB API called `sqlaintp`. Figure 4-6 contains the prototype for this error message function.

The `sqlaintp` API retrieves the message associated with an error condition specified by the `sqlcode` field of the SQLCA structure. You must allocate a buffer to store the message string prior to calling `sqlaintp`.

```
SQL_API_RC SQL_API_FN
sqlaintp        (
char *            pBuffer,
short             BufferSize,
short             LineWidth,
struct sqlca *    pSqlca);
```

Figure 4-6 Syntax of message retrieval DB2 UDB API (C syntax).

4.2.7 SQLCODE vs. SQLSTATE

SQLCODE is an integer value, and therefore it is easy to check for a negative or positive value. However, the SQLCODE for an error condition may not be standard across the entire DB2 family of database products. To help alleviate this problem, the SQLSTATE field contains a standardized error consistent across IBM DB2 database products and across SQL92-conforming database managers.

4.2.8 Program Logic for Error Handling

Application modules can contain numerous SQL statements for processing. The application should verify the success of each SQL statement by checking the SQLCA contents. This may require unusual coding techniques, because the program's flow of control may be interrupted by an SQL error. To avoid coding a call to an error-checking routine after each SQL statement, you can use the statement:

```
EXEC SQL  WHENEVER SQLERROR GO TO label;
```

This embedded SQL statement only needs to be defined once in your source module, but must appear before the SQL statements you want to affect. Every statement that returns with a negative SQLCODE will cause execution to transfer to the statement immediately following the specified `label`.

There are other variations on the usage of the WHENEVER statement. These include:

```
EXEC SQL WHENEVER NOT FOUND GO TO LASTROW;
EXEC SQL WHENEVER SQLWARNING CONTINUE;
```

When processing a multirow result set, you may want to implement a common display routine. This can be accomplished as in the above example, which checks the NOT FOUND condition (SQLCODE=100). If positive values are returned in the SQLCODE, you may go to a specific label or, as in our example, continue program execution using the CONTINUE keyword.

You should note that we chose not to implement these common error handling routines in the DB2CERT application (see Appendix B). We decided to check the SQLCODE following each SQL statement and used an error handling routine if the SQLCODE was negative. The error-handling routine writes data to the db2cert.err file.

4.2.9 Indicator Variables

An *indicator* variable is a special type of host variable that is used to indicate if a column value is null or not. It is not applicable for Java applications, which can compare the value of the host variable to the Java null. When the host variable is used as input into the database, it should be set by the application before the SQL statement is executed. When the host variable is used as output from the database, the indicator is defined by the application, but it is updated by DB2 UDB and returned. The application should then check the value of the indicator variable after the result has been returned.

```
SELECT SALE_PRICE INTO :hv1 INDICATOR :hvind
    FROM PRODUCT;
SELECT SALE_PRICE INTO :hv1 :hvind
    FROM PRODUCT
```

Figure 4-7 General host variable use in SQL.

Figure 4-7 shows two examples of populating an indicator variable. Both of the queries return the value for the SALE_PRICE column. We have defined two host variables, one called hv1 and the other is called hvind. Both host variables are identified by the colon (:). The hv1 host variable must represent a compatible host language data type for the SALE_PRICE column.

The second host variable, hvind, is used to indicate the nullability of the value retrieved into host variable hv1. The indicator host variable is either identified using the keyword INDICATOR, or simply by a blank space as shown in the second SELECT INTO statement in Figure 4-7. All indicator host variables are defined using the host language data type that corresponds to the DB2 UDB data type SMALLINT.

> **Note**
> In C, a variable of type short should be used for an indicator variable.

Null indicators must be checked when an application is retrieving data from a nullable column.

> **Note**
> There are no commas between the column host variable and its corresponding null indicator host variable.

The return of a null value into an application is different than querying the null status of a column within SQL. As an application developer, it is important to note any nullable columns and always use and check the null indicator host variable in the application.

Interpreting an indicator host variable requires that you test its value. If the indicator host variable is negative, then the column contains a null value and the contents of the corresponding host variable are ignored. If the indicator host variable is a nonnegative value, then the input or output host variable contains a nonnull value.

> **Note**
> When an indicator variable is used with an LOB locator, the indicator variable will indicate whether the LOB represented by the LOB locator is null or not.

If the application does not provide a null indicator host variable, an SQL error could be returned by DB2 UDB on subsequent processing of the host variable. When nullable columns are referenced during UPDATE or INSERT statements, the column will be set to null if the indicator variable is negative and the column is nullable.

4.2.10 Data Retrieval Methods

Many of the SQL statements used in database applications are used to retrieve data from the database. The SELECT statement is used to perform data retrieval by returning a set of rows. There is no method of determining the number of rows that will be returned from any given SELECT statement.

When coding a `SELECT` statement in an application, the data must be handled by the application. Therefore, the data is returned into native language host variables. In static SQL programs, methods of retrieving the data include:

- Use the `SELECT INTO` or `VALUES INTO` clause.
- Use a cursor and the `FETCH INTO` clause.

4.2.10.1   Single-Row Results—SELECT INTO

When the result of an SQL statement is a single row, the application can store the data directly into host variables. The `SELECT` statement requires the phrase `INTO` followed by an equal number of host variables for the number of columns being retrieved.

It is important to remember that a single row must be returned (otherwise an error will arise). Specific situations relating to `SELECT INTO` to make note of include:

- If the number of host variables do not match the number of columns specified, a warning flag in the SQLCA will be set.
- If the row does not exist, `SQLCODE +100` or `SQLSTATE 02000` is returned.
- If the result set contains more than one row, an `SQLCODE -811` is returned.

A `SELECT INTO` statement should be used if an equality predicate is specified on a primary key column. This action will always retrieve a single-row result.

4.2.10.2   Single-Row Result—VALUES INTO

The structure of a SELECT statement is easily understood. It has a logical form that reads much like a language: "I want the book from the bookstore in the `DB2MALL` called *DB2 UDB Administration Guide: Performance*." This translates into the following `SELECT` statement:

```
SELECT PRODUCT_NAME
    FROM PRODUCT
    WHERE PRODUCT_NAME = 'DB2 UDB Administration Guide:
Performance' AND STORE = 'bookstore'
```

The structure of a `VALUES INTO` statement is different from the `SELECT` statement because the information being retrieved are not database objects, but special registers, constants, and host variables. *Special registers* are used to contain current information about the application that can be referenced in SQL statements. Some DB2 UDB special registers are shown in Table 4-6.

To obtain the value of any of these special registers, using the `VALUES INTO` statement as shown in Figure 4-8 is one possible method. You can also use them in a `SELECT` statement.

Table 4-6 Special Registers

Name	Description
CURRENT DATE	Specifies the date when the SQL statement is executed on the application server.
CURRENT EXPLAIN MODE	A VARCHAR(254) value that controls the behavior of the Explain facility with respect to eligible dynamic SQL statements. (This is similar to the BIND option EXPLAIN.)
CURRENT EXPLAIN SNAPSHOT	Contains an 8-character string that controls the behavior of the Explain Snapshot facility. (This is similar to the BIND option EXPLSNAP.)
CURRENT PATH	Contains a variable-length string of up to 254 characters that identifies the "SQL path" to be used to resolve function references and data type references for dynamically prepared SQL statements. (Similar to the BIND option FUNCPATH.)
CURRENT QUERY OPTIMIZATION	Contains an integer value that represents the class of query optimization performed by DB2 UDB when preparing dynamic SQL statements. (Similar to the BIND option QUERYOPT.)
CURRENT SERVER	Contains a variable-length string of up to 18 characters that represents the current application server.
CURRENT SCHEMA	A VARCHAR(128) identifying the schema name to be used to qualify unqualified database object references.
CURRENT TIME	Contains the time on the application server when the SQL statement is being executed.
CURRENT TIMESTAMP	Contains a complete timestamp based on a reading of the time-of-day clock at the application server.
USER	Contains the runtime authorization identifier passed to the database manager when an application starts on a database. This is a VARCHAR(128).

```
VALUES CURRENT DATE INTO :hvdate
VALUES CURRENT SERVER INTO :svrName
```

Figure 4-8 Using the VALUES INTO clause.

The VALUES clause can also be used with constants in the INSERT statement or when constant values need to be included in the result set. For example:

```
SELECT PRODUCT_ID
    FROM PRODUCT
UNION VALUES ('999')
```

This query will always return at least one row with the value of 999 for product_id, even if the PRODUCT table is empty. As you can see, the VALUES clause is similar to a SELECT statement. It also provides an easy-to-use interface to invoke User-Defined Functions (UDFs).

```
            VALUES (CUSTOMER_BALANCE (CUSTOMER_ID,BALANCE))
```
Figure 4-9 Using VALUES to invoke a UDF.

In Figure 4-9, the statement invokes a UDF called `customer_balance` and passes the column values of `customer_id` and `balance` to the function. The result of the UDF is a single result (scalar value).

4.2.10.3   Multiple-Row Results

When the `SELECT` statement does not resolve to exactly one row, the application must be written to handle an arbitrary number of rows. A *cursor* is used to retrieve the results from the `SELECT` statement. A cursor is associated with an SQL statement using the `DECLARE` cursor statement in the application. The `DECLARE` statement defines and names the cursor, identifying the set of rows to be retrieved using a `SELECT` statement.

```
            DECLARE c1 CURSOR FOR
            SELECT CUSTOMER_ID, CUSTOMER_NAME
            FROM CUSTOMER
            WHERE CUSTOMER_NAME IN (:hvCusName)
```
Figure 4-10 Cursor declaration with an input host variable.

In Figure 4-10, the cursor `c1` is declared to retrieve the test candidate IDs and first and last names according to an input host variable called `hvCusName`. Since the predicate (WHERE clause) is not an equality predicate using the customer ID (`CUSTOMER_ID`), it must be assumed that the result of this statement could be 0, 1, or more rows (depending on the value of `hvCusName` during the OPEN cursor processing).

4.2.11   Using Cursors

Cursors are used to process a multirow result set. The processing can involve simply retrieving data using a `SELECT`. It also can involve a cursor-positioned `DELETE` or `UPDATE`. As an example, when the DB2 UDB Command Line Processor (CLP) is used, each SQL statement is dynamically prepared and each resulting row is displayed via multiple fetch operations using a cursor.

Generally cursors within DB2 UDB embedded SQL programs can only be used in one direction. Since DB2 Universal Database V6.1, it is possible to have forward, backward, and scrollable cursors. However, backward and scrollable cursors are supported only with the DB2 CLI, ODBC, JDBC, and SQLJ interfaces.

It is important to remember that the result set of the `SELECT` statement is usually determined during the processing of the open cursor. Multiple cursors can be open on the same result set and positioned independently. This can be useful to provide backwardlike scrolling for embedded SQL programs that do not have the support for backward cursors. If a cursor is reopened, its current position is at the beginning of the result set.

Static Embedded SQL

The name of a cursor is only known by the application that declared it. It cannot be a host variable. The cursor name must be unique within the application module.

The steps involved in the usage of cursors are as follows:

1. DECLARE the cursor, specifying its name and type. The location of the DECLARE statement in the application must be anyplace before the usage of the cursor. It associates the cursor to a query.
2. OPEN the cursor to retrieve the matching rows of the result set. The locks, depending upon isolation level, are placed at this time. The input host variables have been evaluated to determine the result set. Following a successful open cursor, the cursor is logically positioned before the first result row.
3. FETCH the results one row at a time. A check should be made to ensure that the end of the set has not been encountered (for example, SQLCODE +100, SQLSTATE 02000). The FETCH statement will initialize the host variables with the last row retrieved, which becomes the current row. It then positions the cursor at the next row. At this time, indicator host variables should also be analyzed.
4. (Optional) Use the DELETE or UPDATE statement to remove or modify the contents of the row the cursor has just retrieved. This is known as cursor-positioned deletes/updates and requires the WHERE CURRENT OF clause in the statement.
5. CLOSE the cursor (by name) to release any resources. The cursor can be opened again.

4.2.11.1 Cursor Types

A cursor type is determined by the declaration of the cursor, its usage, and the record-blocking BIND parameters. There are three categories of cursors:

1. Read-Only—The SELECT statement is a read-only SELECT statement (for example, SELECT customer_id FROM customer). There can be performance advantages, especially when the data is retrieved across a network, because it is likely that record blocking will be performed.
2. Updatable—The rows can be updated. The FOR UPDATE clause is used during the cursor declaration. Only a single table or view can be referenced in the SELECT statement.
3. Ambiguous—The cursor type cannot be determined by its declaration or the SELECT statement being used. The amount of record blocking for these types of cursors is determined by the BIND parameter.

If the cursor is going to be used in an UPDATE WHERE CURRENT OF statement, specify the FOR UPDATE clause during the cursor declaration. The optimizer will pick the best possible access path. Also, if you know that the cursor is only used to retrieve data, add the clause FOR READ ONLY or FOR FETCH ONLY. This will encourage record blocking to occur and avoid extra locks on the result set.

The phrases FOR UPDATE ONLY, FOR FETCH ONLY, and FOR READ ONLY are actually part of the SQL statement and not part of the DECLARE cursor syntax. Let's look at an example cursor declaration and usage.

In Figure 4-11, all of the host variables are initialized in the BEGIN DECLARE SECTION. The cursor is then defined. The cursor type is defined within the SELECT statement. The cursor here is defined as a read-only cursor. The phrase FOR FETCH ONLY is specified at the end of the SQL statement.

We could have specified the WITH HOLD option to maintain the cursor position across transactions. Since we did not specify this option, the cursor will no longer be accessible following a COMMIT statement. Cursors specified as WITH HOLD are useful when a large number of rows need to be examined and modified. However, the application cannot afford to lock all of the rows over the entire unit of work. At commit, a cursor WITH HOLD has all locks released except those protecting the current cursor position.

Let's examine the cursor-specific phrases in the SELECT statement. In Figure 4-12, the FOR UPDATE clause shows that it is possible to specify the column name to update.

> **Note**
>
> The column name in the FOR UPDATE clause must be unqualified and it must identify a column or view identified in the first FROM clause if a full select. If no column names are specified, all updatable columns of the table or view are included.

If no UPDATE or DELETE on a row based on the cursor position is to be done, then add the phrase FOR FETCH ONLY or FOR READ ONLY to the end of the statement instead.

4.2.11.2 Cursor Positioning

A cursor, regardless of type, can have three positions depending on its current state:

1. An open cursor prior to the first fetch is positioned before the first record of the result set and the contents of the output host variables are undefined at this point.
2. Following a fetch, the cursor is considered on record. The output host variables contain the values of the current row. This is the row that will be changed if a positioned UPDATE or DELETE is performed at this time.
3. The third possible cursor position is following the last row. At this point, the host variables contain the values of the current (last) row and the SQLCA contains the value of (SQLCODE +100 , SQLSTATE '02000').

```
        EXEC SQL BEGIN DECLARE SECTION;
          long iCustomer_id;
          char szCName[30];
          char szPhone[12];
          char szStreet[50];
          char szCity[15];
          char szProvState[2];
          char szCode[7];
          char szCountry[15];
          char szCitySearch2[21];
        EXEC SQL END DECLARE SECTION;

        EXEC SQL DECLARE c1 CURSOR FOR
              SELECT
                      CUSTOMER_ID,CUSTOMER_NAME,ADDR_STREET,
                      ADDR_CITY,ADDR_STATE,ADDR_ZIP,
                      ADDR_COUNTRY,CUSTOMER_PHONE
              FROM
                      CUSTOMER
              WHERE
                      CHAR(CITY) LIKE :szCitySearch2
              FOR FETCH ONLY;
        EXEC SQL OPEN c1;
            EXEC SQL FETCH c1 INTO :icustomer_id,
                      :szCName,
                      :szStreet,
                      :szCity,
                      :szProvState,
                      :szCountry,
                      :szCode,
                      :szPhone;
            if (SQLCODE == SQL_RC_OK) {
               printf ("Customer ID\t:%s\n",iCustomer_id);
               printf ("Customer Name\t:%s\n",szCName);
               printf ("City\t\t:%s\n",szCity);
            }
        EXEC SQL CLOSE c1;
        EXEC SQL COMMIT;
```

Figure 4-11 Using cursors.

```
EXEC SQL DECLARE c1 CURSOR FOR
    SELECT
        CUSTOMER_ID,CUSTOMER_NAME,ADDR_STREET,
        ADDR_CITY,ADDR_STATE,ADDR_ZIP,ADDR_COUNTRY,
        CUSTOMER_PHONE,DATE_ENTERED
    FROM
        CUSTOMER
    WHERE
        CHAR(CITY) LIKE :szCitySearch2
    FOR UPDATE OF DATE_ENTERED;
```

Figure 4-12 Updatable cursor declaration.

> **Note**
>
> Remember to COMMIT or ROLLBACK transactions even if they involve read-only cursors, because there are locks held for the SELECT statement.

In Figure 4-13, the result set contains seven test candidates. The candidates are in no particular order because there is no ORDER BY clause in the SQL statement. Examine the three cursor positions shown in the figure. The cursor is either before a record, on a record, or after the last record. Since the example is a read-only cursor, a positioned update or delete would result in an SQL error. The only valid operation on a closed cursor is OPEN.

Let's examine cursor positioning when a cursor is declared as a WITH HOLD cursor. This type of cursor will maintain its position since the last fetch operation, even after the transaction has been committed. This allows you to commit changes for other applications to read without losing your current cursor position.

If the UOW is completed using a ROLLBACK statement, all of the open cursors, including any WITH HOLD cursors, are closed and the resources are released. If the UOW ends in a COMMIT, then the WITH HOLD cursors will remain open as in Figure 4-14. If a CLOSE is issued before a COMMIT, the cursor is no longer accessible. CLOSE does not cause a COMMIT or ROLLBACK.

In the example in Figure 4-14, a positioned UPDATE is being performed on the second row fetched from the result set. The update of the date_entered for customer KEVIN is committed, and then the loop is terminated. The new date_entered will then be accessible by all other applications, since the UPDATE has been committed. Since the cursor was not closed, we can still fetch data using the cursor.

4.2.11.3 Advanced Cursor Usage

Scrolling in a single direction through data is the main way that cursors are used. But how can an application allow more flexible scrolling techniques? Usually, advanced scrolling techniques involve multiple cursors and/or keeping a copy of the retrieved data in application memory.

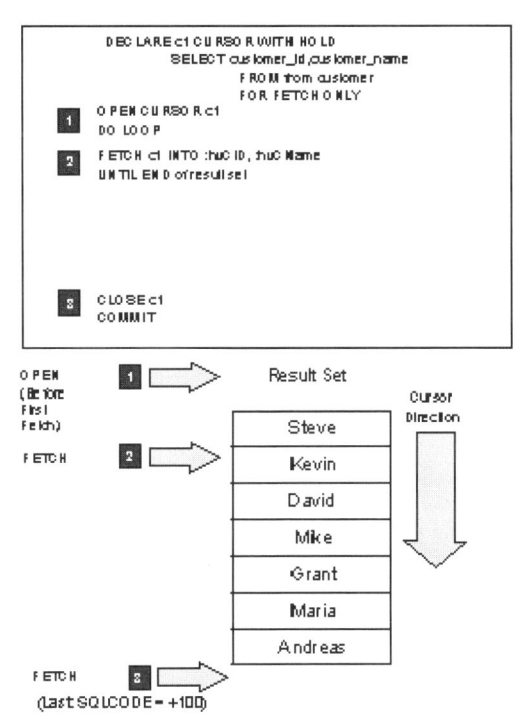

Figure 4-13 Cursor positioning (not `WITH HOLD`).

DB2 UDB V6.1 and later now support scrollable cursors as discussed previously. Here we briefly discuss how an embedded SQL application can do a similar task. Using multiple cursors allows the end-user to reposition the cursors within the data being retrieved. Let's say that an application provides the end-user with the ability to examine Record 1 and then Record 2. Then the application allows a modification of Record 1. With a single nonscrollable cursor, this would be difficult, as the cursor would have to be reopened to position the cursor to Record 1, and the record at position one may have been already modified by another application.

Suppose two cursors are declared for the same result set. The second cursor is always one record behind the first cursor. By using this two-cursor technique, the end-user could update the previous record without closing the first cursor.

Note
Keep in mind that the order of a result set without an ORDER BY clause is arbitrary.

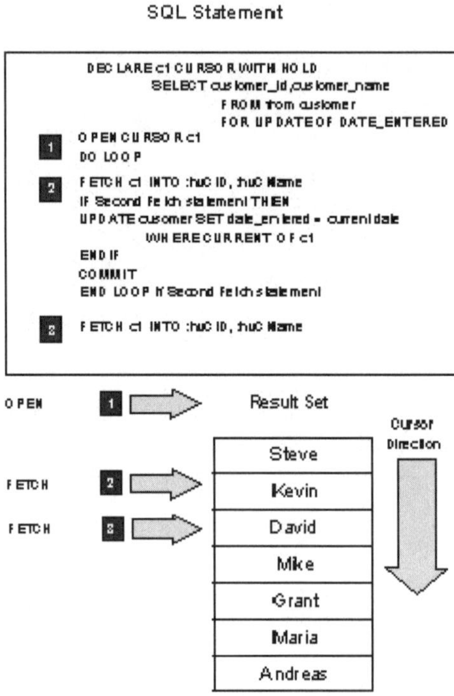

```
                    SQL Statement

        DECLARE c1 CURSOR WITH HOLD
            SELECT customer_id, customer_name
                FROM tom customer
                FOR UPDATE OF DATE_ENTERED
   [1]  OPEN CURSOR c1
        DO LOOP
   [2]  FETCH c1 INTO :huC ID, :huC Name
        IF Second Fetch statement THEN
           UPDATE customer SET date_entered = currentdate
                WHERE CURRENT OF c1
        END IF
        COMMIT
        END LOOP if Second Fetch statement
   [3]  FETCH c1 INTO :huC ID, :huC Name
```

```
OPEN    [1] =>    Result Set
                                       Cursor
                                       Direction
                   | Steve   |
FETCH   [2] =>    | Kevin   |
FETCH   [3] =>    | David   |
                   | Mike    |
                   | Grant   |
                   | Maria   |
                   | Andreas |
```

Figure 4-14 Cursor positioning (WITH HOLD).

Keeping a copy of the data in application memory does not guarantee that the application is displaying the current data values. However, it does provide the embedded SQL application developer with the most flexibility to scroll through data. Usually this technique involves a buffer (storage area) within the application. The end-user is allowed to examine all of the contents of this buffer. When the end-user wants to change the contents of the buffer, an update is attempted. There is no guarantee that the update will be successful. To ensure that the contents will not change, either explicitly lock the table using the LOCK TABLE statement or use an appropriate isolation level. The isolation level should use appropriate locking semantics, such as Repeatable Read.

4.2.12 Application-Level Locking

Locking semantics are usually specified by choosing the isolation level for the application during the bind process. The isolation level affects the number of locks and period of time they are held.

The LOCK TABLE statement can be used to enforce a table-level lock in either exclusive (X) or share (S) mode. As with all types of database locking, the larger the object being locked, the less concurrency available.

> **Note**
> Concurrency is usually a high priority for transaction-processing database applications.

Obtaining an explicit table lock can improve performance for batch applications that involve changes to a large percentage of the table. If a table lock is acquired, row locks on the table will not be acquired.

All locks use approximately the same amount of storage in the locklist. Remember that the locklist is shared by all applications accessing the database. An explicit table lock will avoid filling the locklist and thus defer lock escalation for other applications.

4.2.13 Searched Updates/Deletes

We discussed positioned UPDATE and DELETE statements using cursors in the previous section. If a row or set of rows can be explicitly identified, then a searched UPDATE or DELETE can be used instead of cursors. Adding an appropriate WHERE clause to the end of an UPDATE or DELETE statement with proper input and/or output host variables can provide enough flexibility for the end-user.

An UPDATE statement requires the application developer to specify the columns and their corresponding values to be updated. A static embedded SQL statement cannot use host variables to represent column names in an UPDATE or SELECT list. Therefore, to avoid having to prepare any single-column UPDATE statement dynamically, we use an UPDATE statement where every column is updated. The previously retrieved values are used for the update. The updated column has a new user input value. This is not the most efficient method of updating records in DB2 UDB, but it is a valid method. We will discuss how to modify this part of the application using dynamic embedded SQL in the following section.

4.3 Dynamic Embedded SQL

We have already examined how to implement embedded static SQL applications. Now we examine how to dynamically prepare SQL statements in a program module. Coding embedded dynamic SQL statements may be complex since a special data structure, known as an SQLDA, must be used to interpret the SQL statement.

If in the development phase of an application every possible SQL statement is known, then static embedded SQL statements could be used for the entire application. This is usually not the case, since the end-user requirements will change before, during, and after the development cycle. The application may also require that an undetermined number of columns be returned. If the columns (SELECT list) being returned are unknown during application development, the developer must dynamically prepare the SQL statement and initialize the appropriate number of return variables.

When a fully defined SQL statement is embedded in an application, it is said to be *statically prepared*. The access plan for a static embedded SQL statement is generated during the precompile process. If *deferred binding* is used during the precompile phase (BINDFILE option used), the access plan is generated when the BIND command is used to bind the package to the database.

During the static preparation phase, all aspects of the SQL statement are known by DB2 UDB. Input host variables are treated as placeholders for portions of the SQL statements. Output host variables are placeholders for return arguments for the results of the SQL statements SELECT INTO, VALUES INTO, and FETCH INTO.

Let's examine the basic components of an SQL statement to understand the benefits and requirements of dynamic and static SQL statements:

```
SELECT <col1>, <col2>,...
FROM <tab1>, <tab2>,....
WHERE <condition1> <expression1> <condition2>...
```

Figure 4-15 SQL SELECT statement.

Figure 4-15 shows the basic parts of a SELECT statement. If there are unknown elements when the statement is prepared, they can be satisfied using host variables, or the statement requires dynamic preparation. Table 4-7 provides a checklist of conditions when the statement would require dynamic preparation.

Table 4-7 Dynamic vs. Static Preparation Checklist

Condition	Requires Dynamic Preparation
The column names/types in the SELECT list are unknown.	YES
The number of columns in the SELECT list are unknown.	YES
The table/view names in the FROM clause are unknown.	YES

There is no requirement to dynamically prepare INSERT statements, assuming that the target of the INSERT and the source of the data are well-defined. INSERT statements operate on all columns of a row, and therefore, the column names/types and number of columns are predefined within the table definition.

If the table or view name is not known during application development, then the SQL statement requires dynamic preparation. In addition, using dynamic SQL statements allows the flexibility of controlling the compilation environment for each SQL statement with special registers, such as CURRENT QUERY OPTIMIZATION.

Consequently, if you are planning to provide the end-user with a flexible interface to the database, some of the program modules may be coded with dynamic SQL statements, either embedded or using a callable SQL interface like CLI.

4.3.1 First Look at Dynamic SQL

Generally speaking, coding a dynamic SQL application requires more complex programming techniques because special data structures must be manipulated. The effort of incorporating dynamic SQL statements may be required to provide the end-user with the flexible interface they require. A good example of a dynamic embedded SQL interface is the DB2 Command Line Processor (CLP) utility. This utility dynamically prepares each SQL statement. If a DB2 UDB command is issued from the CLP interface, an appropriate DB2 UDB API is invoked. All of the DB2 UDB APIs are documented in the *DB2 UDB V7 Administrative API Reference*.

Every dynamically prepared SQL statement is optimized and compiled during query processing. This is an important consideration, since it can directly affect the end-user's response time for an SQL query. The more complicated the SQL statement, the more time is required to optimize and compile the query. If the same query was embedded into an application and statically prepared, the query compilation time would have occurred when the PREP or BIND command was issued.

> **Note**
>
> Query compilation (optimization) for static embedded SQL statements occurs during application development using the PREP or BIND command. Query compilation (optimization) for dynamic SQL statements (embedded or callable SQL) occurs during query processing.

In Figure 4-16, the static embedded SQL application development environment and program execution are shown. The end-user is executing SQL statements, known as *sections*, within a *package* stored in the database during the prep or bind phase. The section contains a fully optimized version of the SQL statement known as an *access plan*.

During the execution of the application in Figure 4-16, host variables may need to be resolved, but the *access plan*, or data access strategy, has already been determined.

> **Note**
>
> Since the access plan is chosen at prep or bind time, ensure that the database statistics are updated prior to issuing the PREP or BIND command. The RUNSTATS command generates the current database statistics.

The bind process performs the following two major functions for embedded static SQL:

- The SQL statement syntax will be checked and the privileges will be verified according to the authorization ID of the individual binding the package.

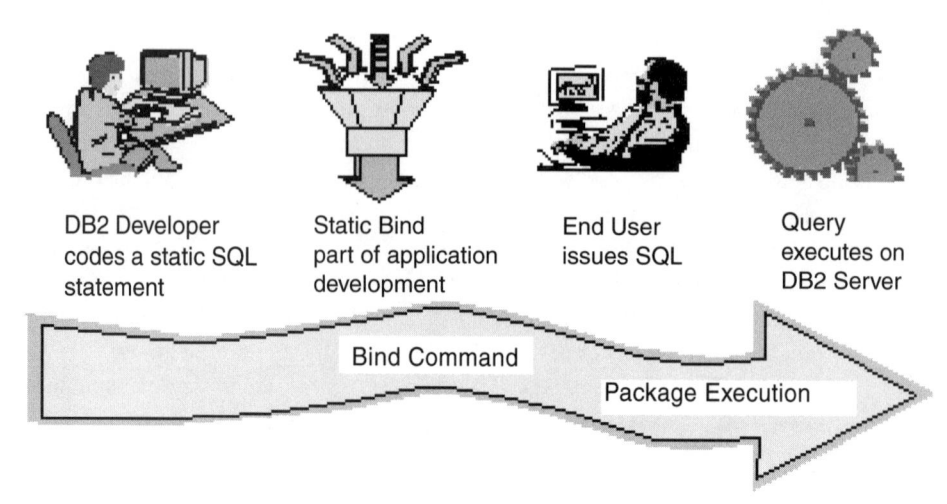

Figure 4-16 Static embedded SQL—query compilation occurs during bind.

- There will be an access plan determined for each SQL statement. This access plan will include index usage and other data access techniques, such as locking strategies. The access plan will be stored as a section within the package, and it is considered a compiled representation of the SQL statement. The term *"compiled"* means that there is no further processing by DB2 UDB required for the statement.

We will now examine the development and execution of an application containing dynamic embedded SQL statements.

In Figure 4-17, the parsing of the SQL statements and the determination of the optimal access plans are performed after the query has been issued by the end-user. Let's look at how the DB2 UDB developer codes an application using dynamically prepared SQL statements.

4.3.2 Dynamic SQL Phases

There are a number of steps that take place when using dynamically prepared SQL statements, starting with the PREPARE statement.

4.3.2.1 PREPARE

If an SQL statement is dynamically prepared, the syntax of the statement must be checked during program execution. The access plan must also be generated during program execution. These two tasks are performed using the PREPARE SQL statement. The PREPARE statement will transform the string representation of an SQL statement into a form that can be executed by an application. The PREPARE statement will create a temporary executable module that is not stored in the database system catalog tables, as is the case for embedded static SQL.

The PREPARE statement can optionally populate a structure known as the SQLDA with information about the SQL statement.

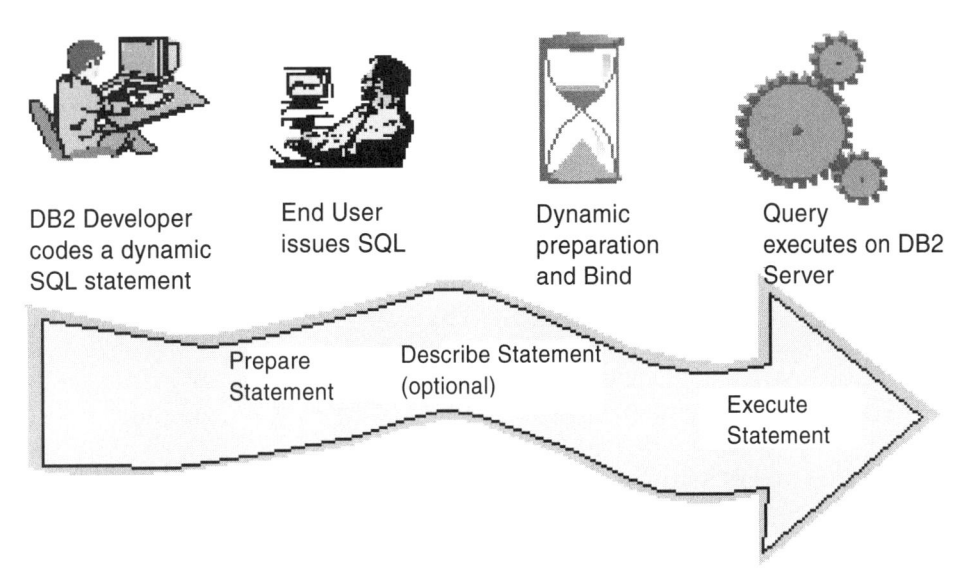

Figure 4-17 Dynamic embedded SQL—query compilation during execution.

4.3.2.2 DESCRIBE

The DESCRIBE statement can be used to provide the application developer with information about an SQL statement that has been previously prepared. For example, a DESCRIBE statement of a previously prepared SELECT statement allows the application developer to determine the amount of storage required to store the query results.

4.3.2.3 EXECUTE

The EXECUTE statement is used to execute a previously prepared SQL statement. Therefore, it is possible for the developer to prepare and describe the statement and never actually execute the statement. This technique can be useful in determining information about the SQL statement without actually executing the statement. Once prepared, a statement can be executed repeatedly within an application.

4.3.2.4 FETCH

The FETCH statement is used to retrieve a single row of data from a result set. It is very similar to the FETCH statement used in embedded static SQL statements. The main difference is that this type of FETCH statement uses a cursor that represents a dynamically prepared SQL statement. The cursor must have been opened prior to the FETCH statement. Data can be retrieved into host variables or a properly allocated SQLDA structure.

4.3.2.5 EXECUTE IMMEDIATE (Optional)

The EXECUTE IMMEDIATE SQL statement is a shortcut to issuing a dynamic SQL statement. An SQL statement that does not require any host variables, parameter markers, or does not return a multirow result set can be executed using the `EXECUTE IMMEDIATE` statement. The statement will be dynamically prepared and executed in a single embedded SQL statement.

4.3.3 Other Concepts

This section details some other concepts to consider when developing applications using dynamic SQL.

4.3.3.1 Deferred Prepare

Deferred prepare improves network traffic performance by combining the SQL `PREPARE` statement flow with the associated `OPEN`, `DESCRIBE`, or `EXECUTE` statement flow. DB2 UDB will defer sending the SQL `PREPARE` statement until the associated `OPEN`, `DESCRIBE`, or `EXECUTE` statement is issued by the application. For example, a `PREPARE` statement that does not have the `INTO <SQLDA>` clause can be deferred until an `OPEN` is issued. Deferred prepare can improve the performance of dynamic SQL and ODBC applications that perform queries, especially in the case where the answer set is small. Deferred prepare can be specified as a precompiler option (`DEFERRED_PREPARE`) or in the Set Client API (`SQL_DEFERRED_PREPARE` setting). The CLP uses deferred prepare.

4.3.3.2 Package Caching

You might have already guessed that dynamically preparing SQL statements can negatively impact query execution time. The access plan chosen for an SQL statement (dynamic or static) will be stored in a special cache, called the *package cache*. This cache is searched prior to query compilation and it allows DB2 UDB to reduce its internal overhead by eliminating the need to access the system catalogs when reloading a package, or in the case of dynamic SQL, eliminating the need for compilation. The package cache is a global cache, storing packages for static and dynamic SQL statements for all applications. Sections are kept in the cache until one of the following occurs:

- The database is shut down.
- The package or dynamic SQL statement is invalidated.
- The cache runs out of space.

If the statement is found in the cache, then the stored access plan is used for the statement. Because the cache is global, this means that two users running the same application can use the same package. This can dramatically decrease the query execution time of dynamically prepared SQL statements, if they are issued more than once by the same application. The execution time of static SQL statements will also be improved because the access plan will not have to be retrieved from the system catalog tables if it is found in the package cache.

The package cache is a configured amount of memory on the database server. If a matching access plan is not found in the package cache, the SQL statement will be either:

- Retrieved from the system catalog tables for static SQL statements.
- Prepared, and an access plan created for dynamic SQL statements.

The size of the package cache is specified within the database configuration using the PCKCACHESZ parameter. The cache is used for all database agents or applications.

> **Note**
> SQL statements prepared and executed dynamically with the EXECUTE IMMEDIATE statement are stored in the same location within the package cache. Therefore, each EXECUTE IMMEDIATE statement will either find an exact match in the cache, or it will create a new access plan and replace the previous EXECUTE IMMEDIATE SQL statement.

4.3.4 Types of Dynamic SQL Statements

There are two major types of dynamic SQL statements:

- Dynamic statements not requiring parameter markers.
- Dynamic statements requiring parameter markers.

4.3.4.1 Parameter Markers

A dynamic SQL statement cannot contain host variables, except for a character string host variable containing the SQL statement to be processed dynamically. (This is because host variable information such as data type and length is only available during application precompilation. At execution time, the host variable information is not present.) Any missing information for a dynamic SQL statement should contain a *parameter marker*. A parameter marker is represented in an SQL statement using the question mark (?) character. In static SQL statements, host variables can only be used as placeholders for certain parts of the statement. Host variables are usually used in the WHERE clause for static SQL statements. Parameter markers are more flexible than host variables. For example, a parameter marker can be used in the FROM clause or the SELECT list, as well as anyplace where static host variables can be used.

A parameter marker is defined in the SQL statement before the statement is prepared. The missing information is supplied in the EXECUTE or OPEN statements using a host variable or SQLDA data structure.

4.3.4.2 Dynamic Statements without Parameter Markers

If the entire SQL statement is known at runtime, then the statement can be dynamically prepared and parameter markers are not required. These statements are fully optimized during the dynamic prepare because there is no missing information.

4.3.4.3 Dynamic Statements with Parameter Markers

Parameter markers are used in dynamic SQL statement processing similar to the way host variables are used in static SQL processing. The statement contains a question mark (?) for each missing element. When the statement is processed, the missing data is substituted using a host variable or SQLDA data structure.

4.3.5 SQLDA Data Structure

The SQLDA data structure is a two-way communications data structure. The SQLDA is used to transfer data back and forth between the application and DB2 UDB. This structure actually contains a number of other structures named SQLVAR . Each SQLVAR data structure corresponds to a single column of data.

> **Note**
>
> When the SELECT list includes a Large Object data type (LOB), the number of SQLVAR entries for the entire SQLDA needs to be doubled.

The SQLDA can be used both as input to SQL statements and output from SQL statements. The SQLDA data structure is defined for C, REXX, FORTRAN, and COBOL.

Before we continue on the subject of embedded dynamic SQL statement processing, we need to examine the SQLDA data structure. This data structure is used as output from DB2 UDB in the following cases:

- During the PREPARE INTO or DESCRIBE statement, since it will contain the required number of SQLVAR elements for the query, or it will populate the SQLDA with the column data type information.
- During the FETCH INTO statements, because the SQLDA can be used as the location for the retrieved rows of data.
- During the EXECUTE statement, because the SQLDA can be used to provide data for the parameter markers of the prepared SQL statement.

In OPEN, FETCH, EXECUTE, and CALL statements, the SQLDA is used to contain input and output host variables. In DESCRIBE and PREPARE INTO statements, the SQLDA is used to describe a column of a result table, including its length and data type.

4.3.6 SQLVAR Elements

There are two types of SQLVAR structures in the SQLDA. First, there are base SQLVARs that contain information regarding the data type, name, length, host variable, and indicator variable for each column in the result set. The base SQLVARs are always present. Secondary SQLVARs

Dynamic Embedded SQL

are only present if the SQLDA has been doubled in size. As noted previously, an SQLDA is doubled in size if the `SELECT` list includes columns defined as LOBs.

The SQLDA header information in Table 4-8 contains information regarding the size of the SQLDA, the number of SQLVARs allocated (`sqln`), and the number of SQLVARs required for the statement (`sqld`). Note that some of the elements of the SQLDA header are initialized by DB2 UDB and others are initialized by the application. The `sqln` element is set by the application and the `sqld` element is set by DB2 UDB.

> **Note**
>
> A `DESCRIBE` or `PREPARE INTO` statement will always populate the `sqld` element with the required number of SQLVARs for an SQL statement.

Table 4-8 SQLDA Header Information

Name of SQL Element	Data Type	Purpose in DESCRIBE and PREPARE	Purpose in FETCH, EXECUTE, and CALL
sqldaid	CHAR(8)	The seventh byte is set to 2 if the SQLDA has been doubled, otherwise it is set to blank.	The seventh byte is set to 2 if the SQLDA is doubled.
sqldabc	INTEGER	The size of the SQLDA structure.	The size of the SQLDA structure.
sqln	SMALLINT	Must be set by the application to equal the number of SQLVARs.	Total number of SQLVARs in the SQLDA structure.
sqld	SMALLINT	Set by DB2 to the number of columns in the result table. If the statement is not a SELECT, the value is zero.	The number of host variables described by occurrences of SQLVAR.

The value of `sqln` needs to be greater than or equal to the value of `sqld` before the SQLDA can be used in a `FETCH`, `EXECUTE`, or `CALL` statement. The `DESCRIBE` will not be successful until the application developer has allocated the proper number (`sqld`) of SQLVAR entries. If there are LOB data types, then twice as many (`2*sqld`) SQLVAR entries must be allocated.

4.3.7 Output SQLDA

If the number of columns defined in an SQL statement is unknown by the application developer, then the application must be ready to accept any number of columns. The maximum number of columns in a SELECT statement is 500 or 1012, depending on whether the page size is 4K or larger. Not only does the application developer need to know the number of columns, they must also know the data type of each column.

In Table 4-9, the SQLVAR structure is shown. The first element, `sqltype`, is used to indicate the data type. If the SQLDA is being used as input using the FETCH, EXECUTE, or CALL statements, the `sqltype` and a compatible host variable must be initialized. The possible values for `sqltype` are defined in the *DB2 UDB V7 SQL Reference*.

Table 4-9 SQLVAR Elements (Basic SQLVAR)

Name of Element	Data Type	Purpose in DESCRIBE and PREPARE INTO Statements	Purpose in FETCH, EXECUTE, and CALL Statements
sqltype	SMALLINT	Contains a number that represents the data type defined for the column in the select list (set by DB2), and if it can contain nulls.	Contains a number representing the data type (set by application) and nullability.
sqllen	SMALLINT	Contains the length attribute of the column (set by DB2).	Contains the length attribute of the host variable (set by application).
sqldata	Pointer (*)	Usually contains the code page (set by DB2) and FOR BIT DATA indication.	Contains the address of the host variable where fetched data will be stored (set by application).
sqlind	Pointer	May contain the code page or the value of 0 (set by DB2).	Contains the address of an associated indicator variable. Not required for NOT NULL columns (set by application).
sqlname	VARCHAR(30)	The unqualified column name (set by DB2).	Used by the CALL statement to access a DRDA application.

A user may supply the entire SQL statement or a portion of the SQL statement. Often, only a portion of the SQL statement is known. Once the entire SQL statement has been determined, the developer must dynamically prepare the statement for execution using the PREPARE statement.

The first example does not contain any parameter markers because the entire statement text is known.

```
szSQLText='SELECT CUSTOMER_ID, CUSTOMER_NAME FROM CUSTOMER'
PREPARE cust1 INTO :minsqlda FROM :szSQLText
```

Figure 4-18 PREPAREing an SQL statement into an SQLDA structure.

Let's examine the example in Figure 4-18, starting from the end of the statement. A host variable called `szSQLText` is referenced. This host variable must contain a valid SQL statement. The host variable should be a string data type and contain the entire SQL statement (there are no parameter markers in this example).

If the SQL statement has any missing parts, they should be represented in the statement text using the (?) character and supplied as host variables during statement execution. The SQL statement is checked for syntax, and information is provided about the number and data types of the columns referenced.

The `PREPARE` statement contains two other user-supplied components. A statement identifier of `cust1` is used to reference the prepared statement during query execution. The `cust1` identifier is not a host variable. It will be used during query execution and row fetching. Another host variable called `minsqlda` is also shown in Figure 4-18. This data structure is used to contain information about the SQL statement. The SQL statement contains two columns of type variable length (VARCHAR).

The SQLDA structure called `minsqlda` contains information about the query being prepared. Like all other host variables, the SQLDA data structure must be initialized prior to its use in an SQL statement. An SQLDA contains a number of SQLVAR data structures. Each SQLVAR data structure corresponds to a single column for each row being processed. Since the nature of the query is unknown by the application developer, the required size of the SQLDA is also unknown.

There are two methods of initializing the SQLDA data structure:

- Allocate an SQLDA with the maximum number of SQLVAR elements.
- Allocate an SQLDA with the minimum number of SQLVAR elements and reinitialize the SQLDA with the proper number of SQLVAR elements following a `DESCRIBE` or a `PREPARE INTO` statement.

The statement being prepared in Figure 4-18 contains a two-column select list. Therefore, an SQLDA structure with at least two SQLVAR elements is required. If the SQLDA does not contain enough SQLVAR elements for the query, the statement cannot be executed. If we decided to declare the maximum SQLDA size, then we would have been wasting memory, but we would have avoided having to reallocate the SQLDA to a larger size. Remember, if any of the columns are defined as LOBs, the number of SQLVAR elements needs to be doubled.

If the SQLDA is not large enough, then additional SQLVAR elements must be allocated and the statement needs to be prepared again, or the `DESCRIBE` statement can be used to acquire the column description. (In the latter case, DB2 UDB returns the number of items detected in the `SELECT` list to the application in the first `PREPARE`.)

> **Note**
>
> A `PREPARE INTO` statement is functionally equivalent to a `PREPARE` followed by a `DESCRIBE` of the statement.

```
PREPARE cust2 FROM :szSQLText2
```
Figure 4-19 Preparing an SQL statement.

In Figure 4-19, the SQL statement defined in the string `szSQLText2` is being dynamically prepared. This will not populate an SQLDA structure. It is not mandatory that every dynamically prepared SQL statement be described using the `PREPARE INTO` or the `DESCRIBE` statements. Remember that the proper SQLDA structure needs to be provided when the statement is executed.

Once the statement (`SELECT * FROM tabname`) has been prepared, it is executed and fetched into an SQLDA data structure. The `DESCRIBE` statement is used to provide detailed information regarding the column name, length, null constraints, and data type.

4.4 Comparing Dynamic SQL with Static SQL

The question of whether to use static or dynamic SQL for performance is usually of great interest to programmers. The answer, of course, is that it all depends on your situation. Refer to Table 4-10 to help you decide whether to use static or dynamic SQL. There may be certain considerations such as security that dictate static SQL, or your environment (such as whether you are using DB2 CLI or the CLP) which dictates dynamic SQL.

When making your decision, consider the following recommendations on whether to choose static or dynamic SQL in a particular situation. In the following table, "Either" means that there is no advantage to either static or dynamic SQL. Note that these are general recommendations only. Your specific application, its intended usage, and working environment dictate the actual choice. When in doubt, prototyping your statements as static SQL, then as dynamic SQL, and then comparing the differences is the best approach.

Table 4-10 Comparing Static and Dynamic SQL

Consideration	Likely Best Choice
Time to run the SQL statement: • Less than 2 seconds • 2 to 10 seconds • More than 10 seconds	 • Static • Either • Dynamic
Data uniformity: • Uniform data distribution • Slight nonuniformity • Highly nonuniform distribution	 • Static • Either • Dynamic

Table 4-10 Comparing Static and Dynamic SQL (Continued)

Range (<,>,BETWEEN,LIKE) predicates: • Very infrequent • Occasional • Frequent	 • Static • Either • Dynamic
Repetitious execution: • Runs many times (10 or more times) • Runs a few times (less than 10 times) • Runs once	 • Either • Either • Static
Nature of query: • Random • Permanent	 • Dynamic • Either
Runtime environment (DML/DDL or Data Manipulation Language/ Data Definition Language): • Transaction Processing (DML only) • Mixed (DML and DDL—DDL affects packages) • Mixed (DML and DDL—DDL does not affect packages)	 • Either • Dynamic • Either
Frequency of RUNSTATS: • Very infrequently • Regularly • Frequently	 • Static • Either • Dynamic

In general, an application using dynamic SQL has a higher start-up (or initial) cost per SQL statement due to the need to compile the SQL statements prior to using them. Once compiled, the execution time for dynamic SQL compared to static SQL should be equivalent and, in some cases, faster due to better access plans being chosen by the optimizer. Each time a dynamic statement is executed, the initial compilation cost becomes less of a factor. If multiple users are running the same dynamic application with the same statements, only the first application to issue the statement realizes the cost of statement compilation.

In a mixed DML and DDL environment, the compilation cost for a dynamic SQL statement may vary as the statement may be implicitly recompiled by the system while the application is running. In a mixed environment, the choice between static and dynamic SQL must also factor in the frequency in which packages are invalidated. If the DDL invalidates packages, dynamic SQL may be more efficient, as only those queries executed are recompiled when they are next used. Others are not recompiled. For static SQL, the entire package is rebound once it has been invalidated.

Now suppose your particular application contains a mixture of the above characteristics and some of these characteristics suggest that you use static, while others suggest dynamic. In this case, there is no clear-cut decision and you should probably use whichever method you have the most experience with, and with which you feel most comfortable. Note that the considerations in the above table are listed roughly in order of importance.

Static and dynamic SQL each come in two types that make a difference to the DB2 optimizer. These are:

1. Static SQL containing no host variables.
   This is an unlikely situation that you may see only for:

   - Initialization code.
   - Novice training examples.

2. This is actually the best combination from a performance perspective in that there is no runtime performance overhead and yet the DB2 optimizer's capabilities can be fully realized.
3. Static SQL containing host variables.
   This is the traditional *legacy* style of DB2 applications. It avoids the runtime overhead of a PREPARE and catalog locks acquired during statement compilation. Unfortunately, the full power of the optimizer cannot be harnessed since it does not know the entire SQL statement. A particular problem exists with highly nonuniform data distributions.
4. Dynamic SQL containing no parameter markers.
   This is the typical style for random query interfaces (such as the CLP) and is the optimizer's preferred flavor of SQL. For complex queries, the overhead of the PREPARE statement is usually worthwhile due to improved execution time..
5. Dynamic SQL containing parameter markers.
   This is the most common type of SQL for CLI applications. The key benefit is that the presence of parameter markers allows the cost of the PREPARE to be amortized over the repeated executions of the statement, typically a SELECT or INSERT. This amortization is true for all repetitive dynamic SQL applications.
6. Unfortunately, just like static SQL with host variables, parts of the DB2 optimizer will not work since complete information is unavailable. The recommendation is to use *static SQL with host variables* or *dynamic SQL without parameter markers* as the most efficient options.

4.5 Summary

The process of creating static embedded SQL program modules was discussed in this chapter. By embedding SQL statements into a programming language, we can manipulate the data contained in a DB2 UDB database. The programming modules containing the SQL statements must be converted from SQL statements to DB2 UDB library APIs. This step is known as the precompilation step, since it is always performed before the programming module is compiled and linked.

There are two types of database connections. The default database connection type is known as a Type 1 connect. This connection only allows a single database to be involved in a transaction, or unit of work (UOW). A Type 2 connection allows establishing connections to multiple databases within the same UOW.

The programming language variables used as input or output for SQL statements are known as host variables. These host variables must be declared to the precompiler and used properly within the embedded SQL statements. An input host variable can be used to define the conditions for the query (predicate) or data values in an INSERT / UPDATE statement. An output host variable can be used to receive the results of a SELECT or VALUES statement.

SQL statements can result in single or multiple rows of data. A single-row result can be retrieved using the INTO clause to specify the output host variable. A multiple-row result set must be manipulated using one or more cursors. A cursor is defined using the DECLARE statement. Once the cursor has been declared, the cursor must be opened using the OPEN statement. An open cursor can populate output host variables corresponding to the current data row. The FETCH statement is used to populate host variables. Multiple cursors can be declared on the same result set.

Data can be deleted or updated using either a condition (predicate) or cursor manipulation. If a data record is to be modified using cursors, it is known as a positioned modification, using the WHERE CURRENT CURSOR phrase.

This chapter also included dynamic embedded SQL programming techniques. The PREPARE, DESCRIBE, EXECUTE, and FETCH steps are required for issuing dynamic SQL statements. Another option is to use EXECUTE IMMEDIATE for statements that do not have any missing elements and do not return more than one row. Instead of using host variables, dynamic statements employ parameter markers, denoted by question marks (?), for specifying missing information. The SQLDA structure is used for exchanging data between the application and database manager.

CHAPTER 5

Administrative APIs

This chapter provides a brief description of the DB2 UDB administrative APIs needed to develop administrative applications such as those that can administer DB2 instances, back up and restore databases, and import and export data.

A complete explanation and syntax of these APIs can be found in the *Administrative API Reference*.

It is assumed that the reader has an understanding of database administration and application programming, plus a knowledge of:

- Structured Query Language (SQL).
- The C, COBOL, FORTRAN, or REXX programming language.
- Application program design.

5.1 DB2 APIs

DB2 APIs are grouped into the following functional categories. See Table 5-1 below for API function names.

- Database Manager Control.
- Database Control.
- Database Directory Management.
- Client/Server Directory Management.
- Network Support.
- Database Configuration.
- Recovery.
- Operational Utilities.

- Database Monitoring.
- Data Utilities.
- General Application Programming.
- Application Preparation.
- Remote Server Utilities.
- Table Space Management.
- Node Management.
- Nodegroup Management.
- Additional APIs.

Table 5-1 DB2 APIs

API Description	Sample Code	`INCLUDE` File
Database Manager Control		
`sqlepstart` - Start database manager.	`makeapi`, `dbstart`	`sqlenv`
`sqlepstp` - Stop database manager.	`makeapi`, `dbstop`	`sqlenv`
`sqlfxsys` - Get database manager configuration.	`dbmconf`	`sqlutil`
`sqlfdsys` - Get database manager configuration defaults.	`d_dbmcon`	`sqlutil`
`sqlfrsys` - Reset database manager configuration.	`dbmconf`	`sqlutil`
`sqlfusys` - Update database manager configuration.	`dbmconf`	`sqlutil`
`sqlesdeg` - Set runtime degree.	`setrundg`	`sqlenv`
Database Control		
`db2DatabaseRestart` - Restart database.	n/a	`db2ApiDf`
`sqlecrea` - Create database.	`dbconf`	`sqlenv`
`sqlecran` - Create database at node.	n/a	`sqlenv`
`sqledrpd` - Drop database.	`dbconf`	`sqlenv`
`sqledpan` - Drop database at node.	n/a	`sqlenv`
`sqlemgdb` - Migrate database.	`migrate`	`sqlenv`
`sqlxphqr` - List in-doubt transactions.	n/a	`sqlxa`
`sqle_activate_db` - Activate database.	n/a	`sqlenv`
`sqle_deactivate_db` - Deactivate database.	n/a	`sqlenv`
`sqlcspqy` - List DRDA in-doubt transactions.	n/a	`sqlxa`

Table 5-1 DB2 APIs (Continued)

API Description	Sample Code	INCLUDE File
Database Directory Management		
sqlecadb - Catalog database.	dbcat	sqlenv
sqleuncd - Uncatalog database.	dbcat	sqlenv
sqlegdad - Catalog DCS database.	dcscat	sqlenv
sqlegdel - Uncatalog DCS database.	dcscat	sqlenv
sqledcgd - Change database comment.	dbcmt	sqlenv
sqledosd - Open database directory scan.	dbcat	sqlenv
sqledgne - Get next database directory entry.	dbcat	sqlenv
sqledcls - Close database directory scan.	dbcat	sqlenv
sqlegdsc - Open DCS directory scan.	dcscat	sqlenv
sqlegdgt - Get DCS directory entries.	dcscat	sqlenv
sqlegdcl - Close DCS directory scan.	dcscat	sqlenv
sqlegdge - Get DCS directory entry for database.	dcscat	sqlenv
Client/Server Directory Management		
sqlectnd - Catalog node.	nodecat	sqlenv
sqleuncn - Uncatalog node.	nodecat	sqlenv
sqlenops - Open node directory scan.	nodecat	sqlenv
sqlengne - Get next node directory entry.	nodecat	sqlenv
sqlencls - Close node directory scan.	nodecat	sqlenv
Network Support		
sqleregs - Register.	regder	sqlenv
sqledreg - Deregister.	regder	sqlenv
db2LdapRegister	n/a	db2ApiDf
db2LdapUpdate	n/a	db2ApiDf
db2LdapDeregister	n/a	db2ApiDf
db2LdapCatalogNode	n/a	db2ApiDf
db2LdapUncatalogNode	n/a	db2ApiDf
db2LdapCatalogDatabase	n/a	db2ApiDf
db2LdapUncatalogDatabase	n/a	db2ApiDf

Table 5-1 DB2 APIs (Continued)

API Description	Sample Code	`INCLUDE` File
Database Configuration		
`sqlfxdb` - Get database configuration.	`dbconf`	`sqlutil`
`sqlfddb` - Get database configuration defaults.	`d_dbconf`	`sqlutil`
`sqlfrdb` - Reset database configuration.	`dbconf`	`sqlutil`
`sqlfudb` - Update database configuration.	`dbconf`	`sqlutil`
Recovery		
`sqlubkp` - Backup Database	`backrest`	`sqlutil`
`sqlurcon` - Reconcile.	n/a	`sqlutil`
`sqlurestore` - Restore database.	`backrest`	`sqlutil`
`sqluroll` - Roll database forward.	`backrest`	`sqlutil`
`db2HistoryOpenScan` - Open recovery history file scan.	n/a	`db2ApiDf`
`db2HistoryGetEntry` - Get next recovery history file entry.	n/a	`db2ApiDf`
`db2HistoryCloseScan` - Close recovery history file scan.	n/a	`db2ApiDf`
`db2Prune`	n/a	`db2ApiDf`
`db2HistoryUpdate` - Update recovery history file.	n/a	`db2ApiDf`
Operational Utilities		
`sqlefrce` - Force application.	`dbstop`	`sqlenv`
`sqlureot` - Reorganize table.	`dbstat`	`sqlutil`
`sqlustat` - RUNSTATS.	`dbstat`	`sqlutil`
Database Monitoring		
`db2GetSnapshotSize` – Estimate size required for `db2GetSnapshot()` output buffer.	`db2mon`	`sqlmon`
`db2MonitorSwitches` - Get/Update monitor switches.	`db2mon`	`sqlmon`
`db2GetSnapshot` - Get snapshot.	n/a	`db2ApiDf`
`db2ResetMonitor` - Reset monitor.	`db2mon`	`sqlmon`
`db2ConvMonStream`	n/a	`db2ApiDf`
Data Utilities		
`sqluexpr` - Export.	`impexp`	`sqlutil`
`sqluimpr` - Import.	`impexp`	`sqlutil`
`sqluload` - Load.	`tload`	`sqlutil`
`db2LoadQuery` - Load query.	`loadqry`	`db2ApiDf`

Table 5-1 DB2 APIs (Continued)

API Description	Sample Code	INCLUDE File
General Application Programming		
db2AutoConfig	autoconf	db2AuCfg
db2AutoConfigFreeMemory	autoconf	db2AuCfg
sqlaintp - Get error message.	util, check err	sql
sqlogstt - Get SQLSTATE message.	util, check err	sql
sqleisig - Install signal handler.	dbcmt	sqlenv
sqleintr - Interrupt.	n/a	sqlenv
sqlgdref - Dereference address.	n/a	sqlutil
sqlgmcpy - Copy memory.	n/a	sqlutil
sqlefmem - Free memory.	tspace	sqlenv
sqlgaddr - Get address.	n/a	sqlutil
Application Preparation		
sqlaprep - Precompile program.	makeapi	sql
sqlabndx - Bind.	makeapi	sql
sqlarbnd - Rebind.	rebind	sql
Remote Server Utilities		
sqleatin - Attach.	dbinst	sqlenv
sqleatcp - Attach and change password.	dbinst	sqlenv
sqledtin - Detach.	dbinst	sqlenv
Table Space Management		
sqlbtcq - Tablespace container query.	tabscont	sqlutil
sqlbotcq - Open tablespace container query.	tabscont	sqlutil
sqlbftcq - Fetch tablespace container query.	tabscont	sqlutil
sqlbctcq - Close tablespace container query.	tabscont	sqlutil
sqlbstsc - Set tablespace containers.	backrest	sqlutil
sqlbmtsq - Tablespace query.	tabspace	sqlutil
sqlbstpq - Single tablespace query.	tabspace	sqlutil
sqlbotsq - Open tablespace query.	tabspace	sqlutil
sqlbftpq - Fetch tablespace query.	tabspace	sqlutil

Table 5-1 DB2 APIs (Continued)

API Description	Sample Code	INCLUDE File
`sqlbctsq` - Close tablespace query.	`tabspace`	`sqlutil`
`sqlbgtss` - Get tablespace statistics.	`tabspace`	`sqlutil`
`sqluvqdp` - Quiesce tablespaces for table.	`tload`	`sqlutil`
Node Management		
`sqleaddn` - Add node.	n/a	`sqlenv`
`sqledrpn` - Drop node verify.	n/a	`sqlenv`
Nodegroup Management		
`sqludrdt` - Redistribute nodegroup.	n/a	`sqlutil`
Additional APIs		
`sqluadau` – Get authorizations.	`dbauth`	`sqlutil`
`sqlegins` - Get instance.	`dbinst`	`sqlenv`
`sqleqryc` - Query client.	`client`	`sqlenv`
`sqleqryi` - Query client information.	`cli_info`	`sqlenv`
`sqlesetc` - Set client.	`client`	`sqlenv`
`sqleseti` - Set client information.	`cli_info`	`sqlenv`
`sqlesact` - Set accounting string.	`setact`	`sqlenv`
`sqlurlog` - Asynchronous read log.	`asynrlog`	`sqlutil`
`sqlugrpn` – Get row partitioning number.	n/a	`sqlutil`
`sqlugtpi` - Get table partitioning information.	n/a	`sqlutil`
`db2AdminMsgWrite`	n/a	`db2ApiDf`

> **Note**
>
> The sample programs can be found in the language-specific directory of the samples subdirectory in the `sqllib` directory (for example, `\Program Files\sqllib\samples\c` for C source code, if DB2 is installed on Windows platforms). The file extensions on sample code depend on the programming language being used. For example, for sample code written in C, the extension is `.c` or `.sqc`. Not all programs are available in all supported programming languages. Not all APIs have sample code (indicated by n/a).
>
> The file extensions on INCLUDE files depend on the programming language being used. For example, an INCLUDE file written for C has a file extension of `.h`. The INCLUDE files can be found in directory `sqllib\include` (directory delimiters are dependant upon the operating system).

5.2 Application Migration Considerations

This section describes issues that should be considered before migrating an application to Version 7.

There are four possible operating scenarios:

1. Running pre-Version 7 applications against databases that have not been migrated.
2. Running pre-Version 7 applications against migrated databases.
3. Updating applications with Version 7 APIs.
4. Running Version 7 applications against migrated databases.

The first and the fourth are consistent operating environments that do not require qualification. The second, in which only the databases have been migrated, should work without changes to any application, because back-level applications are supported. However, as with any new version, a small number of incompatibilities can occur, and these are described in the administration guide. For the third scenario, in which applications are to be updated with Version 7 APIs, the following points should be considered:

- All pre-Version 7 APIs that have been discontinued in Version 7 are still defined in the Version 7 header files so that older applications will compile and link with Version 7 headers.
- Discontinued APIs should be removed from applications as soon as possible to enable these applications to take full advantage of the new functions available in Version 7, and to position the applications for future enhancements.

The names of the APIs listed below have changed because of new functions in Version 7. Users should scan for these names in their application source code to identify the changes required following Version 7 migration of an application. APIs that are not listed do not require changes following migration of an application.

Note that an application may contain the generic version of an API call, depending on the application programming language being used. In all cases, the generic version of the API name is identical to the C version of the name, with the exception that the fourth character is always "g."

5.2.1 Changed APIs and Data Structures

Table 5-2 shows a correlation between older and newer versions of APIs.

5.3 Context Management APIs

In the default implementation of threaded applications against a DB2 database, serialization of access to the database is enforced by the database APIs. If one thread performs a database call that is blocked for some reason (that is, the table is already in exclusive use), all other threads

Table 5-2 Back-level Supported APIs

API (Version)	Descriptive Name	New API (Version)
`sqlbftsq` (V2)	Fetch tablespace query.	`sqlbftpq` (V5)
`sqlbstsq` (V2)	Single tablespace query.	`sqlbstpq` (V5)
`sqlbtsq` (V2)	Tablespace query.	`sqlbmtsq` (V5)
`sqlectdd` (V2)	Catalog database.	`sqlecadb` (V5)
`sqlepstr` (V2)	Start database manager (DB2 Parallel Edition Version 1.2).	`sqlepstart` (V5)
`sqlestar` (V2)	Start database manager (DB2 Version 2).	`sqlepstart` (V5)
`sqlestop` (V2)	Stop database manager.	`sqlepstp` (V5)
`sqlerstd` (V5)	Restart database.	`db2DatabaseRestart` (V6)
`sqlmon` (V6)	Get/Update monitor switches.	`db2MonitorSwitches` (V7)
`sqlmonss` (V5)	Get snapshot.	`db2GetSnapshot` (V6)
`sqlmonsz` (V6)	Estimate size required for `sqlmonss()` output buffer.	`db2GetSnapshotSize` (V7)
`sqlmrset` (V6)	Reset monitor.	`db2ResetMonitorData` (V7)
`sqlubkup` (V2)	Backup database.	`sqlubkp` (V5)
`sqlugrpi` (V2)	Get row partitioning information (DB2 Parallel Edition Version 1.x).	`sqlugrpn` (V5)
`sqluhcls` (V5)	Close recovery history file scan.	`db2HistoryCloseScan` (V6)
`sqluhget` (V5)	Retrieve DDL information from the history file.	`db2HistoryGetEntry` (V6)
`sqluhgne` (V5)	Get next recovery history file entry.	`db2HistoryGetEntry` (V6)
`sqluhops` (V5)	Open recovery history file scan.	`db2HistoryOpenScan` (V6)
`sqluhprn` (V5)	Prune recovery history file.	`db2Prune` (V6)
`sqluhupd` (V5)	Update recovery history file.	`db2HistoryUpdate` (V6)
`sqluqry` (V5)	Load query.	`db2LoadQuery` (V6)
`sqlursto` (V2)	Restore database.	`sqlurst` (V5)
`sqlxhcom` (V2)	Commit an in-doubt transaction.	`sqlxphcm` (V5)
`sqlxhqry` (V2)	List in-doubt transactions.	`sqlxphqr` (V5)
`sqlxhrol` (V2)	Roll back an in-doubt transaction.	`sqlxphrl` (V5)
`SQLB-TBSQRY-DATA` (V2)	Tablespace data structure.	`SQLB-TBSPQRY-DATA` (V5)
`SQLEDBSTRTOPT` (V2)	Start database manager data structure (DB2 Parallel Edition Version 1.2).	`SQLE-START-OPTIONS` (V5)
`SQLUHINFO` and `SQLUHADM` (V5)	History file data structures.	`db2HistData` (V6)

will be blocked as well. In addition, all threads within a process share a commit scope. True concurrent access to a database can only be achieved through separate processes, or by using the Context Management APIs, shown in Table 5-3 below. Refer to the *Administrative API Reference* for their use and syntax.

These APIs can be used to allocate and manipulate separate environments (contexts) for the use of database APIs and embedded SQL. Each context is a separate entity, and any connection or attachment using one context is independent of all other contexts (and thus all other connections or attachments within a process). For work to be done on a context, it must first be associated with a thread. A thread must always have a context when making database API calls or when using embedded SQL. If these APIs to manipulate contexts are not used, all threads within a process share the same context. If these APIs are used, each thread can have its own context. It will have a separate connection to a database or attachment to an instance, and will have its own commit scope.

Table 5-3 Context Management APIs

API Name	Description
SqleAttachToCtx	Attach to context.
sqleBeginCtx	Create and attach to an application context.
sqleDetachFromCtx	Detach from context.
sqleEndCtx	Detach and destroy application context.
sqleGetCurrentCtx	Get current context.
sqleInterruptCtx	Interrupt context.
sqleSetTypeCtx	Set application context type.

Contexts need not be associated with a given thread for the duration of a connection or attachment. One thread can attach to a context, connect to a database, detach from the context, and then a second thread can attach to the context and continue doing work using the existing database connection. Contexts can be passed around among threads in a process, but not among processes.

If the new APIs are not used, the old behavior is in effect, and existing applications need not change. Even if the new APIs are used, the following APIs continue to be serialized:

- sqlabndx—Bind.
- sqlaprep—Precompile Program.
- sqluexpr—Export.
- sqluimpr—Import.

The new APIs can be used with embedded SQL and transaction APIs.

These APIs have no effect (that is, they are no-ops) on platforms that do not support application threading.

> **Note**
>
> The Command Line Interface, or CLI, automatically uses the new scheme (it creates a new context for each incoming connection), and it is up to the user to disable this explicitly. For more information, see the *CLI Guide and Reference*.

By default, AIX does not permit more than 10 shared memory segments per process, thus limiting the number of local DB2 connections per process to 10. When this limit is reached, DB2 returns SQLCODE -1224 on an SQL CONNECT. DB2 Connect also has the 10-connections limitation if local users are running two-phase commit over SNA (Systems Network Architecture), or two-phase commit with a TP (Transaction Processing) Monitor (SNA or TCP/IP).

> **TIP** On AIX Version 4.2.1 or greater, the environment variable EXTSHM(=ON) can be used to enhance the number of shared memory regions to which a process can attach.
>
> On AIX prior to Version 4.2.1, there are no operating system-based solutions. An alternative is to move the local database or DB2 Connect into another machine and to access it remotely, or to access the local database or DB2 Connect database with TCP/IP loop-back by cataloging it as a remote node that has the TCP/IP address of the local machine.

5.4 Summary

DB2 instances, databases, and data can be administered not only from the Command Line Processor (CLP), Control Center, and DB2 scripts, but by using the administrative APIs made available for ambitious programmers.

Programmers can now code their applications in such a way so that serialization of database access is avoided. This is done by the use of context APIs. CLI applications, however, do not have to worry about context management as the CLI driver manages contexts at the driver level and no context management is necessary at the application level.

References

DB2 UDB Administrative API Reference

DB2 UDB CLI Guide and Reference

CHAPTER 6

CLI/ODBC and OLE DB Programming

In this chapter, we're going to take a look at call-level interfaces as provided by IBM's DB2 Call Level Interface (CLI) and Microsoft's Open Database Connectivity (ODBC). IBM's CLI provides a library (or driver) of DBMS functions that can be used to access a DB2 database. Microsoft's ODBC provides a standard of functions that can be used to access a vendor's DBMS (Database Management System) such as DB2. Both CLI and ODBC were originally based on parts of the X/Open CLI Standard. Much of the X/Open CLI Standard has been accepted as part of the ISO CLI Standard (ISO/IEC 9075-3:1995 SQL/CLI). ODBC 3.0 does contain considerable functionality that is not part of the ISO standard, much of which is being added to the next draft.

6.1 Objectives

After reading this chapter, you should:

- Be able to set up the environment needed to develop or run ODBC, CLI, and OLE DB (Object Linking and Embedding Database) applications.
- Understand the basic program flow for developing these types of applications.
- Understand initialization and termination phases within these applications.
- Handle diagnostic and error processing.
- Know the different methods of transaction processing, including preparing and executing SQL statements and fetching the results from the database.
- Understand some advanced programming features.
- Recognize and know when to make use of different cursor types that are available to CLI.
- Be aware of the catalog functions available for accessing database system information such as listing available tables.

- Be able to bind arrays of parameters.
- Be able to insert arrays of data into the database.
- Know the main objects available for OLE DB programming.
- Be introduced to the advance feature of OLE Automation with DB2's User-Defined Functions (UDFs) and stored procedures.

6.2 CLI and ODBC Overview

How do ODBC and CLI fit together? IBM's CLI driver implements most of the function set that is defined by Microsoft's ODBC. Microsoft supplies a Driver Manager that manages many different vendors' drivers such as IBM's CLI for the Windows environment. A Window application that wants to use ODBC to access a database will be dynamically linked to the ODBC Driver Manager and make a function call to it such as `SQLConnect()`. The Driver Manager then finds this function in the appropriate vendor-supplied driver, such as IBM's CLI driver, and uses it to communicate to the DBMS; in this case, it connects to a database.

A program does not necessarily need to be dynamically linked to the ODBC Driver Manager to access a DB2 database. It could, alternatively, be linked with the CLI driver. This process removes a layer of function calls that would otherwise be required, and makes available CLI-specific calls that are not available through the Driver Manager. A disadvantage of this is that the application becomes DB2-specific and can no longer be used to access a different database such as Oracle. Another disadvantage is that the application no longer has access to specific features found within the Driver Manager such as connection pooling. Figure 6-1 illustrates the relationship between the application and DB2 in both the ODBC and CLI environments.

So far we've been primarily talking about the Windows environment, but ODBC Driver Managers are also available for O2 and many UNIX platforms. Visigenic is one such supplier of a Driver Manager for UNIX operating systems. Of course, DB2 provides a CLI driver for all platforms that DB2 UDB is available for. Be aware, though, DB2 does not provide a Driver Manager for UNIX platforms. These often come with third-party products or else have to be purchased separately. It is possible to rename the CLI driver to the name of an ODBC Driver Manager so that applications can load that driver instead. So long as the application is only accessing a DB2 database, this practice should be safe.

6.2.1 Advantages of CLI

Often accessing a database through DB2 CLI is compared against accessing it through embedded SQL. The DB2 CLI interface has several key advantages over embedded SQL:

- It is ideally suited for a client server environment, in which the target database is not known when the application is built. It provides a consistent interface for executing SQL statements, regardless of which database server the application is connected to.

CLI and ODBC Overview

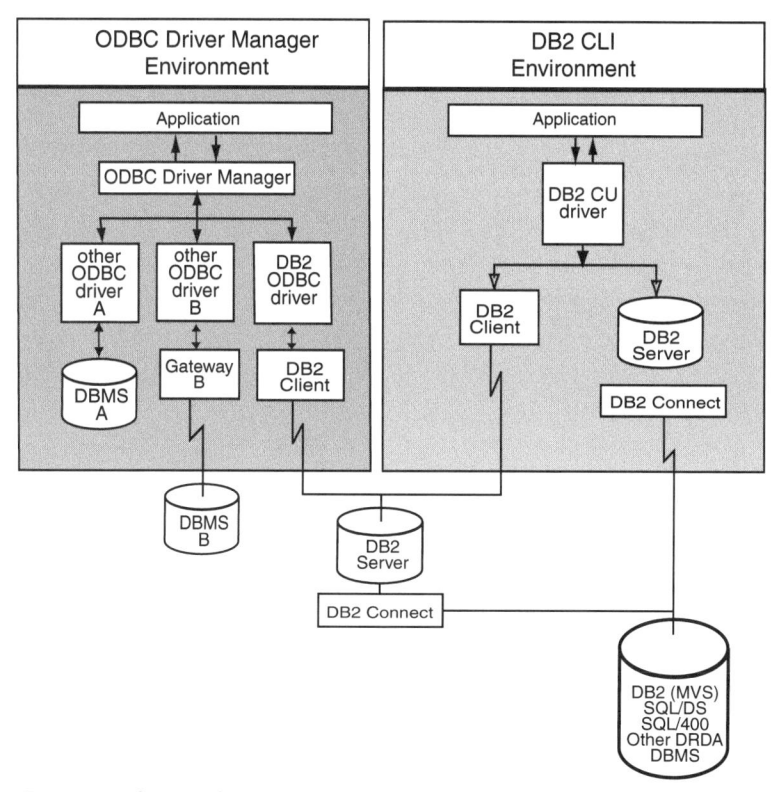

Figure 6-1 DB2 UDB CLI vs. ODBC.

- It increases the portability of applications by removing the dependence on precompilers. Applications are distributed not as embedded SQL source code, which must be preprocessed for each database product, but as compiled applications or runtime libraries.
- Individual DB2 CLI applications do not need to be bound to each database; only bind files shipped with DB2 CLI need to be bound once for all DB2 CLI applications. This can significantly reduce the amount of management required for the application once it is in general use.
- DB2 CLI applications can connect to multiple databases, including multiple connections to the same database, all from the same application.
- Each connection has its own commit scope. This is much simpler (using CLI) than using embedded SQL, where the application must make use of multithreading to achieve the same result.
- DB2 CLI eliminates the need for application-controlled, often complex, data areas such as the SQLDA and SQLCA, which are typically associated with embedded SQL applications. Instead, DB2 CLI allocates and controls the necessary data structures and provides a handle for the application to reference them.

- DB2 CLI enables the development of multithreaded, thread-safe applications where each thread can have its own connection and a separate commit scope from the rest. DB2 CLI achieves this by eliminating the data areas described above and associating all such data structures that are accessible to the application with a specific handle.
- Unlike embedded SQL, a multithreaded CLI application does not need to call any of the context management DB2 APIs; this is handled by the DB2 CLI driver automatically.
- DB2 CLI provides enhanced parameter input and fetching capability, allowing arrays of data to be specified on input, retrieving multiple rows of a result set directly into an array, and executing statements that generate multiple result sets.
- DB2 CLI provides a consistent interface to query catalog (tables, columns, foreign keys, primary keys, etc.) information contained in the various DBMS catalog tables. The result sets returned are consistent across DBMSs. This shields the application from catalog changes across releases of database servers, as well as catalog differences among different database servers, thereby saving applications from writing version-specific and server-specific catalog queries.
- Extended data conversion is also provided by DB2 CLI, requiring less application code when converting information between various SQL and C data types.
- DB2 CLI incorporates the ODBC and X/Open CLI functions, both of which are accepted industry specifications. DB2 CLI is also aligned with the emerging ISO CLI standard. Knowledge that application developers invest in these specifications can be applied directly to DB2 CLI development, and vice versa. This interface is intuitive to grasp for those programmers who are familiar with function libraries but know little about product-specific methods of embedding SQL statements into a host language.
- DB2 CLI provides the ability to retrieve multiple rows and result sets generated from a stored procedure residing on a DB2 UDB (or DB2 for MVS/ESA version 5 or later) server. However, note that this capability exists for V5 DB2 UDB clients using embedded SQL if the stored procedure resides on a server accessible from a DataJoiner Version 2 server.
- DB2 CLI supports server-side scrollable cursors that can be used in conjunction with array output. This is useful in GUI applications that display database information in scroll boxes that make use of the Page Up, Page Down, Home, and End keys. You can declare a read-only cursor as scrollable, then move forward or backward through the result set by one or more rows. You can also fetch rows by specifying an offset from:

    - The current row.
    - The beginning or end of the result set.
    - A specific row you have previously set with a bookmark.

- DB2 CLI applications can dynamically describe parameters in an SQL statement the same way that CLI and embedded SQL applications describe result sets. This enables CLI applications to dynamically process SQL statements that contain parameter markers without knowing the data type of those parameter markers in advance. When the SQL statement is prepared, describe information is returned, detailing the data types of the parameters.

6.3 Setting Up the CLI Environment

There are several steps involved with setting up a DB2 UDB CLI environment. Slight differences are necessary depending on whether a development environment is needed or just the runtime environment. However, the basic steps are as follows:

- The appropriate DB2 UDB package must be installed. If a developer's environment is needed, then the Software Developer's Kit (SDK) is necessary; otherwise, at a minimum, the DB2 UDB Client Application Environment (CAE) is needed.
- The database being accessed is cataloged properly. If the database is remote, a node must also be cataloged.
- DB2 UDB CLI bind files must be bound to the database.
- The CLI environment is configured using the Client Configuration Assistant (CCA) or by editing the db2cli.ini file directly. It is important to remember to examine the CLI environment settings in the db2cli.ini file or by using the CCA. The settings affect the execution behavior of all CLI applications executing on the system.

6.3.1 DB2 UDB Installation

The *DB2 UDB Quick Beginnings Guide* is a very good reference for installing DB2 UDB, the specifics of which are outside the scope of this book. All that we need to concern ourselves with here is that the appropriate DB2 UDB product is installed so that a CLI or ODBC application can be either developed or executed. As has already been mentioned, to execute the application, at a minimum the DB2 UDB CAE must be installed. Alternatively, the entire DB2 UDB server can be installed, including the DB2 UDB SDK.

To develop a CLI application, we must install the DB2 UDB SDK. All of the CLI APIs are contained in a static library. The names of the libraries on the various DB2 UDB development operating systems are:

- db2cli.lib on OS/2 and Windows platforms.
- libdb2.a or libdb2.so on UNIX platforms.

Also, the SDK includes various header files that are needed for CLI development. These include sqlcli.h and sqlcli1.h.

To develop ODBC applications, an ODBC SDK must also be installed in addition to (at minimum) the DB2 CAE. The DB2 SDK is not needed as the ODBC SDK provides its own static libraries and header files for successful compilation of an application. On Windows, Microsoft supplies this kit. For its configuration for use with DB2 UDB, please see the section ahead entitled, "Accessing a DB2 Database via ODBC."

6.3.2 Database Cataloging

Again, the *DB2 UDB Quick Beginnings Guide* is an excellent reference for cataloging a local or remote database. This can be accomplished by either using the command line prompt with DB2 commands or the CCA. The details of which will be left to that manual. The exception to this is cataloging a database for use with ODBC. See the section ahead entitled, "Accessing a DB2 Database via ODBC."

6.3.3 CLI Bind Files

The bind files required for CLI applications will be automatically bound when the first CLI application connects to the database. (An exception to this case is when the first application connects from a Runtime Client. This environment does not include DB2 bind files.) The bind may not be successful if the user does not have BINDADD authority on the database. Therefore, the Database Administrator (DBA) may be required to bind the necessary files manually using the DB2 UDB BIND command or the CCA. Each supported DB2 server used different bind files (see Table 6-1).

Table 6-1 CLI Bind List Files

Bind File	DB2 Server
db2cli.lst	DB2 UDB (OS/2, Windows, UNIX)
ddcsvm.lst	DB2 for VM (SQL/DS)
ddcsvse.lst	DB2 for VSE (SQL/DS)
ddcsmvs.lst	DB2 for OS/390 (MVS/ESA)
ddcs400.lst	DB2 for OS/400

For example, to manually bind the CLI packages from a DB2 UDB Command Window on Windows NT against a DB2 UDB for AIX database, you would issue the following command after connecting to the database:

```
DB2 BIND @db2cli.lst MESSAGES db2cli.msg GRANT PUBLIC
```

Likewise, if the DB2 database resides on OS/390, you could use the command:

```
DB2 BIND @ddcsmvs.lst BLOCKING ALL SQLERROR CONTINUE
MESSAGES mvsbind.msg GRANT PUBLIC
```

The syntax for the BIND command can be obtained from the *DB2 UDB Command Reference Guide*.

6.3.4 Configuring CLI

Usually it is not necessary to modify the DB2 UDB CLI configuration file (`db2cli.ini`). It is important to understand that the file exists and may require small modifications. Some of the reasons for modifying the CLI configuration file include:

- Increase CLI application performance.
- Change default CLI behavior.
- Enable workarounds for specific applications.

The `db2cli.ini` file is located in the `sqllib/cfg` directory of the instance owner in UNIX systems, or the `sqllib` directory for OS/2 and Windows operating systems.

An example `db2cli.ini` file is shown below. There are many more options that can be specified in the CLI configuration file.

```
; Comment goes here
[DB2MALL]
CURSORHOLD=0
DEFERREDPREPARE=1
PATCH1=2
```

The first line is a comment about the section of the file. Multiple databases may be configured in this file. The second line contains the database alias name in the brackets, `[DB2MALL]`. The DB2MALL database can still be accessed from a DB2 UDB CLI application without an entry in the `db2cli.ini` file, but if there is no section for the DB2MALL database, all of the default values for the parameters will be used. This may not be desirable. The three lines below the database name contain keywords and corresponding values. The supported keywords are defined in the *DB2 UDB Call Level Interface Guide and Reference*.

The DB2 UDB CCA or ODBC Administration Tool on Windows and OS/2 platforms allow you to configure the CLI environment without editing the `db2cli.ini` file directly. The interface is easy to use and explains each parameter that can be modified.

6.3.5 Accessing a DB2 Database via ODBC

To access a DB2 database from ODBC, the following are required on the DB2 UDB client where the ODBC application executes:

- DB2 UDB Runtime Client or server must be installed. If the database is on a remote DB2 system, it should be cataloged correctly and be accessible for connection.
- The ODBC Driver Manager must be installed.
- An ODBC driver for DB2 UDB must be installed and registered with the ODBC Driver Manager.
- The DB2 database must be registered as an ODBC data source with the Driver Manager.

There must be an ODBC Driver Manager installed on the computer where the ODBC application has been installed. For all Microsoft operating systems, Microsoft provides the ODBC Driver Manager.

The IBM DB2 UDB ODBC driver or another ODBC driver for DB2 must be installed and registered. The Microsoft ODBC Driver Manager and DB2 UDB ODBC driver are automatically installed on the Windows platforms during DB2 UDB installation as long as the ODBC component, highlighted by default, is not unchecked. The DB2 UDB ODBC driver is also registered with the Driver Manager during installation of DB2 UDB on Windows platforms. On Windows platforms you can run the Microsoft ODBC Administrator from the Control Panel to verify that "IBM DB2 ODBC Driver" is shown on the list. On UNIX platforms, the DB2 UDB ODBC driver and databases available through it are specified using odbc.ini and .odbcinst.ini files in the home directory of the user running the ODBC application.

The database must be identified to the ODBC Driver Manager as an available data source. The data source can be made available to all users of the system (a system data source), or only for the current user (a user data source). On Windows, you can register the data source with the Driver Manager using the CCA. Databases configured through the CCA are selected as system ODBC data sources by default, unless you explicitly uncheck the selection. For non-Windows platforms, this is accomplished by using the appropriate ODBC Administration Tool or by configuring the Driver Manager manually. For the exact configuration methods, refer to the documentation provided with the ODBC Driver Manager.

6.3.6 ODBC Development Considerations

For ODBC application development, you must obtain an ODBC SDK, similar to setting up a development environment for CLI applications. The steps of binding CLI packages and customizing CLI using db2cli.ini or the CCA are also applicable to ODBC applications that will access DB2 data sources. These steps are performed in the same way as for CLI applications.

6.4 Basic Program Flow for a CLI Application

Coding CLI applications involves writing C/C++ modules that contain DB2 UDB CLI functions. All of the available function calls are described in detail in the *DB2 UDB Call Level Interface Guide and Reference*. Coding ODBC applications is very similar to CLI applications because the function calls made are essentially the same. The primary difference is in the way the application is linked. CLI applications are linked using the DB2 UDB-supplied libraries and ODBC applications are linked with ODBC libraries. There are some functions that are supported by CLI and not by ODBC, and vice versa, but we will not be covering any of those functions here.

All CLI applications contain three main tasks; initialization, transaction processing, and termination. There are also general tasks that exist throughout an application such as message processing. Initialization involves allocating and initializing environment and connection handles as well as connecting to one or more databases. Transaction processing consists of the main

Basic Program Flow for a CLI Application

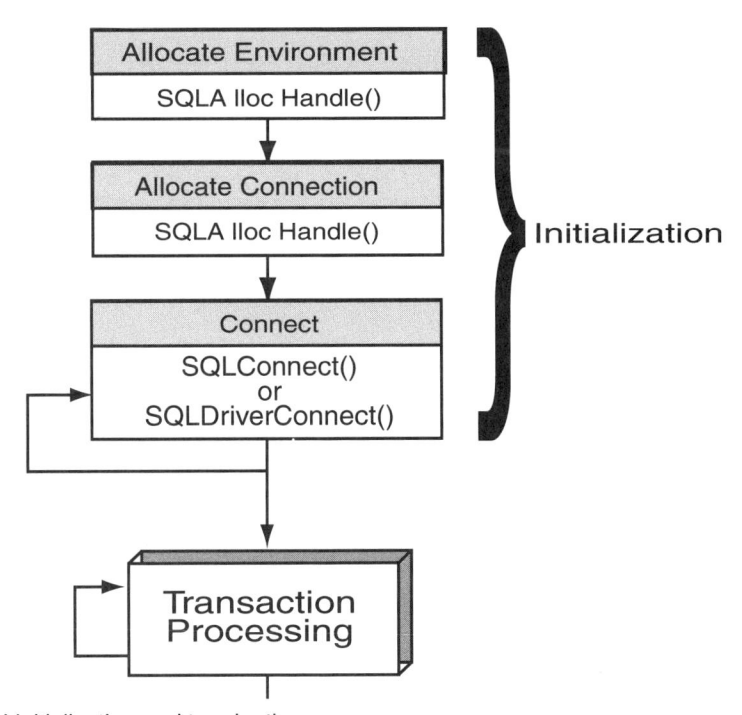

Figure 6-2 CLI initialization and termination.

tasks of the application; SQL statements are passed to DB2 to query and modify data against a database. Finally, the termination phase involves disconnecting the application from the database and freeing allocated resources. Figure 6-2 shows the basic function call sequences for the initialization and termination tasks. The transaction processing task is illustrated later in Figure 6-3.

6.4.1 Initializing Handle Types and Connecting

The initialization task consists of the allocation and initialization of environment and connection handles (which are later freed in the termination task). An application then passes the appropriate handle when it calls other DB2 CLI functions. A handle is a variable that refers to a data object controlled by DB2 CLI. Using handles relieves the application from having to allocate and manage global variables or data structures, such as the SQLDA or SQLCA, used in IBM's embedded SQL interfaces.

The `SQLAllocHandle()` function is called with a handle type and parent handle arguments to create environment, connection, statement, or descriptor handles. The function `SQLFreeHandle()` is used to free the resources allocated to a handle.

There are four types of handles:

- **Environment handle**—The environment handle refers to the data object that contains information regarding the global state of the application, such as attributes and connections. An environment handle must be allocated before a connection handle can be allocated.
- **Connection handle**—A connection handle refers to a data object that contains information associated with a connection to a particular data source (database). This includes connection attributes, general status information, transaction status, and diagnostic information.

    An application can be connected to several servers at the same time, and can establish several distinct connections to the same server. An application requires a connection handle for each concurrent connection to a database server. For information on multiple connections, refer to "Connecting to One or More Data Sources."

    Call `SQLGetInfo()` to determine if a user-imposed limit on the number of connector handles has been set.
- **Statement Handle(s)**—Statement handles are discussed in the next section, "Transaction Processing."
- **Descriptor Handle(s)**—A descriptor handle refers to a data object that contains information about:
    - Columns in a result set.
    - Dynamic parameters in an SQL statement.

6.4.2 Connecting to One or More Data Sources

To connect concurrently to one or more data sources (or multiple concurrent connections to the same data source), an application calls `SQLAllocHandle()`, with a HandleType of `SQL_HANDLE_DBC`, once for each connection. The subsequent connection handle is used with `SQLConnect()` to request a database connection, and with `SQLAllocHandle()`, with a HandleType of `SQL_HANDLE_STMT`, to allocate statement handles for use within that connection. There is also an extended connect function, `SQLDriverConnect()`, which allows for additional connect options and the ability to directly open a connection dialog box in environments that support a Graphical User Interface (GUI). The function `SQLBrowseConnect()` can be used to discover all of the attributes and attribute values required to connect to a data source.

The use of connection handles ensures that multithreaded applications that utilize one connection per thread are thread-safe since separate data structures are allocated and maintained by DB2 CLI for each connection.

6.4.3 Disconnecting and Termination

The termination phase involves disconnecting your application from the database(s) and freeing allocated resources after transaction processing has completed. The `SQLDisconnect()` API closes a connection. The corresponding connection handle can then be freed using `SQLFreeHandle()` with the argument `SQL_HANDLE_DBC`. Once all the connection handles have been freed, the `SQLFreeHandle()` function can be called with the argument `SQL_HANDLE_ENV` to successfully free the environment handle.

6.4.4 Transaction Processing

The main task of the application is accomplished during the transaction processing phase. SQL statements are passed to DB2 CLI to query and modify the data using a five-step process (see Figure 6-3):

1. Allocating statement handle(s).
2. Preparing and executing SQL statements.
3. Processing results.
4. Ending the transaction.
5. Freeing statement handle(s).

6.4.4.1 Allocation Statement Handle(s)

Statement handles need to be allocated before any SQL statement can be executed. A statement handle refers to the data object that is used to track the execution of a single statement. This includes information such as statement attributes, SQL statement text, cursor information, result values, and status information. The API `SQLAllocHandle()` is called with a HandleType of `SQL_HANDLE_STMT` to allocate a statement handle.

6.4.4.2 Preparing and Executing SQL Statements

Once a statement handle has been allocated, SQL statements can be specified and executed using one of two methods:

1. Execute directly, which combines the prepare and execute steps into one. You would use this method if the statement will be executed only once or if the column information is not needed prior to statement execution. The function `SQLExecDirect()` is used for executing statements directly.
2. Prepare then execute, which splits the preparation of the statement from the execution. This method is useful if the statement will be executed repeatedly, usually with different parameter values. This avoids having to prepare the same statement more than once. The subsequent executions make use of the access plans already generated by the prepare. The prepare followed by execute is accomplished by the function calls `SQLPrepare()` and `SQLExecute()`.

```
                    ┌─────────────────────────┐
                    │   Allocate a Statement  │
              ┌────▶│    SQLAllocHandle()     │
              │     └─────────────────────────┘
              │            │            │
              │            ▼            ▼
              │    ┌──────────────┐  ┌──────────────────┐
              │    │ Prepare a    │  │ Directly Execute │
              │    │ Statement    │  │ a Statement      │
              │    │ SQLPrepare() │  │ SQLBindParameter()│
              │    │ SQLBindParameter() │ SQLExecDirect()│
              │    └──────────────┘  └──────────────────┘
              │            │                   │
              │            ▼                   │
              │    ┌──────────────────┐        │
              │    │ Execute a Statement│      │
         ┌───▶│    │ SQLExecute()      │      │
         │    │    └──────────────────┘        │
         │    │            │                   │
         │    │   ┌────────┼────────┐          │
         │    │   ▼        ▼        ▼          ▼
```

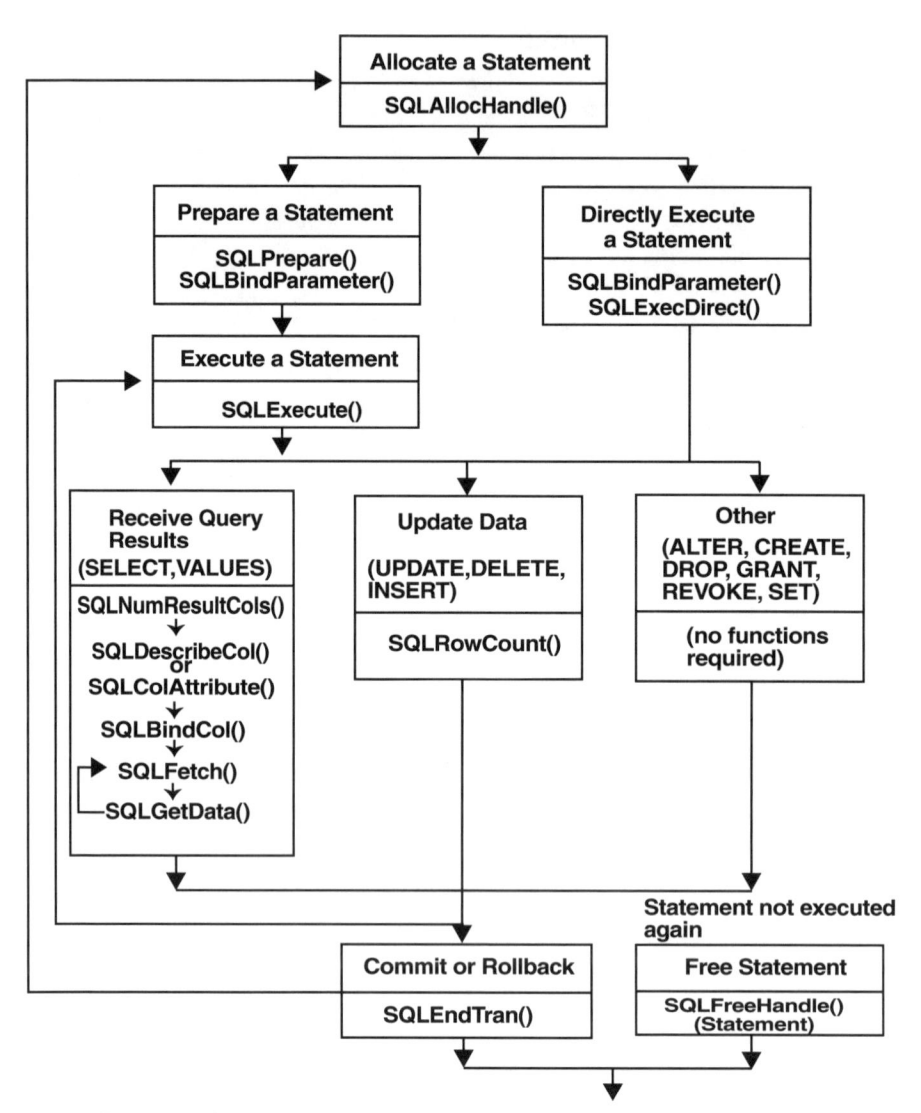

Figure 6-3 Overview of transaction processing in CLI applications.

Like in dynamic embedded SQL, it may be necessary to include parameter markers, denoted by a question mark (?), within an SQL statement. An application variable is associated or bound with a parameter marker using the SQLBindParameter() function. For example, if a statement like the one below is to be executed repeatedly with different values, it can be prepared once using the parameter marker, and the new value can be bound to the parameter marker before each execution.

```
SELECT column1 from table WHERE column2 = ?
```

Basic Program Flow for a CLI Application

DB2 provides dynamic statement caching at the server. Applications that repeatedly execute the same SQL statement across multiple transactions can realize better performance by preparing these statements once at the beginning of the application and then executing the statements as many times as needed throughout the application.

6.4.4.3 Processing Results

The next step after the statement has been executed depends on the type of the SQL statement. If the statement does not query or modify data, no action may be required other than the normal check for diagnostic messages. Such could be the case for SQL that creates or drops a table. For statements that update data, for example UPDATE, DELETE, and INSERT statements, the function SQLRowCount() can be used to obtain the number of rows affected by the SQL statement.

```
int main( ) {
   SQLHANDLE henv;
   SQLHANDLE hdbc;
   SQLHANDLE hstmt;
   SQLCHAR * sqlstmt = (SQLCHAR *)"SELECT col1
                       FROM table1 WHERE col2 = ?";
   SQLCHAR value1[30];
   SQLINTEGER ind;
/*************** Initialization ***************/
/* allocate henv, hdbc, connect to database   */
/************* End of Initialization **********/
...
/********* Start Transaction Processing ********/
/* allocate statement handle */
SQLAllocHandle( SQL_HANDLE_STMT, hdbc, &hstmt);
/* prepare the statement */
SQLPrepare( hstmt, sqlstmt, SQL_NTS);
/* bind a value to parameter marker in sqlstmt */
SQLBindParameter( hstmt, 1, SQL_PARAM_INPUT,
               SQL_C_CHAR, SQL_CHAR, 9, 0,
               "data", 4, NULL);
/* execute the statement */
SQLExecute( hstmt);

/* For the sake of simplicity we will leave out */
/* steps to find out the structure of the       */
/* result set.                                  */
/* Bind the first (col1) column of the result   */
SQLBindCol( hstmt, 1, SQL_C_CHAR, value1, 30, &ind);
/* fetch and print each row */
while( SQLFetch(hstmt) == SQL_SUCCESS)
   printf( "%s\n", firstname);
```

```
            /* explicitly commit or roll back the transaction */
            SQLEndTran( SQL_HANDLE_DBC, hdbc, SQL_ROLLBACK);
            /* free the statement handle */
            SQLFreeHandle( SQL_HANDLE_STMT, hstmt);
            /********** End Transaction Processing **********/

            /**************** Termination ****************/
            /* disconnect free connection and environment  */
            /* handles                                     */
            return( SQL_SUCCESS);
}
```

If the statement is a query, you usually need to perform the following steps to retrieve each row of the result set:

1. The first step requires establishing or describing the structure of the result set. The number of columns on the result set is found using SQLNumResultCols(). Information about the columns in the result set, like name, column type, or length, is obtained using SQLDescribeCol() or SQLColAttributes().
2. To receive data into the application, one option is to bind the application variables to columns in the result set using SQLBindCol().
3. The third step is to call SQLFetch() to fetch the first or next row of the result set. If any columns have been bound in the second step, data is retrieved into the bound application variables.
4. If the application does not bind any columns in the second step, as in the case when it needs to retrieve columns of long data pieces, it can use SQLGetData() after the fetch.

Both the SQLBindCol() and SQLGetData() techniques can be combined if some columns are bound and some are unbound.

6.4.4.4 Ending the Transaction

The transaction ends when it is either implicitly or explicitly committed or rolled back. DB2 CLI applications can switch between two commit modes, *auto-commit* and *manual-commit*. In auto-commit mode, every SQL statement is a complete transaction, and a commit is issued implicitly at the end of each statement execution, which for query statements is the point when the cursor is freed. Typically, a query-only application may wish to use auto-commit mode, which is the default.

In manual-commit mode, a transaction can span execution of multiple SQL statements. In this mode, an explicit commit or rollback using the SQLEndTran() function needs to be issued to end the transaction. Calling SQLEndTran() affects all statements of a specified connection, since each connection is considered as having only one outstanding transaction.

6.4.5 Diagnostics and Error Processing

Every CLI function returns a function return code. This provides basic diagnostic information to the application. The application should examine the return code before proceeding to the next function call. Table 6-2 lists the possible CLI return codes. Not all return codes are applicable to each CLI function. If the application encounters an unexpected return code from a function call, typically anything other than `SQL_SUCCESS`, it can call `SQLGetDiagRec()` or `SQLGetDiagField()` to retrieve detailed diagnostic information. The details include `SQLSTATE`, the native error or `SQLCODE`, and the message text.

Table 6-2 DB2 CLI Function Return Codes

Return Code	Explanation
`SQL_SUCCESS`	The function completed successfully, no additional `SQLSTATE` information is available.
`SQL_SUCCESS_WITH_INFO`	The function completed successfully, with a warning or other information. Call `SQLGetDiagRec()` to receive the `SQLSTATE` and any other informational messages or warnings.
`SQL_STILL_EXECUTING`	The function is running asynchronously and has not yet completed. The DB2 CLI driver has returned control to the application after calling the function, but the function has not yet finished executing.
`SQL_NO_DATA_FOUND`	The function returned successfully, but no relevant data was found. When this is returned after the execution of an SQL statement, additional information may be available and can be obtained by calling `SQLGetDiagRec()`.
`SQL_NEED_DATA`	The application tried to execute an SQL statement, but DB2 CLI lacks parameter data that the application indicated would be passed at execute time.
`SQL_ERROR`	The function failed. Call `SQLGetDiagRec()` to receive the `SQLSTATE` and any other error information.
`SQL_INVALID_HANDLE`	The function failed due to an invalid input handle (environment, connection, or statement handle). This is a programming error. No further information is available.

Embedded SQL applications rely on the SQLCA for all diagnostic information. DB2 CLI applications can retrieve much of the same information by using `SQLGetDiagRec()`, hence it is not necessary to examine the SQLCA in most cases. However, if you need to examine the SQLCA from within a CLI application, the `SQLGetSQLC()` function can be used. `SQLGetSQLCA()` should never be used as a substitute for `SQLGetDiagRec()` or `SQLGetDiagField()`.

The following example contains sample code to illustrate error handling and retrieval of diagnostic information by a CLI application:

```
/* Call a CLI function , for example: */
rc = SQLConnect( hdbc, "DB2MALL", SQL_NTS, "baduid",
                 SQL_NTS, "badpwd", SQL_NTS );
/* If not successful, call an error checking routine */
if ( rc != SQL_SUCCESS )
errprint( SQL_HANDLE_DBC, hdbc, rc);
...
/* Example of a simple error routine to print the error: */
SQLRETURN errprint( SQLSMALLINT htype,    /* A handle type */
                    SQLHANDLE   hndl,     /* A handle */
                    SQLRETURN   erc )     /* Return code */
{
    SQLCHAR    buffer[SQL_MAX_MESSAGE_LENGTH + 1];
    SQLCHAR    sqlstate[SQL_SQLSTATE_SIZE + 1];

    SQLINTEGER  sqlcode;
    SQLSMALLINT length, i=1;

    printf( ">--- ERROR -- RC = %d ------------\n", erc);
    while ( SQLGetDiagrec( htype, hndl, i, sqlstate
                           &sqlcode, buffer,
                           SQL_MAX_MESSAGE_LENGTH + 1,
                           &length) == SQL_SUCCESS )
    {
    printf( "         SQLSTATE: %s\n", sqlstate );
    printf( "Native error code: %ld\n", sqlcode );
    printf( "%s \n", buffer );
    i++;
    }
       return( SQL_ERROR );
}
```

In the above example, we check to see whether the CLI call to connect to the database returned successfully. If the wrong userid/password is specified, an error condition occurs and the `errprint()` function is called to print out the diagnostic information. Here is the sample output of this routine:

```
         >--- ERROR -- RC = -1 ------------
                 SQLSTATE: 08004
         Native error code: -1403
  [IBM][CLI Driver] SQL1403N  The username and/or password sup-
  plied is incorrect.  SQLSTATE=08004
```

You can include additional logic for your error handling. For instance, since in our example the call for connecting to the database failed, we could have exited the program or prompted the user to supply the userid and password again.

6.5 Advanced Programming Features

6.5.1 Supported Cursor Types

DB2 CLI supports scrollable cursors, which provides the ability to scroll through a result set:

- Forward by one or more rows.
- Backward by one or more rows.
- From the first row by one or more rows.
- From the last row by one or more rows.
- From a previously stored location in the cursor

There are two types of scrollable cursors supported by DB2 CLI:

- Static, read-only cursor.
- Keyset-driven cursor

6.5.1.1 Static, Read-Only Cursor

This type of scrollable cursor is static; once it is created, no rows will be added or removed, and no values in any rows will change. The cursor is not affected by other applications accessing the same data.

The cursor is also read-only. It is not possible for the application to change any values. How the rows of the cursor are locked, if at all, is determined by the isolation level of the statement used to create the cursor. Refer to the *DB2 UDB SQL Reference Guide* for a complete discussion of isolation levels and their effects.

6.5.1.2 Keyset-Driven Cursor

This type of scrollable cursor adds two features that static cursors do not have: the ability to detect changes to the underlying data, and the ability to use the cursor to make changes to the underlying data.

When a keyset-driven cursor is first opened, it stores the keys in a keyset for the life of the entire result set. This is used to determine the order and set of rows that are included in the cursor. As the cursor scrolls through the result set, it uses the keys in this keyset to retrieve the current data values for each row. Each time the cursor refetches the row, it retrieves the most recent values in the database, not the values that existed when the cursor was first opened. For this reason, no changes will be reflected in a row until the application scrolls past the row.

There are various types of changes to the underlying data that a keyset-driven cursor may or may not reflect:

- **Changed values in existing rows**—The cursor will reflect these types of changes. Because the cursor refetches the row from the database each time it is required, keyset-driven cursors always detect changes made by themselves and others.
- **Deleted rows**—The cursor will also reflect these types of changes. If a row in the rowset is deleted after the keyset is generated, it will appear as a "hole" in the cursor. When the cursor goes to refetch the row from the database, it will realize that it is no longer there.
- **Added rows**—The cursor will NOT reflect these types of changes. The set of rows is determined once, when the cursor is first opened. It does not reissue the `SELECT` statement to see if new rows have been added that should be included.

Keyset-driven cursors can also be used to modify the rows in a result set with calls to either `SQLBulkOperations()` or `SQLSetPos()`.

6.5.1.3 Deciding on Which Cursor Type to Use

The first decision to make is between a static cursor and a scrollable cursor. If your application does not need the additional features of a scrollable cursor, then a static cursor should be used.

If a scrollable cursor is required, then you have to decide between a static or keyset-driven cursor. A static cursor involves the least overhead. If the application does not need the additional features of a keyset-driven cursor, then a static cursor should be used.

If the application needs to detect changes to the underlying data, or needs to add, update, or delete data from the result set, then it must use a keyset-driven cursor.

To determine the types of cursors supported by the driver and DBMS, the application should call `SQLGetInfo()`.

6.5.2 Catalog Functions

Often, one of the first tasks an application performs is to display to the user a list of tables from which one or more tables are selected by the user to work with. Although the application can issue its own queries against the database system catalog to get this type of catalog information, it is best that the application calls the DB2 CLI catalog functions instead. These catalog functions provide a generic interface to issue queries and return consistent result sets across the DB2 family of servers. This allows the application to avoid server-specific and release-specific catalog queries.

The catalog functions operate by returning to the application a result set through a statement handle. After calling these functions, the application can fetch individual rows of the result set as it would process column data from an ordinary `SQLFetch()`. The DB2 CLI catalog functions are listed in Table 6-3.

The result sets returned by these functions are defined in the descriptions for each catalog function in the *DB2 UDB Call Level Interface Guide and Reference*. The columns are defined in a specified order. In future releases, other columns may be added to the end of each defined result set; therefore, applications should be written in a way that would not be affected by such changes.

Advanced Programming Features

Table 6-3 Available Catalog Functions

Function	Description
SQLColumnPrivileges	Get privileges associated with the columns of a table.
SQLColumns	Get column information for a table.
SQLForeignKeys	Get the list of foreign key columns.
SQLPrimaryKeys	Get primary key columns of a table.
SQLProcedureColumns	Get input/output parameter information for a procedure.
SQLProcedures	Get list of procedure names.
SQLSpecialColumns	Get special (row identifier) columns.
SQLStatistics	Get index and statistics information for a base table.
SQLTablePrivileges	Get privileges associated with a table.
SQLTables	Get table information.
SQLGetTypeInfo	Get data type information.

Some catalog functions result in execution of fairly complex queries, and for this reason, should only be called when needed. It is recommended that the application save the information returned rather than making repeated calls to get the same information.

6.5.3 Executing Statements

6.5.3.1 Preparing

An SQL statement can either be executed directly (SQLExecDirect()) or it can first be prepared (SQLPrepare()) and then executed (SQLExecute()). Statements that are executed directly are sent to the server to be prepared and processed as a single step. This method allows for ease of use for the programmer and performs satisfactorily if the statement being executed is only going to be performed once.

```
SQLREAL     var1;
SQLUINTEGER var2;
SQLINTEGER  var1Ind=0, var2Ind=0;

/* Prepare a statement to insert data into a table */
SQLPrepare(hstmt, "INSERT into table1 values (?,?)",
           SQL_NTS);

/* Bind the data to the parameter markers */
SQLBindParameter(hstmt, 1, SQL_PARAM_INPUT,
                 SQL_C_FLOAT, SQL_REAL, 7, 0,
                 &var1, 0, &var1Ind);
SQLBindParameter(hstmt, 2, SQL_PARAM_INPUT,
                 SQL_C_ULONG, SQL_INTEGER, 10, 0,
```

```
            &var2, 0, &var1Ind);

    /* Repeatedly execute the statement */
    while(GetData(&var1, &var1Ind, &var2, &var2Ind))
SQLExecute(hstmt);
```

If the statement is to be executed more than once, then it is better to prepare the statement first and then execute it multiple times. This action causes the access plans to be generated only once (during the prepare phase) and results in faster subsequent execution of the statement. It is not necessary that the statement being processed multiple times be exactly the same, just that it have the same structure. For example, a statement that inserts values into a database will have the same statement structure but may insert different values upon each execution.

To achieve this, parameter markers are used in the statement and then host variables are bound to these markers. In this way, CLI will use the values from the bound parameters during SQL statement processing, but will have bound the statement only once during the `SQLPrepare()`.

6.5.3.2 Binding Parameters

As was seen in the example in the previous section, each parameter marker in the SQL statement must be associated with a variable. This association is called binding and is established with the `SQLBindParameter()` function call. This function describes the variable from the application as well as the SQL data in the SQL statement. For the variable, it gives the address, C data type, and NULL indicator. For the SQL data, it describes the SQL data type and precision. These two descriptions must be compatible with each other as data conversion may occur.

For SQL statements, only input parameters (`SQL_PARAM_INPUT`) for the SQL statement are allowed. For `CALL` statements to a stored procedure, output parameters and input output parameters are allowed. To bind a variable to a parameter, identification of the parameter must be established. This can be accomplished by specifying the parameter's position, as is shown in the previous example. All parameters are positioned within the SQL statement from left to right, starting with position number 1.

Parameters can be bound or rebound as many times as the application likes before the statement is executed. Also, a parameter can be rebound after the statement is executed once and before it is executed a second time.

6.5.3.3 Arrays of Parameters

For some data entry and update applications (especially graphical), users may often insert, delete, or change many cells in a data entry form and then ask for the data to be sent to the database. For these situations of bulk insert, delete, or update, DB2 CLI provides an array input method to save the application from having to call `SQLExecute()` repeatedly on the same `INSERT`, `DELETE`, or `UPDATE` statement. In addition, there are significant savings in network flows.

Advanced Programming Features

There are two ways an application can bind the parameter markers in an SQL statement to arrays:

- **Column-wise array insert (uses column-wise binding)**—A different array is bound to each parameter.
- **Row-wise array insert (uses row-wise binding)**—A structure is created to store a complete set of parameters for a statement. An array of these structures is created and bound to the parameters. Parameter binding offsets (described in the next section) can only be used with row-wise bindings.

SQLBindParameter() is still used to bind buffers to parameters, the only difference is that the addresses passed are array addresses, not single-variable addresses. The application must also set the SQL_ATTR_PARAM_BIND_TYPE statement attribute to specify whether column-wise or row-wise binding will be used.

Column-wise Array Insert   This method involves the binding of parameter marker(s) to array(s) of storage locations via the SQLBindParameter() call. For character and binary input data, the application uses the maximum input buffer size argument (BufferLength) on an SQLBindParameter() call to indicate to DB2 CLI the location of values in the input array. For other input data types, the length of each element in the array is assumed to be the size of the C data type. The statement attribute SQL_ATTR_PARAMSET_SIZE must be set (with a call to SQLSetStmtAttr()) to the size of the array before the execution of the SQL statement.

Suppose for Figure 6-4 there is an application that allows the user to change values in the col1 and col2 columns of a data entry form. Also suppose that the primary key of the underlying table1 table is col3. The application can then request to prepare the following SQL statement:

```
UPDATE table1 SET col1= ? and col2= ? WHERE col3=?
```

When the user has entered all the changes, the application counts that n rows are to change and allocates m=3 arrays to store the changed data and primary key. Then it calls SQLBindParameter() to bind the three parameter markers to the locations of three arrays in memory. Next it sets the statement attribute SQL_ATTR_PARAMSET_SIZE (with a call to SQLSetStmtAttr()) to specify the number of rows to change (the size of the array). Then it calls SQLExecute() once and all the updates are sent to the database. This is the flow shown on the right side of Figure 6-4.

The basic method is shown on the left side of Figure 6-4, where SQLBindParameter() is called to bind the three parameter markers to the location of three variables in memory. SQLExecute() is called to send the first set of changes to the database. The variables are updated to reflect values for the next row of changes and again SQLExecute() is called. Note that this method has *n-1* extra SQLExecute() calls.

```
                    ↓
         ┌──────────────────┐
         │  SQLAllocHandle  │
         │   (Statement)    │
         └──────────────────┘
                    ↓
         ┌──────────────────┐
         │    SQLPrepare    │
         └──────────────────┘
              ↙         ↘
   ┌──────────────────┐  ┌──────────────────┐
   │ SQLBindParameter │  │ SQLBindParameter │
   └──────────────────┘  └──────────────────┘
              ↓                   ↓
   ┌──────────────────┐  ┌──────────────────────┐
   │    SQLExecute    │  │    SQLSetStmtAttr    │
   └──────────────────┘  │(SQL_ATTR_PARAMSET_SIZE)│
         n Iterations    └──────────────────────┘
                                   ↓
                         ┌──────────────────┐
                         │    SQLExecute    │
                         └──────────────────┘
                    if statement is not executed again
                         ┌──────────────────┐
                         │  SQLFreeHandle   │
                         │   (Statement)    │
                         └──────────────────┘
                                   ↓
```

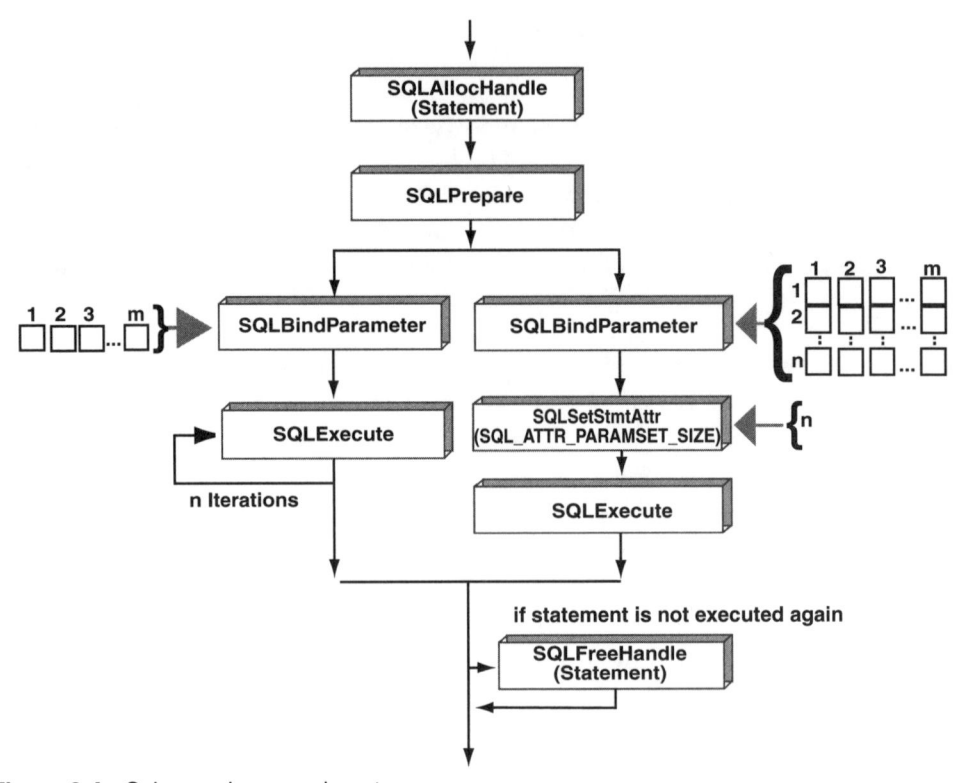

Figure 6-4 Column-wise array insert.

See the subsequent section, "Retrieving Diagnostic Information," for information on errors that can be accessed by the application.

Row-wise Array Insert The first step when using row-wise array insert is to create a structure that contains two elements for each parameter. The first element for each parameter holds the length/indicator buffer, and the second element holds the value itself. Once the structure is defined, the application must allocate an array of these structures. The number of rows in the array corresponds to the number of values that will be used for each parameter.

```
struct { SQLINTEGER La; SQLINTEGER A;   /* Information for
parameter A */
         SQLINTEGER Lb; SQLCHAR B[4];   /* Information
for parameter B */
         SQLINTEGER Lc; SQLCHAR C[11];  /* Information
for parameter C */
       } R[n];
```

Figure 6-5 shows the structure R with three parameters in an array of *n* rows. The array can then be populated with the appropriate data.

Once the array is created and populated, the application must indicate that row-wise binding is going to be used. It does this by setting the statement attribute SQL_ATTR_-PARAM_BIND_TYPE to the length of the structure created. The statement attribute SQL_-ATTR_PARAMSET_SIZE must also be set to the number of rows in the array.

Each parameter can now be bound to the appropriate two elements of the structure (in the first row of the array) using SQLBindParameter().

```
/* Parameter A */
rc = SQLBindParameter(hstmt, 1, SQL_PARAM_INPUT,
    SQL_C_LONG, SQL_INTEGER,
        5, 0, &R[0].A, 0, &R.La);

/* Parameter B */
rc = SQLBindParameter(hstmt, 2, SQL_PARAM_INPUT,
    SQL_C_CHAR, SQL_CHAR,
        10, 0, R[0].B, 10, &R.Lb);

/* Parameter C */
rc = SQLBindParameter(hstmt, 3, SQL_PARAM_INPUT,
    SQL_C_CHAR, SQL_CHAR,
        3, 0, R[0].C, 3, &R.Lc);
```

At this point, the application can call SQLExecute() once and all of the updates are sent to the database.

See the subsequent section, "Retrieving Diagnostic Information," for information on errors that can be accessed by the application.

Retrieving Diagnostic Information A parameter status array can be populated after the SQLExecute() or SQLExecDirect() call. The array contains information about the processing of each set of parameters. See the statement attribute SQL_ATTR_-PARAM_STATUS_PTR or the corresponding Implementation Parameter Descriptor (IPD) field SQL_DESC_ARRAY_STATUS_PTR for complete details.

The statement attribute SQL_ATTR_PARAMS_PROCESSED or the corresponding IPD descriptor header field SQL_DESC_ROWS_PROCESSED_PTR can be used to return the number of sets of parameters that have been processed. See these attributes in the description of SQLSetStmtAttr() or SQLSetDescField().

Once the application has determined what parameters had errors, it can use the statement attribute SQL_ATTR_PARAM_OPERATION_PTR or the corresponding Application Parameter Descriptor (APD) field SQL_DESC_ARRAY_STATUS_PTR (both of which point to an array of values) to control which sets of parameters are ignored in a second call to SQLExecute() or SQLExecDirect(). See these attributes in the description of SQLSetStmtAttr() or SQLSetDescField().

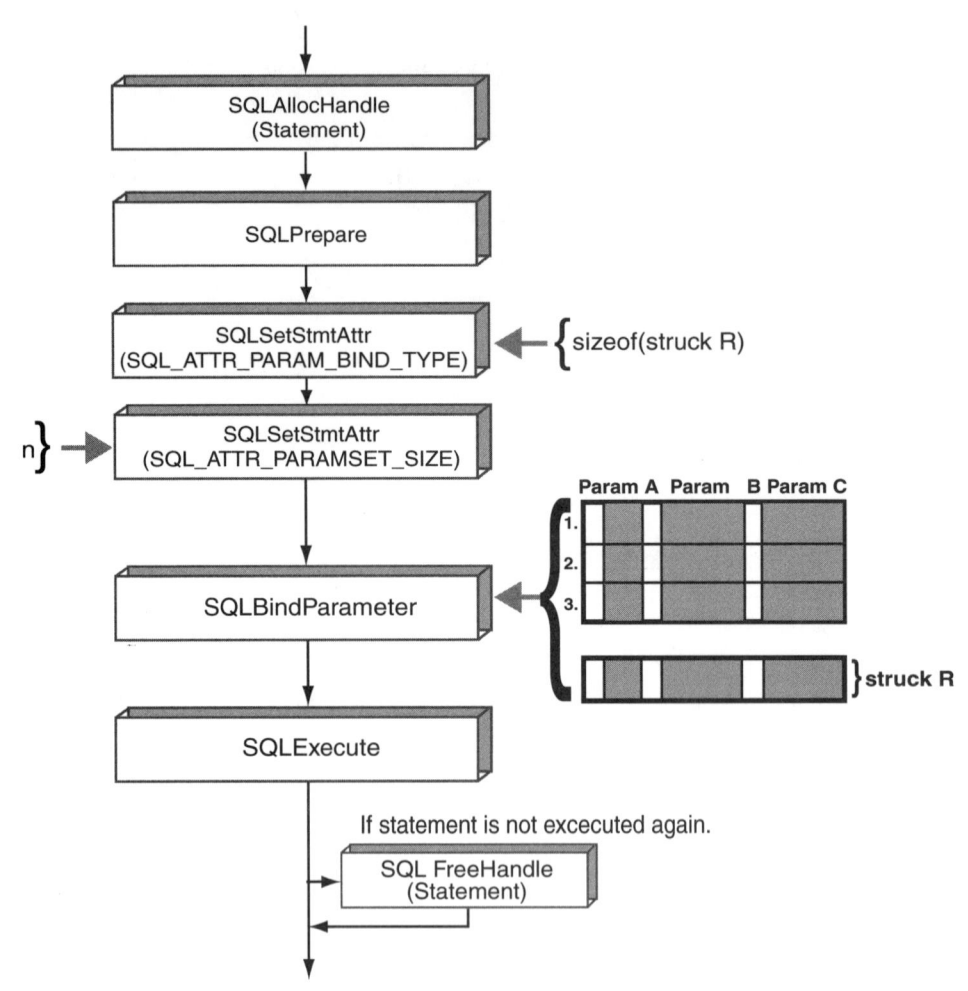

Figure 6-5 Row-wise array insert.

6.5.4 Retrieving Results with Scrollable Cursors

Previously, in the section "Processing Transactions," we saw an example that illustrated the use of SQLBindCol() to bind data from a result set prior to SQLFetch() to fetch each row from the result set. This example illustrated sequential fetching, or retrieving rows starting with the first row and ending with the last row. What if you have an application whereby you want to allow the user to scroll through a set of data? You may want to allow the user the ability to scroll forwards and backwards through this list as well as jump to the end or the beginning of the list. To accomplish this, we can use scrollable cursors with the use of SQLScrollFetch(). Let's first define the meaning of some terms before we look at an example of scrollable cursors:

- **Result set**—The complete set of rows generated by the SQL SELECT statement. Once created, a result will not change.
- **Rowset**—The subset of rows from the result set that is returned after each fetch. The application indicates the size of the rowset before the first fetch of data, and can modify the size before each subsequent fetch. Each call to SQLFetchScroll() populates the rowset with the appropriate rows from the result set.
- **Bookmark**—It is possible to store a pointer to a specific row in the result set, a bookmark. Once stored, the application can continue to move throughout the result set, then return to the bookmarked row to generate a rowset. See the section, "Bookmarks with Scrollable Cursors," for complete details.

If we have a screen-based application that displays *n* rows of data at a time, we may wish to allow the user to jump through this display using the cursor keys or the Page Up and Page Down keys. To accomplish this, we need to be able to position the rowset within the result set as dictated by the user's actions.

The position of the rowset within the result set is specified in the call to SQLFetchScroll(). For example, the following call would generate a rowset starting on the 11th row in the result set (Step 5 in Figure 6-6):

```
SQLFetchScroll(hstmt,         /* Statement handle */
    SQL_FETCH_ABSOLUTE,       /* FetchOrientation value */
    11);                      /* Offset value */
```

Scroll bar operations of a screen-based application can be mapped directly to the positioning of a rowset. By setting the rowset size to the number of lines displayed on the screen, the application can map the movement of the scroll bar to calls to SQLFetchScroll() (refer to Table 6-4).

The following figure demonstrates a number of calls to SQLFetchScroll() using various FetchOrientation values. The result set includes all of the rows (from 1 to *n*), and the rowset size is 3. The order of the calls is indicated on the left, and the FetchOrientation values are indicated on the right.

The statement attribute SQL_ATTR_ROW_ARRAY_SIZE is used to declare the number of rows in the rowset. For example, to declare a rowset size of 35 rows, the following call would be used:

```
/*...*/
#define ROWSET_SIZE 35
/*...*/
    rc = SQLSetStmtAttr(
            hstmt,
            SQL_ATTR_ROW_ARRAY_SIZE,
            (SQLPOINTER) ROWSET_SIZE,
            0);
```

Table 6-4 Cursor positions after calls to `SQLScrollFetch()`

Rowset Retrieved	Fetch Orientation Value	Scroll Bar
First rowset	`SQL_FETCH_FIRST`	Home: Scroll bar at the top
Last rowset	`SQL_FETCH_LAST`	End: Scroll bar at the bottom
Next rowset	`SQL_FETCH_NEXT` (same as calling `SQLFetch()`)	Page Down
Previous rowset	`SQL_FETCH_PRIOR`	Page Up
Rowset starting on next row	`SQL_FETCH_RELATIVE` with `FetchOffset` set to 1	Line Down
Rowset starting on previous row	`SQL_FETCH_RELATIVE` with `FetchOffset` set to -1	Line Up
Rowset starting on specific row	`SQL_FETCH_ABSOLUTE` with `FetchOffset` set to an offset from the start (a positive value) or the end (a negative value) of the result set	Application-generated
Rowset starting on previously bookmarked row	`SQL_FETCH_BOOKMARK` with `FetchOffset` set to a positive or negative offset from the bookmarked row (see "Using Bookmarks with Scrollable Cursors" for more information)	Application-generated

The application cannot assume that the entire rowset will contain data. It must check the rowset size after each rowset is created because there are instances where the rowset will not contain a complete set of rows. For instance, consider the case where the rowset size is set to 10 and `SQLFetchScroll()` is called using `SQL_FETCH_ABSOLUTE` and `FetchOffset` set to -3. This will attempt to return 10 rows, starting 3 rows from the end of the result set.

Only the first three rows of the rowset will contain meaningful data, however, and the application must ignore the rest of the rows.

6.5.4.1 Typical Scrollable Cursor Application

Each application that will make use of scrollable cursors must complete the following steps, in the following order:

1. **Set up the environment.**
   The following additional statement attributes are required when using scrollable cursors in DB2 CLI applications:

Advanced Programming Features

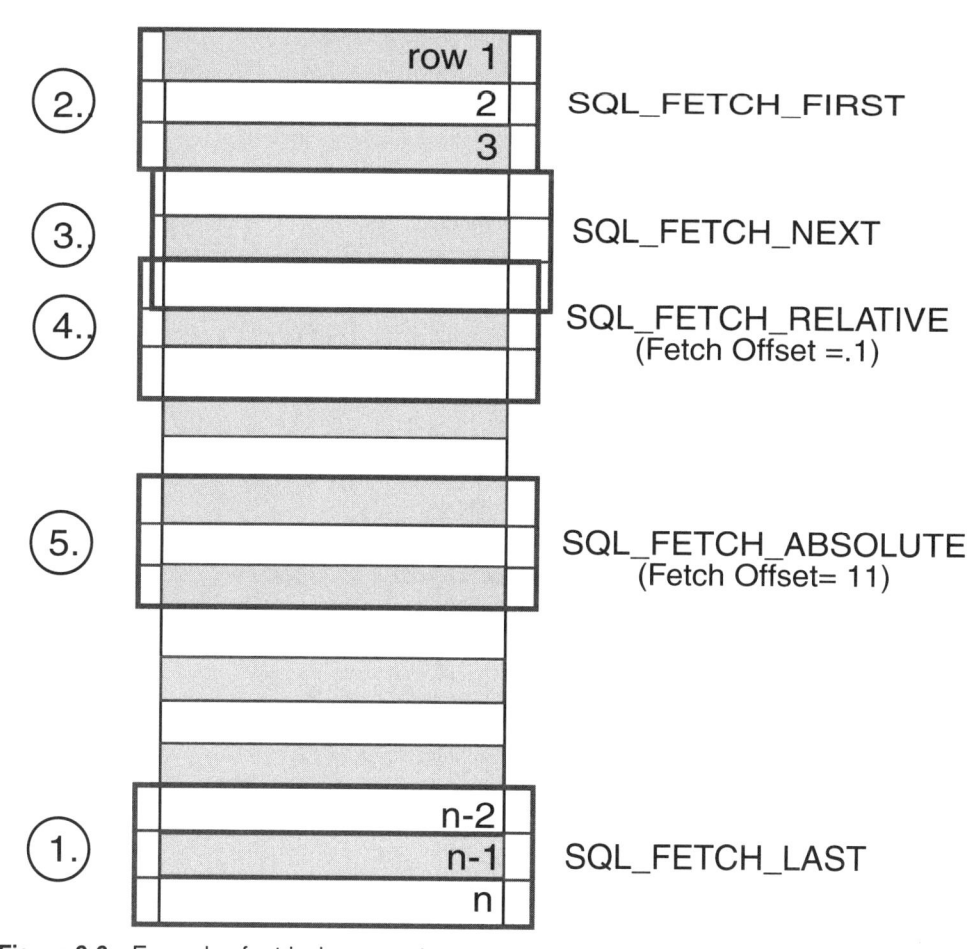

Figure 6-6 Example of retrieving rowsets.

Setting the rowset size—Set the SQL_ATTR_ROW_ARRAY_SIZE statement attribute to the number of rows that you want returned from each call to SQLFetchScroll(). The default value is 1.

Type of scrollable cursor—DB2 CLI supports static, read-only, or keyset-driven cursors. Use SQLSetStmtAttr() to set the SQL_ATTR_CURSOR_TYPE statement attribute to either SQL_CURSOR_STATIC or SQL_CURSOR_KEYSET_DRIVEN. ODBC defines other scrollable cursor types, but they cannot be used with DB2 CLI. This value must be set or the default value of SQL_CURSOR_FORWARD_ONLY will be used.

Location to store number of rows returned—The application needs a way to determine how many rows were returned in the rowset from each call to SQLFetchScroll(). The number of rows returned in the rowset can at times be

less than the maximum size of the rowset that was set using
SQL_ATTR_ROW_ARRAY_SIZE. Set the SQL_ATTR_ROWS_FETCHED_PTR
statement attribute as a pointer to a SQLUINTEGER variable. This variable will then
contain the number of rows returned in the rowset after each call to
SQLFetchScroll().

Array to use for the row status—Set the SQL_ATTR_ROW_STATUS_PTR
statement attribute as a pointer to the SQLUSMALLINT array that is used to store the
row status. This array will then be updated after each call to SQLFetchScroll().

Will bookmarks be used?—If you plan on using bookmarks in your scrollable
cursor, then you must set the SQL_ATTR_USE_BOOKMARKS statement attribute to
SQL_UB_VARIABLE.

The following example demonstrates the required calls to SQLSetStmtAttr():

```
/* ... */

    /* Set the number of rows in the rowset */
    rc = SQLSetStmtAttr(
             hstmt,
             SQL_ATTR_ROW_ARRAY_SIZE,
             (SQLPOINTER) ROWSET_SIZE,
             0);
    CHECK_STMT(hstmt, rc);

    /* Set the SQL_ATTR_ROWS_FETCHED_PTR statement attribute
to */
    /* point to the variable numrowsfetched: */
    rc = SQLSetStmtAttr(
             hstmt,
             SQL_ATTR_ROWS_FETCHED_PTR,
             &numrowsfetched,
             0);
    CHECK_STMT(hstmt, rc);

    /* Set a pointer to the array to use for the row status
*/
    rc = SQLSetStmtAttr(
             hstmt,
             SQL_ATTR_ROW_STATUS_PTR,
             (SQLPOINTER) row_status,
             0);
    CHECK_STMT(hstmt, rc);

    /* Set the cursor type */
```

Advanced Programming Features

```
          rc = SQLSetStmtAttr(
                    hstmt,
                    SQL_ATTR_CURSOR_TYPE,
                    (SQLPOINTER) SQL_CURSOR_STATIC,
                    0);
          CHECK_STMT(hstmt, rc);

          /* Indicate that we will use bookmarks by setting the */
          /* SQL_ATTR_USE_BOOKMARKS statement attribute to
       SQL_UB_VARIABLE: */
          rc = SQLSetStmtAttr(
                    hstmt,
                    SQL_ATTR_USE_BOOKMARKS,
                    (SQLPOINTER) SQL_UB_VARIABLE,
                    0);
          CHECK_STMT(hstmt, rc);
```
`/* ... */`

2. **Execute SQL SELECT statement and bind the results.**
   Follow the usual DB2 CLI process for executing an SQL statement and binding the result set. The application can call `SQLRowCount()` to determine the number of rows in the overall result set. Scrollable cursors support the use of both column-wise and row-wise binding.

3. **Fetch a rowset of rows at a time from the result set.**
   At this point, the application can read information from the result set using the following steps:

   1. Use `SQLFetchScroll()` to fetch a rowset of data from the result set. The `FetchOrientation` argument is used to indicate the location of the rowset in the result set. A typical call to `SQLFetchScroll()` to retrieve the first rowset of data would be as follows:

             `SQLFetchScroll(hstmt, SQL_FETCH_FIRST, 0);`

   2. Calculate the number of rows returned in the result set. This value is set automatically after each call to `SQLFetchScroll()`. In the example above, we set the statement attribute `SQL_ATTR_ROWS_FETCHED_PTR` to the variable `numrowsfetched` that will therefore contain the number of rows fetched after each `SQLFetchScroll()` call. If you set the `SQL_ATTR_ROW_STATUS_PTR` statement attribute, then the row status array will also be updated for each possible row in the rowset.

   3. Display or manipulate the data in the rows returned.

   4. Free the statement, which then closes the result set.

Once the application has finished retrieving information, it should follow the usual DB2 CLI process for freeing a statement handle.

6.5.4.2 Bookmarks with Scrollable Cursors

You can save a pointer to any row in the result set as a bookmark. The application can then use that bookmark as a relative position to retrieve a rowset of information. You can retrieve a rowset starting from the bookmarked row, or specify a positive or negative offset.

Once you have positioned the cursor to a row in a rowset using `SQLSetPos()`, you can obtain the bookmark value from column 0 using `SQLGetData()`. In most cases, you will not want to bind column 0 and retrieve the bookmark value for every row, but use `SQLGetData()` to retrieve the bookmark value for the specific row you require.

A bookmark is only valid within the result set in which it was created. The bookmark value will be different if you select the same row from the same result set in two different cursors.

The only valid comparison is a byte-by-byte comparison between two bookmark values obtained from the same result set. If they are the same, they both point to the same row. Any other mathematical calculations or comparisons between bookmarks will not provide any useful information, including comparing bookmark values within a result set and between result sets.

To make use of bookmarks, the following steps must be employed in addition to the steps described above for use with scrollable cursors:

1. **Set up the environment.**
   To use bookmarks, you must set the `SQL_ATTR_USE_BOOKMARKS` statement attribute to `SQL_UB_VARIABLE` in addition to the other statement attributes required for scrollable cursors.

   ODBC defines both variable-, and fixed-length bookmarks. DB2 CLI only supports the newer variable-length bookmarks, however.

2. **Get the bookmark value from the desired row in a rowset.**
   The application must execute the `SQL SELECT` statement and use `SQLFetchScroll()` to retrieve a rowset with the desired row. `SQLSetPos()` is then used to position the cursor within the rowset. Finally, the bookmark value is obtained from column 0 using `SQLGetData()` and stored in a variable.

3. **Set the bookmark value statement attribute.**
   The statement attribute `SQL_ATTR_FETCH_BOOKMARK_PTR` is used to store the location for the next call to `SQLFetchScroll()` that uses a bookmark.

   Once you have the bookmark value using `SQLGetData()` (the variable `abookmark` below), call `SQLSetStmtAttr()` as follows:

```
rc = SQLSetStmtAttr(
        hstmt,
        SQL_ATTR_FETCH_BOOKMARK_PTR,
```

```
                    (SQLPOINTER) abookmark,
         0);
```

4. **Retrieve a rowset based on the bookmark.**
   Once the bookmark value is stored, the application can continue to use `SQLFetchScroll()` to retrieve data from the result set. The application can then move throughout the result set, but still retrieve a rowset based on the location of the bookmarked row at any point before the cursor is closed.

   The following call to `SQLFetchScroll()` will retrieve a rowset starting with the bookmarked row:

   ```
   rc = SQLFetchScroll(hstmt, SQL_FETCH_BOOKMARK, 0);
   ```

   The value 0 specifies the offset. You would specify -3 to begin the rowset 3 rows before the bookmarked row, or specify 4 to begin 4 rows after.

   Note that the variable used to store the bookmark value is not specified in the `SQLFetchScroll()` call. It was set in the previous step using the statement attribute `SQL_ATTR_FETCH_BOOKMARK_PTR`.

6.5.4.3　Retrieving a Result Set into an Array

One of the most common tasks performed by an application is to issue a query statement and then fetch each row of the result set into application variables that have been bound using `SQLBindCol()`. If the application requires that each column or each row of the result set be stored in an array, each fetch must be followed by either a data copy operation or a new set of `SQLBindCol()` calls to assign new storage areas for the next fetch.

Alternatively, applications can eliminate the overhead of extra data copies or extra `SQLBindCol()` calls by retrieving multiple rows of data (called a rowset) at a time into an array.

> **Note**
>
> A third method of reducing overhead, which can be used on its own or with arrays, is to specify a binding offset. Rather than rebinding each time, an offset can be used to specify new buffer and length/indicator addresses that will be used in a subsequent call to `SQLFetch()` or `SQLFetchScroll()`. This can only be used with row offset binding and is described in "Column Binding Offsets."

When retrieving a result set into an array, `SQLBindCol()` is also used to assign storage for application array variables. By default, the binding of rows is in column-wise fashion. This is symmetrical to using `SQLBindParameter()` to bind arrays of input parameter values as described in the previous section.

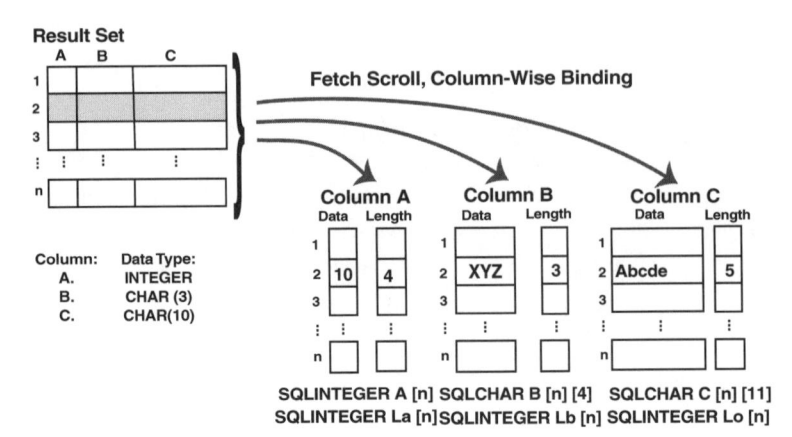

Figure 6-7 Column-wise binding.

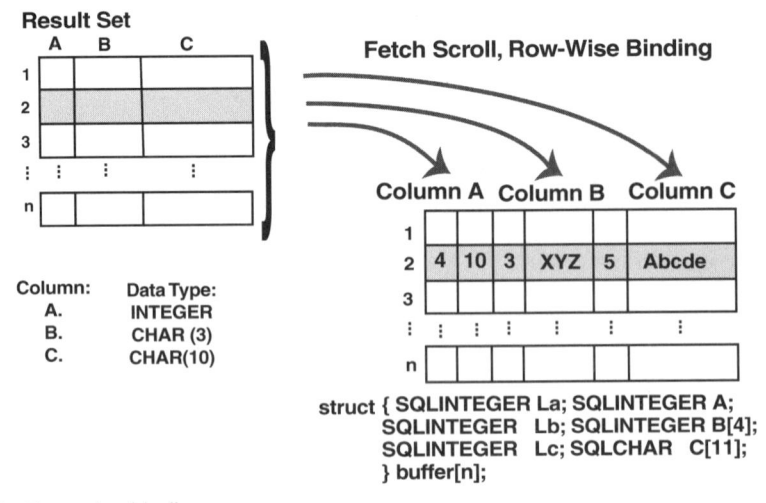

Figure 6-8 Row-wise binding.

`SQLFetchScroll()` supports scrollable cursors, the ability to move forwards and backwards from any position in the result set. This can be used with both column-wise and row-wise binding. See "Scrollable Cursors" for more information.

Returning Array Data for Column-wise Bound Data Figure 6-7 is a logical view of column-wise binding. The right side of Figure 6-7 shows the function flows for column-wise retrieval.

To specify column-wise array retrieval, the application calls `SQLSetStmtAttr()` with the `SQL_ATTR_ROW_ARRAY_SIZE` attribute to indicate how many rows to retrieve at a time. When the value of the `SQL_ATTR_ROW_ARRAY_SIZE` attribute is greater than 1, DB2 CLI knows to treat the deferred output data pointer and length pointer as pointers to arrays of data and length rather than to one single element of data and the length of a result set column.

The application then calls SQLFetchScroll() to retrieve the data. When returning data, DB2 CLI uses the maximum buffer size argument (BufferLength) on SQLBindCol() to determine where to store successive rows of data in the array; the number of bytes available for return for each element is stored in the deferred length array. If the number of rows in the result set is greater than the SQL_ATTR_ROW_ARRAY_SIZE attribute value, multiple calls to SQLFetchScroll() are required to retrieve all the rows.

Returning Array Data for Row-wise Bound Data The application can also do row-wise binding, which associates an entire row of the result set with a structure. In this case, the rowset is retrieved into an array of structures, each of which holds the data in one row and the associated length fields. Figure 6-8 gives a pictorial view of row-wise binding.

To perform row-wise array retrieval, the application needs to call SQLSetStmtAttr() with the SQL_ATTR_ROW_ARRAY_SIZE attribute to indicate how many rows to retrieve at a time. In addition, it must call SQLSetStmtAttr() with the SQL_ATTR_ROW_BIND_TYPE attribute value set to the size of the structure to which the result columns will be bound. DB2 CLI treats the deferred output data pointer of SQLBindCol() as the address of the data field for the column in the first element of the array of these structures. It treats the deferred output length pointer as the address of the associated length field of the column.

The application then calls SQLFetchScroll() to retrieve the data. When returning data, DB2 CLI uses the structure size provided with the SQL_ATTR_ROW_BIND_TYPE attribute to determine where to store successive rows in the array of structures.

Figure 6-9 shows the required functions for each method. The left side shows n rows being selected and retrieved one row at a time into m application variables. The right side shows the same n rows being selected and retrieved directly into an array.

The diagram shows m columns bound, so m calls to SQLBindCol() are required in both cases. If arrays of less than n elements had been allocated, then multiple SQLFetchScroll() calls would be required.

Column Binding Offsets When an application needs to change bindings (for a subsequent fetch, for example), it can call SQLBindCol() a second time. This will change the buffer address and length/indicator pointer used.

Instead of multiple calls to SQLBindCol(), DB2 CLI also supports column binding offsets. Rather than rebinding each time, an offset can be used to specify new buffer and length/indicator addresses, which will be used in a subsequent call to SQLFetch() or SQLFetchScroll(). This can only be used with row-wise binding, but will work whether the application retrieves a single row or multiple rows at a time.

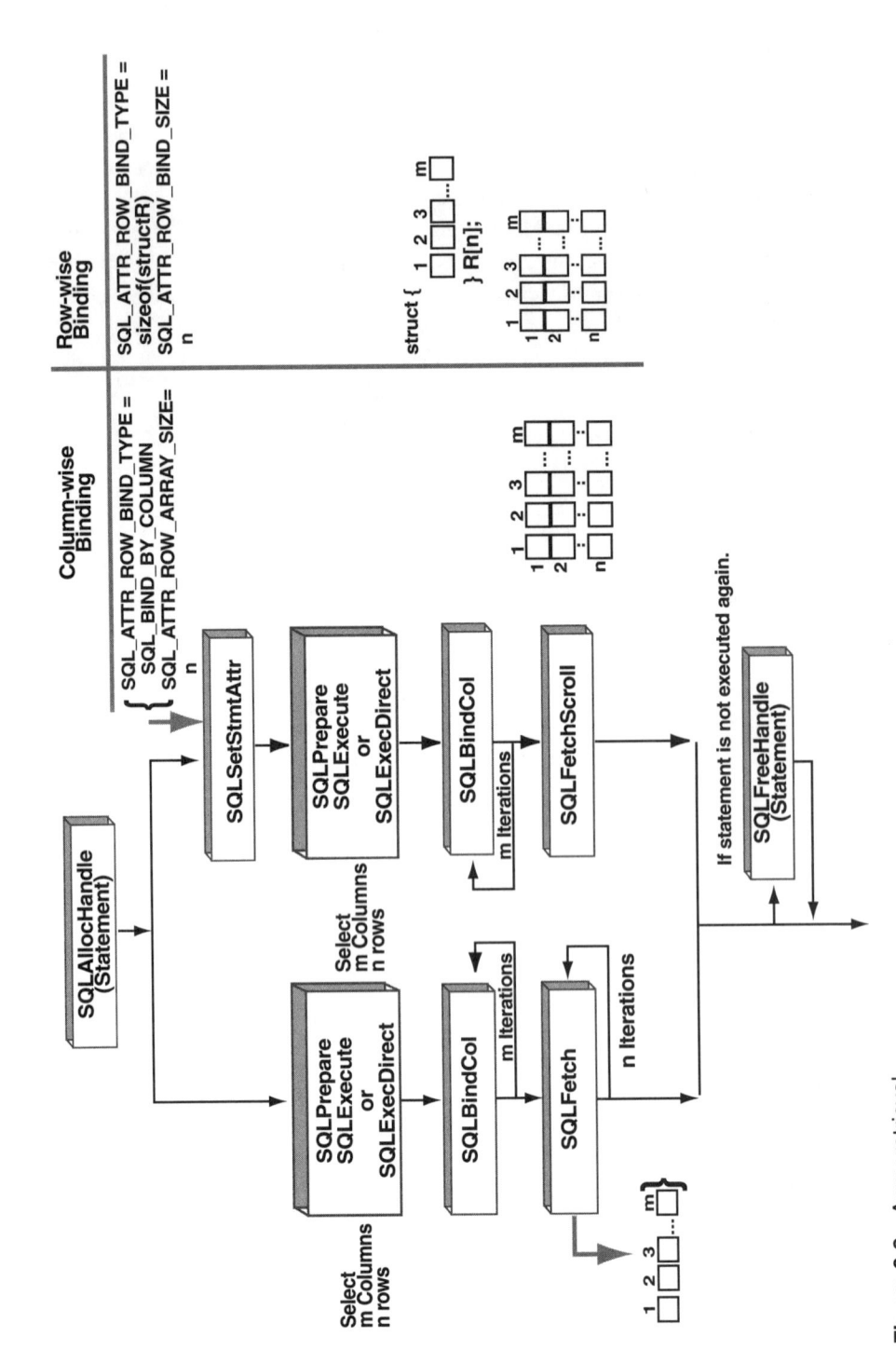

Figure 6-9 Array retrieval.

To make use of column binding offsets, an application would follow these steps:

1. Call SQLBindCol() as usual. The first set of bound data buffers and length/indicator buffer addresses will act as a template. The application will then move this template to different memory locations using the offset.
2. Call SQLFetch() or SQLFetchScroll() as usual. The data returned will be stored in the locations bound above.
3. Set up a variable to hold the memory offset value. The statement attribute SQL_ATTR_ROW_BIND_OFFSET_PTR points to the address of an SQLINTEGER buffer where the offset will be stored. This address must remain valid until the cursor is closed. This extra level of indirection enables the use of a single memory variable to store the offset for multiple sets of bindings on different statement handles. The application needs only set this one memory variable and all of the offsets will be changed.
4. Store an offset value (number of bytes) in the memory location pointed to by the statement attribute set in the previous step. The offset value is always added to the memory location of the originally bound value. This sum must point to a valid memory address.
5. Call SQLFetch() or SQLFetchScroll() again. CLI will add the offset specified above to the locations used in the original call to SQLBindCol() to determine where in memory to store the results.
6. Repeat Steps 4 and 5 above as required.

6.6 DB2 OLE DB Driver

Microsoft is now looking at moving from the ODBC standard for accessing databases to a new Object Linking and Embedding (OLE) standard. The OLE standard encapsulates much of the functionality that ODBC provides, but takes it one step further. The main purpose of the new standard is to provide access to any data, whether that data is managed by a Relational DBMS (RDBMS), a spreadsheet, flat file, or even an e-mail. Many ODBC vendors are starting off by supplying bridges from an OLE application to their ODBC drivers. DB2 has developed its own OLE driver known as the DB2 OLE DB driver.

DB2 UDB V7.1 does not ship with the DB2 OLE driver. Instead, this driver is available for download from the IBM DB2 Web site. (Actually, DB2 UDB V7.1 does ship with a beta version of this driver, but it is strongly recommended that you download the latest driver from IBM's Internet site.)

OLE defines a set of standard interfaces through which an application can access the services of another (for example, the DB2 DBMS). Each interface defines a set of functions (also sometimes called methods) that allows the application access to these services. For a service to provide an interface, it must fully define all functions for that service. Thus if an application determines that an interface is supported, it will then know how to use that interface. A service is capable of providing additional interfaces that augment the standard set.

Since service providers must provide all of the functionality for an interface, interfaces are broken down by functionality. Thus, if an OLE DB service provider provides the ability to read data from its DBMS but not to write to it, then an application can discover this by querying the server for the existence of the appropriate interfaces.

The core object model for OLE DB can be broken down into the following four objects:

- **Data source object**—The data source object is the initial object generated when an instance is defined for a given OLE DB data provider's unique Class Identifier (CLSID). It encapsulates much of the functionality of the ODBC environment, including connection and informational properties.
- **Session object**—The session object defines the scope for a transaction and generates the rowsets from the data source. This object also supports interfaces for describing schema information. The session object also encapsulates the functionality of the ODBC connection for which multiple connections can exist.
- **Command object**—The command object is generated from a session object. It can be used for issuing commands against the OLE DB provider, such as SQL statements. These statements can be defined, prepared, and executed. There may be multiple command objects for a single session object.
- **Rowset object**—The rowset object is a shared data object used for returning data, such as a result set returned by executing a query. The rowset object is the minimal interface that providers must support. Rowsets are used for returning results from schema functions and command functions. There may be multiple rowsets associated with a single session or command object.

Other objects defined for OLE DB include:

- **Enumerator object**—This object provides a list of available data sources.
- **Transaction object**—This object supports various transaction capabilities.
- **Error object**—This object gives access to error codes and messages during processing. This is similar to the ODBC function `SQLGetDiagRec()`.

6.6.1 DB2 OLE Automation

OLE automation is part of the OLE 2.0 architecture from Microsoft Corporation. With OLE automation, your applications, regardless of the language in which they are written, can expose their properties and methods in OLE automation objects. Other applications, such as Lotus Notes or Microsoft Exchange®, can then integrate these objects by taking advantage of these properties and methods through OLE automation.

The applications exposing the properties and methods are called OLE automation servers or objects, and the applications that access those properties and methods are called OLE automation controllers. OLE automation servers are COM (Component Object Model) components

DB2 OLE DB Driver 151

(objects) that implement the OLE IDispatch interface. An OLE automation controller is a COM client that communicates with the automation server through its IDispatch interface. COM is the foundation of OLE. For OLE automation User-Defined Functions (UDFs) or Stored Procedures (SPs), DB2 acts as an OLE automation controller. Through this mechanism, DB2 can invoke methods of OLE automation objects as external UDFs or SPs.

For an overview of OLE automation, refer to *Microsoft Corporation: The Component Object Model Specification*, October 1995. For details on OLE automation, refer to *OLE Automation Programmer's Reference*, Microsoft Press, 1996, ISBN 1-55615-851-3.

OLE automation UDFs and SPs are implemented as public methods of OLE automation objects. The OLE automation objects must be externally creatable by an OLE automation controller, in this case DB2, and support late binding (also called IDispatch-based binding). OLE automation objects must be registered in the Windows registration database (registry) with a class identifier (CLSID), and optionally an OLE programmatic ID (progID) to identify the automation object. The progID can identify an in-process (.DLL) or local (.EXE) OLE automation server, or a remote server through DCOM (Distributed COM). OLE automation UDFs can be scalar functions or table functions.

For automation UDFs, you need to register the methods of the object as UDFs using the `SQL CREATE FUNCTION` statement. Registering an OLE automation UDF is very similar to registering any external C or C++ UDF, but you must use the following options:

- `LANGUAGE OLE`.
- `FENCED`, since OLE automation UDFs must run in FENCED mode.

The external name consists of the OLE progID identifying the OLE automation object and the method name separated by ! (exclamation mark):

```
CREATE FUNCTION bcounter () RETURNS INTEGER
EXTERNAL NAME 'bert.bcounter!increment'
LANGUAGE OLE
FENCED
SCRATCHPAD
FINAL CALL
NOT DETERMINISTIC
NULL CALL
PARAMETER STYLE DB2SQL
NO SQL
NO EXTERNAL ACTION
DISALLOW PARALLEL;
```

For automation SPs, you must register the methods of the object as SPs using the `CREATE PROCEDURE` statement. To register an OLE automation SP, issue a `CREATE PROCEDURE` statement with the `LANGUAGE OLE` clause. The external name consists of the OLE progID identifying the OLE automation object and the method name separated by ! (exclamation mark).

```
CREATE PROCEDURE median (INOUT sal DOUBLE)
       EXTERNAL NAME 'db2mall.price!median'
       LANGUAGE OLE
       FENCED
       PARAMETER STYLE DB2SQL
```

The calling conventions for OLE method implementations are identical to the conventions for functions written in C or C++. An implementation of the above method in the BASIC language looks like the following (notice that in BASIC, the parameters are by default defined as calls by reference):

```
Public Sub increment(output As Long, _
                    indicator As Integer, _
                    sqlstate As String, _
                    fname As String, _
                    fspecname As String, _
                    sqlmsg As String, _
                    scratchpad() As Byte, _
                    calltype As Long)
```

6.6.2 Installing the OLE DB Driver

Once you have installed DB2 UDB V7.1 on a Windows 32-bit operating system, you must perform the following steps to use the IBM OLE DB Provider for DB2 (IBMDADB2) in your DB2 applications:

1. Download the updated `ibmdadb2.dll` driver from the FTP site:
   `ftp://ftp.software.ibm.com/ps/products/db2/tools/`
2. Make sure that you rename the old `ibmdadb2.dll` in your `sqllib\bin` directory to `ibmdadb2.bak` before overwriting it with the new file.
3. Copy `ibmdadb2.dll` into `sqllib\bin\`.

A link to download the OLE DB driver is also located at the IBM DB2 OLE DB Web site, `http://www.software.ibm.com/data/db2/udb/ad/v71/oledb.html`. Be sure to visit this Web site and read the document available there. The OLE DB driver is continuously being updated with improved functionality, so make sure that you understand what features may or may not be available with your current driver.

6.7 Summary

A lot was covered in this chapter, and still there is so much more that could have been discussed. Early in the chapter, we discussed the basic program flow for a CLI/ODBC application and defined it as consisting of three phases: initialization, transaction processing, and termination. The initialization phase consists of allocating the various handles and resources needed to establish a connection to the database and to make that connection. The termination phase does quite

Summary

the opposite and is needed to disconnect from the database and free all of the allocated resources needed to access the database.

The transaction processing phase is the largest and most complex of these phases. In its basic form, it is the phase whereby an SQL statement is executed against the database. This may be to execute a simple query such as an `INSERT` statement or a more complex query that binds parameter markers to an SQL statement and then retrieves data from result sets returned by the database. This phase can involve complex processing such as column-wise or row-wise array inserts, or column-wise or row-rise binding of parameters to an SQL statement.

The available cursors for the transaction processing phase were also reviewed. Cursors are used when handling result sets that are made available by the database. These result sets can be retrieved as part of an SQL `SELECT` statement against the database, or more sophisticated cursors can be used to also update rows within the database. One such cursor is the keyset cursor.

There are two types of basic cursors available: a static cursor, or read-only cursor and a dynamic cursor, or updatable cursor. Some cursors allow you to scroll through the result set and specify which rowset you can read or update. With this cursor type (keyset, for example), you can move the current rowset to the beginning, end, or to an absolute or relative position within the result set.

At the end of the chapter, we took a look at the OLE DB driver and described how to set this up and where the latest driver could be found. The main OLE DB objects were discussed and identified. These include the data source object—used to determine available data source names; the Session Object—used to generate the rowsets from the data source; the command object—for issuing SQL commands against the database; and the rowset object—used for returning data from the database.

References

DB2 UDB Call Level Interface Guide and Reference

DB2 UDB Application Development Guide

IBM DB2 Online Documentation Web Site:
   http://software.ibm.com/data/db2/library

Microsoft ODBC Web Site:
   http://www.microsoft.com/data/odbc/

Microsoft OLE DB Web Start Page:
   http://msdn.microsoft.com/library/psdk/dasdk/oled0cs7.htm

DB2 UDB OLE DB Web Site:
   http://www-4.ibm.com/software/data/db2/udb/ad/v71/oledb.html

CHAPTER 7

Java Programming

Java's "Write once, run anywhere" philosophy allows you to distribute your application over multiple Intel and UNIX platforms. Java programs can access DB2 databases from standalone applications, applets running within a Web browser, and servlets run from powerful Web application servers such as IBM WebSphere. DB2 also has both static and dynamic SQL programming support for Java, allowing you to maximize your performance and offer you flexibility as needed.

DB2 provides Java Database Connectivity (JDBC) drivers to write dynamic SQL programs in Java. Similarly, DB2 comes with an SQLj driver so that you can embed static SQL statements into your Java code. The beauty of SQLj is that it uses JDBC for all of its runtime operations. This allows you to easily write mixed applications that use both JDBC and SQLj. You can also write stored procedures for DB2 using either of these interfaces, as well as external UDFs (User-Defined Functions) that you can call in your SQL queries from any client program.

7.1 Objectives

Before reading this chapter, you should be familiar with the Java programming language and how to write Java applications and applets. After reading this chapter, you should understand:

- Types of JDBC drivers supported by DB2.
- JDBC interfaces and program flow.
- Differences between JDBC 1.22 and JDBC 2.0.
- Advanced JDBC 2.0 techniques.
- SQLj program design and flow.
- SQLj source precompilation and binding.

- JDBC and SQLj stored procedures.
- Java UDFs

7.2 JDBC Programming

JDBC is Java's programming interface for universal data access, largely inspired by ODBC. Many JDBC calls have direct equivalents in ODBC. While ODBC is designed for C and is a procedural interface, JDBC's architecture is object-oriented. Similar to ODBC, a good JDBC application should work with any DBMS vendor product using the same code since all JDBC drivers implement the interfaces in the `java.sql` and optionally the `javax.sql` packages.

In addition, any well-architected interface for Java must be object-oriented, and JDBC is designed with this in mind. Different aspects of application-database interaction are maintained and controlled using Java objects, defined by classes that implement the JDBC interface specifications. JDBC drivers are initially registered with a noninstantiable `DriverManager` class, which is used to obtain database connections by specifying a Uniform Resource Locator (URL). Each connection is represented using a `Connection` object. A `Connection` object provides methods to obtain and set connection-level properties and to create `Statement` objects, which are used to execute SQL queries. Queries that return a result set have their cursor operations encapsulated in a `ResultSet` object. If an error occurs during processing, an `SQLException` is thrown, which the application must then handle.

It is important to note that JDBC is an extensive API, and there are additional objects to consider. First, we describe the fundamental ones mentioned above, and introduce others as necessary when we discuss more advanced topics. Except for `DriverManager`, which is a class, each of the JDBC API members we name herein are formally defined as Java interfaces in the `java.sql` package.

The DB2 JDBC driver classes implement these interfaces and have their own DB2-specific names. Because of the object-oriented programming concept known as polymorphism, your applications do not need to refer to the vendor-specific class names for the DB2 JDBC driver types. Instead, your Java programs should always declare objects using the JDBC API interface names.

There are different types of JDBC drivers designed to fulfill specific development needs. They are divided into four classes based on their underlying implementation and capabilities. They are presented here with reference to DB2 as follows:

- **Type I:** *JDBC-ODBC bridge plus ODBC driver*—The JDBC-ODBC Bridge Driver is supplied with the Java runtime libraries. This driver translates calls from a Java application into corresponding ODBC calls and issues them against an ODBC Driver Manager. Using the data source name, the ODBC Driver Manager then routes each ODBC call to the corresponding ODBC driver. While this driver can be used with DB2, its intended use is with DBMS vendors that do not provide their own JDBC driver. The ODBC Driver Manager

and a corresponding ODBC driver for the DBMS must be installed and configured for the JDBC-ODBC Bridge Driver to be used.
- **Type II:** *Partly Java driver using native API*—These drivers translate JDBC calls into DBMS-specific native-API calls. In DB2 V7.1 and earlier, the Type II driver provided is `COM.ibm.db2.jdbc.app.DB2Driver`, located in `sqllib/java/db2java.zip`. This driver translates JDBC calls into corresponding DB2 CLI calls via the Java Native Interface (JNI) and is known as the DB2 JDBC application or "app" driver.
- **Type III:** *JDBC net pure Java driver*—Drivers that connect to a middleware process that perform DBMS-specific native-API calls fit into this category. The Type III JDBC driver in DB2 V7.1 is known as the DB2 JDBC applet or net driver. It is defined in the class `COM.ibm.db2.jdbc.net.DB2Driver`, located in `sqllib/java/db2java.zip`. This driver communicates with a DB2 Java Daemon process, which translates calls into DB2 CLI.
- **Type IV:** *Pure Java driver using native protocol*—Type IV drivers are written in pure Java, and directly establish a network connection to a DBMS and submit requests using a vendor-specific or standardized protocol. For example, Distributed Relational Database Architecture (DRDA) is an industry-standard protocol for communicating with a DBMS. A Type IV JDBC driver could communicate directly over the network to a DBMS using DRDA. Currently, there is no Type IV JDBC driver supplied with DB2; however, there are plans to introduce this in DB2 V8.

We will explore the app driver and net driver in greater detail a little later, so you will become thoroughly acquainted with the intended use of each. You can also use the JDBC-ODBC bridge that is provided as part of the JDK (Java Development Kit) or Java 2 SDK (Software Developer's Kit); however, this driver is designed to work with all vendors, and so it does not take into account additional performance benefits that DB2-specific JDBC drivers do.

7.2.1 DB2 JDBC Driver Versions

JDBC is an evolving interface. The current level of the specification is JDBC 2.0, and the previous specification was JDBC 1.22. DB2 V7.1 includes JDBC 1.22 and JDBC 2.0 drivers for Intel and UNIX platforms. JDBC 2.0 provides significant feature enhancements from JDBC 1.22, such as scrollable cursors, batch updates, connection pooling, distributed transactions (using the Java Transaction API), and better large object support. DB2's JDBC 2.0 drivers support this functionality; however, they do not provide all of the features in the JDBC 2.0 specification. For example, DB2 does not have an ARRAY data type, thus there is no support for use of SQL3 data types such as ARRAY.

It is important to note that the functionality of the JDBC 1.22 specification is also included in JDBC 2.0, with the exception of how Large Objects (LOBs) are handled. Therefore, we will begin by describing basic JDBC concepts that apply to both versions, and then discuss the enhanced features of the DB2 JDBC 2.0 drivers, and note differences between driver versions as necessary.

7.2.2 Changing between DB2 JDBC Driver Versions

By default, DB2 V7.1 is configured to use the JDBC 1.22 drivers. On Windows platforms, since the `sqllib` directory is shared among all instances, your entire system can only use either JDBC 1.22 or JDBC 2.0 at one time. On UNIX platforms, each Java application can have its own configuration. To switch between versions of DB2 JDBC drivers, DB2 provides two scripts, `usejdbc1` and `usejdbc2` (batch files on Windows), located in `sqllib/java12`. The `usejdbc2` script allows you to switch to the JDBC 2.0 drivers, and the `usejdbc1` script switches back to JDBC 1.22. Running the batch files on Windows physically copies the active JDBC driver version into the `sqllib\java directory`.

> **Note**
>
> On Windows, it is important to shut down any processes that use DB2 JDBC libraries and any active DB2 Java Daemon processes before running either of these scripts. Otherwise, since the files are in use, a share violation will occur and files in use won't be replaced. Files not in use, however, will be replaced, thus leading to the possibility of mixed levels of code.

The same scripts are available on UNIX systems, but running them only changes the settings for certain environment variables, and no files are copied. To run either script on a UNIX platform using the Korn shell, use the following syntax:

```
usejdbc2
```

7.2.3 DB2 JDBC Development Prerequisites

On Windows, the classes for the DB2 JDBC app and net drivers for the JDBC version currently in use are all in the `db2java.zip` file, located in the `sqllib\java` directory. On UNIX, there is a `db2java.zip` file for each version of JDBC. The JDBC 2.0 drivers are located in `sqllib/java12`, and the JDBC 1.22 drivers are in `sqllib/java`. These classes implement the JDBC interface specifications laid out in the `java.sql` package of the Java API. To access the JDBC drivers for DB2, the `db2java.zip` file must be included in your `CLASSPATH`. You can specify the `CLASSPATH` when you invoke the Java Virtual Machine (JVM) or by setting the corresponding environment variable.

To develop JDBC 1.22 applications, you must have the JDK 1.1.8 or greater installed on your system. For JDBC 2.0 applications, you must install the Java 2 SDK Standard Edition (JDK 1.2.2 or greater). The Standard Edition of the Java 2 SDK will provide the `java.sql` packages, which comprise the JDBC 2.0 core API. Functionality such as connection pooling and dis-

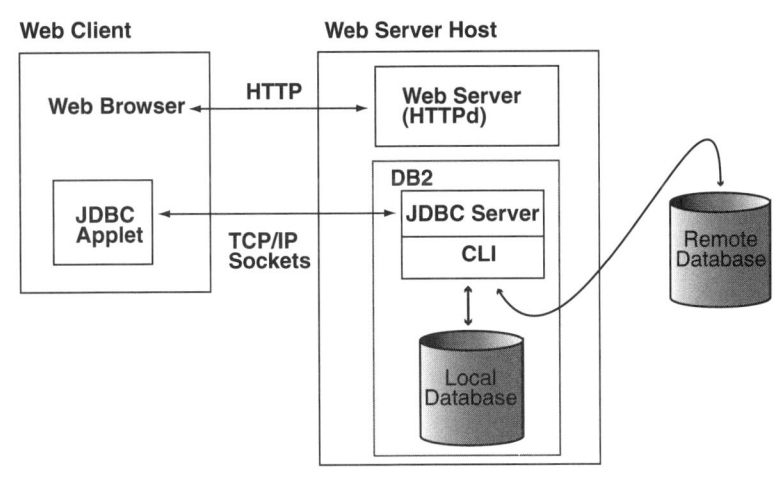

Figure 7-1 DB2 net driver software layers.

tributed transactions are specified in the JDBC 2.0 Standard Extension API, which requires the `javax.sql` packages. In addition, JDBC 2.0 applications often use the `javax.transaction`, `javax.transaction.xa`, and `javax.naming` packages, which define the Java Transaction API (JTA) and the Java Naming and Directory Interface (JNDI). All of the `javax` packages mentioned are part of the Java 2 SDK Enterprise Edition.

7.2.4 DB2 JDBC Applet (or net) Driver

The DB2 JDBC applet or "net" driver is designed for use in Java applets that access DB2 databases. First, the client Web browser downloads `db2java.zip` prior to running the applet. Then, the DB2 net driver establishes a TCP/IP connection with a DB2 Java Daemon process running on the system where the Web page was served. The DB2 Java Daemon is simply a DB2 CLI application, which fulfills database requests on behalf of the applet (see Figure 7-1). You can start a DB2 Java Daemon process by running the command:

```
db2jstrt [port]
```

You can optionally specify the port number for the DB2 Java Daemon to listen for TCP/IP connections. If no port is specified, the default port is 6789. It is possible to run multiple DB2 Java Daemon processes on the same system as long as each listens on a different port.

> **Note**
> The DB2 Java Daemon is also known as the DB2 JDBC (Applet) Server.

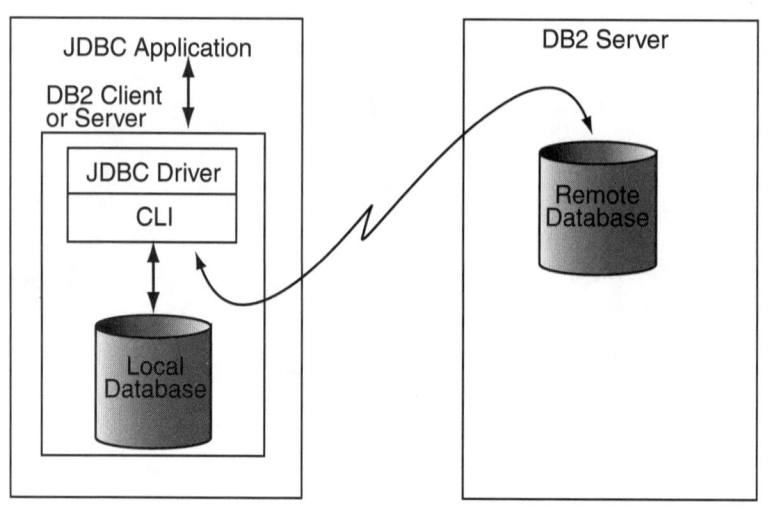

Figure 7-2 DB2 app driver software layers.

Although the intended use for the net driver is with Java applets, it can also be used with Java applications and servlets. The benefit to this is that you don't need to install a DB2 client on the system where the Java program is running, and since the net driver is written entirely in Java, you can avoid the use of JNI. However, this is generally slower than using the app driver since the net driver needs to communicate with a middleware process to fulfill database requests.

7.2.5 DB2 JDBC Application (or app) Driver

The DB2 JDBC application or "app" driver is intended for use with Java applications and servlets, or more generally, whenever the DB2 Client libraries are installed on the system where the JDBC program is running (see Figure 7-2). The app driver communicates directly with a DB2 server using CLI calls made through the DB2 client libraries, and provides much better performance than the net driver since there is no DB2 Java Daemon middleware process.

In addition, use of the DB2 net driver requires at least two network flows per flow that occurs using the app driver. This is because with the net driver, there is one flow from the program to the Java Daemon, and a second from the Java Daemon to the DB2 server (or IPC (Inter-Process Communication) in the latter case if the DB2 Java Daemon is running locally on a DB2 server). In comparison, the app driver requires a single network or IPC flow through the DB2 client libraries. Thus, the app driver should be used whenever possible.

It is not possible to use the app driver with Java applets because an applet is run on a client browser and most clients who view a Web page will not have the DB2 libraries installed on their system.

7.2.6 JDBC Driver Registration

Before a JDBC driver can be used in a Java program, it must be registered with a JDBC class known as the `DriverManager`. This only needs to be done once per driver in the application by instantiating a DB2 JDBC driver object using the `Class.forName()` method and specifying the fully-qualified driver name. For the app driver, use the following syntax:

```
Class.forName("COM.ibm.db2.jdbc.app.DB2Driver");
```

Similarly, for the net driver, use the syntax:

```
Class.forName("COM.ibm.db2.jdbc.net.DB2Driver");5
```

> **Note**
>
> On OS/2, `Class.forName(String className)` does not instantiate a new object of the specified class. The `newInstance()` method must be invoked to do this. Thus, use the syntax `Class.forName(String className).newInstance()`.

You can register a JDBC driver in a static initializer within the class definition or within the runtime code. The former technique ensures that the driver is registered as soon as the class using it is loaded by the JVM. A static initializer can be written as follows:

```
Class MyClass {
    static {
        try {
            Class.forName("COM.ibm.db2.jdbc.app.DB2Driver");
            Class.forName("COM.ibm.db2.jdbc.net.DB2Driver");
        } catch (Exception e) {
            e.printStackTrace();
        }
    }
    // Additional class definition
}
```

In this example, we are registering both DB2 JDBC drivers. You can have as many JDBC drivers in your Java programs as you want, using the prescribed method. In addition to registering these drivers, ensure that you have imported all of the necessary JDBC packages. Here is an all-inclusive series of `import` commands:

```
import java.sql.*;
import javax.sql.*;
import javax.transaction.*;
import javax.transaction.xa.*;
import javax.naming.*;
```

It is not always necessary to import all of these packages into your class. For example, if you are only using the JDBC 1.22 API or the JDBC 2.0 Core API, you do not need the `javax` packages. These latter packages are used with the JDBC 2.0 Standard Extension API, the JTA, and the JNDI, which require the Java 2 SDK Enterprise Edition to be installed.

7.2.7 Supported Data Types

SQL data types need to be mapped to corresponding programming language data types to be accessed by an application. In Java, this is fairly straightforward. Every SQL data type has a corresponding JDBC type and a Java type. The JDBC types are defined in the `java.sql.Types` class and map to standard Java primitive types or class objects (see Table 7-1).

Table 7-1 DB2 SQL to JDBC and Java Data Type Mappings

SQL Type	JDBC Type	Java Type	
BLOB	BLOB	`java.sql.Blob`	(JDBC 2.0)
		`byte [ ]`	(JDBC 1.22)
CLOB	CLOB	`java.sql.Clob`	(JDBC 2.0)
		`String`	(JDBC 1.22)
DBCLOB	CLOB	`java.sql.Clob`	(JDBC 2.0)
		`String`	(JDBC 1.22)
LONG VARCHAR FOR BIT DATA	LONGVARBINARY	`byte[ ]`	
VARCHAR FOR BIT DATA	VARBINARY	`byte[ ]`	
CHARACTER FOR BIT DATA	BINARY	`byte[ ]`	
LONG VARCHAR	LONGVARCHAR	`String`	
CHARACTER	CHAR	`String`	
VARCHAR	VARCHAR	`String`	
NUMERIC	NUMERIC	`java.math.BigDecimal`	
DECIMAL	DECIMAL	`java.math.BigDecimal`	
INTEGER	INTEGER	`int`	
SMALLINT	SMALLINT	`short`	
BIGINT	BIGINT	`long`	
REAL	REAL	`float`	
FLOAT	FLOAT	`double`	
FLOAT	DOUBLE	`double`	
DATE	DATE	`java.sql.Date`	
TIME	TIME	`java.sql.Time`	
TIMESTAMP	TIMESTAMP	`java.sql.Timestamp`	

Most character data is mapped into the Java `String` type, and binary data is mapped into the Java `byte[]` type. JDBC also defines several data types of its own to handle `DATE`, `TIME`, and `TIMESTAMP` data types, as well as `BLOB` and `CLOB` data.

Most types correspond to individual `getXXX()` and `setXXX()` methods in the `ResultSet` and `PreparedStatement` interfaces, which you use when retrieving values from result sets and when binding statement parameters, respectively. We distinguish `getXXX()` and `setXXX()` methods from regular get and set methods. We use "XXX" as a variable term to indicate that a Java-type name should be substituted for retrieval or binding an output column or parameter, respectively, for an SQL query.

7.2.8 JDBC Interfaces

We now discuss the JDBC interface specifications in detail, with a listing of many commonly used methods in each class or interface. However, for a complete reference of the JDBC API, please download the Java 2 SDK documentation for JDBC 2.0 and JDK 1.1.x API documentation for JDBC 1.22. You can also view the documents online at the Sun Microsystems site for Java. The links at the end of the chapter include these sites as well as others.

7.2.9 `DriverManager`

The JDBC DriverManager class is included in the `java.sql` package. JDBC drivers register themselves with the `DriverManager` when they are instantiated using the `Class.forName()` syntax we discussed earlier. A JDBC application then calls a `DriverManager.getConnection()` method to obtain a database connection. The database connection information is specified using a URL. A valid URL for the DB2 app driver has the form:

```
jdbc:db2:<dbname>
```

The first part of the URL specifies the protocol, which in this case is JDBC; the second specifies the subprotocol, which corresponds to a DB2 database connection; and the third is the data source name. Only the third needs to be uniquely supplied by the application. For example, here is how you would connect locally to the DB2MALL database using the app driver:

```
String url = "jdbc:db2:db2mall";
Connection con = DriverManager.getConnection(url);
```

The database connection is returned in the form of a JDBC `Connection` object. The URL for the net driver is a little more complicated. It has the following form:

```
jdbc:db2://<server>:<port>/<dbname>
```

Following the protocol and subprotocol, the // symbol indicates a TCP/IP connection, followed by the server name. After this, the DB2 Java Daemon listener port may optionally be specified. If no port is specified, then the default port, 6789, is used. Finally, we indicate the database name by preceding it with a slash (/).

For example, using the net driver, we would connect to the `DB2MALL` database on a system known as `sanya11` using a DB2 Java Daemon listening on TCP/IP port `7000` as follows:

```
String url = "jdbc:db2://sanya11:7000/db2mall";
String uid = "steve";
String pwd = "mypassword";
Connection con = DriverManager.getConnection(url, uid, pwd);
```

Here, we used a slightly different form of the `getConnection()` method, but still received a `Connection` object. You have probably guessed that the `Connection` returned by the net driver is different from the one returned by the app driver, since they have different implementations. However, we can polymorphically consider them the same type of object, even though the actual classes are different. We've described the various forms of the `getConnection()` method in the following API section.

> **TIP** When a connection to DB2 using the net driver occurs within an applet, the DB2 JDBC server hostname in the connection URL must match the hostname of the Web page served to the browser. This is because of the security restriction within applets that only allows them to establish a network connection to the system where the Web page was originally served.

`DriverManager` methods:

- `Connection getConnection(String url)` — Connects and returns a `Connection` object. Connecting with only a URL is valid for local database connections and for remote connections when DB2 server authentication type is set to `CLIENT`.
- `Connection getConnection(String url, String userid, String passwd)` — Connects and returns a `Connection` object. URL, userid, and password are all specified.
- `Connection getConnection(String url, Properties info)` — Connects and returns a `Connection` object. The user and password keys are specified in a `Properties` object.

7.2.10 Connection

All connection-level operations such as transaction control and setting the isolation level are accomplished by calling methods in a `Connection` object. In addition, since every SQL query must reference a specific connection, JDBC `Statement` objects are also obtained by invoking methods in a `Connection` object. As we just described, a DB2 `Connection` object is obtained by calling a `DriverManager.getConnection()` method with a valid DB2 database URL. We present many useful methods in this section, but leave examples until the next section, so that we can combine them with our discussion of `Statement` and `ResultSet` objects.

Connection methods:

- `void close()` — Closes the connection and deallocates resources for this `Connection` object.
- `void commit()` — Commits the current transaction.
- `void rollback()` — Rolls back the current transaction.
- `void setTransactionIsolation(int level)` — Sets the isolation level.
- `void setAutoCommit(boolean enableAutoCommit)` — Turns auto-commit mode on or off. When auto-commit is on, every SQL `Statement` results in a commit flow to the DB2 server.
- `Statement createStatement()` — Returns a `Statement` object that can be executed.
- `PreparedStatement prepareStatement(String sql)` — Prepares a statement for execution and returns the corresponding `PreparedStatement` object. A `Prepared Statement` can be executed multiple times with different input parameters.
- `CallableStatement prepareCall(String sql)` — Prepares a stored procedure call and returns a `CallableStatement` object.

> **TIP** It is always better to call an object's `close()` method explicitly, to ensure its resources are immediately cleaned up. Otherwise, the JVM's garbage collector thread will do the cleanup, which is not immediate and less efficient since it requires checking by the JVM.

7.2.11 Statement

A `Statement` object lets you execute an SQL query using the corresponding JDBC `Connection`. When all of the values in your query can be specified literally, a `Statement` object will suffice. To dynamically prepare and execute statements, however, JDBC supplies the `PreparedStatement` interface, which extends `Statement`. `PreparedStatement` allows you to bind parameter markers, consistent with a dynamic SQL PREPARE operation. You can rebind these parameters and execute the same query many times with different sets of parameters this way, without having to perform a PREPARE operation each time. Recall that this is an obvious performance improvement, since query preparation has the cost of generating an access plan.

In addition, the `CallableStatement` interface extends the interface defined by `PreparedStatement`. `CallableStatement` objects are used to call stored procedures that have output parameters. Thus, consistent with object-oriented inheritance concepts, `PreparedStatement` objects inherit the functionality of `Statement` objects, and `CallableStatement` objects inherit the functionality of both `PreparedStatement` and `Statement`.

Here are some of the commonly used methods in the `Statement` interface. We provide similar references for `PreparedStatement` and `CallableStatement` when we discuss their use in greater detail.

`Statement` methods:

- `void addBatch(String sql)` **(JDBC 2.0)**—Adds `sql` to this object's list of commands for batch execution.
- `void cancel()`—Cancels this statement's execution.
- `void close()`—Releases this statement's resources immediately.
- `boolean getMoreResults()`—Returns `true` if there are more results to be returned by this statement. This method is used when a stored procedure was executed.
- `ResultSet getResultSet()`—Returns the current result set. This is used to retrieve multiple result sets when a stored procedure was executed.
- `boolean execute(String sql)`—Executes an SQL statement that returns more than one result set. If no result sets are returned, then `false` is returned. This method is used for calling stored procedures.
- `int [] executeBatch()` **(JDBC 2.0)**—Executes a batch of queries and returns an array whose length is equal to the number of queries. Each entry contains the number of rows affected by the corresponding query execution.
- `ResultSet executeQuery(String sql)`—Executes `sql` and returns the corresponding `ResultSet` object.
- `int executeUpdate(String sql)`—Executes INSERT, UPDATE, or DELETE query and returns the number of rows affected.
- `void setQueryTimeout(int seconds)`—Sets the number of seconds before a query will time out during execution.

7.2.12 `ResultSet`

When a query is executed and produces a result set, the corresponding `Statement` object returns a `ResultSet` object. A `ResultSet` object manipulates a cursor and allows you to retrieve values for each column. In DB2, forward-only result sets can use updateable cursors. The DB2 JDBC 2.0 driver also introduces read-only scrollable result sets.

> **Note**
>
> DB2 V7.1 JDBC 2.0 drivers do not support the use of the `updateXXX()` methods in the `ResultSet` interface. To update a row in a `ResultSet` using an updateable cursor, you must use JDBC 1.22 techniques, which are described later in this chapter.

JDBC Programming

ResultSet methods:

- `boolean absolute(int row)` **(JDBC 2.0)**—Moves cursor position to specified row. If row is negative, then specified from end of result set. If the row number does not exist, then `false` is returned.
- `void close()`—Closes the cursor for this result set.
- `int getInt(int columnNumber)`—Returns an `int` value for the column specified by `columnNumber`.
- `int getInt(String columnName)`—Returns an `int` value for the output column specified by `columnName`. Requires additional lookup, so this is slower than the form of this method that specifies column number.
- `boolean next()`—Fetches the next row in the result set, and returns `false` if there are no more rows.
- `boolean previous()` **(JDBC 2.0)**—Fetches the previous row in the result set.
- `boolean relative(int rows)` **(JDBC 2.0)**—Fetches the row specified, relative to the current row.
- `boolean wasNull()`—Returns `true` if the last value was a NULL value.

7.2.13 SQLException

Dealing with errors is greatly facilitated in JDBC applications since the JDBC driver does all error checking. If an error occurs, the driver will throw an `SQLException`, which the application must catch. This is cleaner than ODBC, where the application must check the return code for every function call and call appropriate error-handling routines when required. JDBC error checking uses standard `try-catch` block syntax as follows:

```
try {
   // JDBC operations
} catch (SQLException e) {
   //Error handling code
}
```

A `try-catch` block like the one above should surround all JDBC sections of your Java code. Otherwise, ensure that methods that perform JDBC operations but do not catch exceptions declare this in a `throws` declaration. For example:

```
void myJDBCMethod() throws SQLException
{
// method contents
}
```

Our fictitious method above declares that it will throw an `SQLException` if one occurs, thus leaving the responsibility to the caller to handle it. There are several useful methods from `SQLException` objects, which we have outlined below. We do not use `try-catch` blocks or method-throw declarations in our samples in this chapter for simplicity and readability, but you should be aware that they are required.

SQLException methods:

- String getSQLState() — Returns the SQLSTATE for the error.
- int getErrorCode() — Returns the DB2-specific SQL code for the error.
- String getMessage() — Returns the error message associated with the error.
- void printStackTrace() — Prints out the Java stack traceback for the error.

7.2.14 Executing Statements

We have already described how to connect to a DB2 database using the DriverManager.getConnection() methods in the previous section. We now describe in detail how to execute SQL queries and process result sets. Our first example updates the product table units_in_stock inventory account column:

```java
// Declare variables
String sql = "UPDATE product " +
             "SET units_in_stock=units_in_stock-10 " +
             "WHERE product_id=123";

Connection con = null;
int rowCount = 0;

// Obtain connection and set autocommit on
con = DriverManager.getConnection("jdbc:db2:db2mall");
con.setAutoCommit(true);

Statement stmt = con.createStatement();
rowCount = stmt.executeUpdate(sql);
stmt.close();

// Disconnect
con.close();
```

Since we knew all of the values in our query beforehand, we hard-coded them, and thus used a Statement object obtained from the connection. In addition, since there was only a single statement in our transaction, we turned on auto-commit. It is on by default, but we used setAutoCommit() for clarity.

We then called the executeUpdate() method of the Statement object to execute our query. This method is used with all INSERT, DELETE, and UPDATE statements, and returns a count of the number of rows affected. We stored this value in the rowCount variable in our example, but we did not use it for processing purposes. Notice that we called the close()

method for each JDBC object, thereby ensuring that we did not continue to use resources we did not need.

If you notice that iterative execution within your application results in increased memory usage each time, be sure that you are closing objects when you are finished with them. Otherwise, your applications will have to wait for Java's garbage collector thread to destroy objects, which is less efficient.

7.2.15 Using Prepared Statements

If we are going to execute the same statement multiple times, we should use a `PreparedStatement` instead of a `Statement` object. This way, we save the overhead of obtaining a new `Statement` object and the PREPARE cost of each additional query. This is possible when the syntax of each query is the same and only parameters in the SET and WHERE clauses differ. We demonstrate how to use `PreparedStatement` objects by modifying our previous example:

```java
// Declare variables
String sql = "UPDATE product " +
             "SET units_in_stock = units_in_stock - ? " +
             "WHERE product_id = ?";
int [] newUnitsInStock = {10, 20, 30};
int [] productIds = {123, 456, 789};
169
Connection con = null;
int rowCount = 0;

// Obtain connection and turn off autocommit
con = DriverManager.getConnection("jdbc:db2:db2mall");
con.setAutoCommit(false);

// Prepare the statement and process each update
PreparedStatement ps = con.prepareStatement(sql);
for(int i=0; i < newUnitsInStock.length; i++)
{
   ps.setInt(1, newUnitsInStock[i]);
   ps.setInt(2, productIds[i]);
   rowCount = ps.executeUpdate();
}

// Commit the transaction
ps.close();
con.commit();

// Disconnect
con.close();
```

Notice that we specify parameter markers using the ? character in our query string this time, and use the `setXXX()` methods in the `PreparedStatement` object to set each parameter's value according to data type. In our example, both parameters were integers, so we used `setInt()`. Also, notice that the `PreparedStatement` object is not closed until after all of the statements have been executed, since we reference the same prepared statement with each execution.

In addition, this time we turned off auto-commit, because we wanted to explicitly commit the transaction only after all three queries were successful. This would make sense, for example, if the customer had purchased multiple items and we needed to ensure that all of the `units_in_stock` columns were updated before the transaction was completed.

Here are some of the popular methods in the `PreparedStatement` interface:

PreparedStatement methods:

- `ResultSet executeQuery()` — Executes the prepared query and returns the corresponding `ResultSet`.
- `boolean execute()` — Returns `true` if the `execute` statement returns one or more result sets. This is used for calling stored procedures.
- `int executeUpdate()` — Executes an INSERT, UPDATE, or DELETE statement and returns the number of affected rows.
- `void setNull(int parameterIndex, int jdbcType)` — Sets the value of the parameter specified by the `parameterIndex` to NULL, using the specified `jdbcType` (for all JDBC types, see the Types class in `java.sql`).
- `setInt(int parameterIndex, int x)` — Sets the value of the parameter specified by the `parameterIndex` to the value x.

7.2.16 Retrieving Result Sets

So far, all of our examples have involved updating data. We now shift our focus to using queries that return a result set. A `ResultSet` object is returned when you execute a query using a `Statement` or `PreparedStatement` object. For example, we can execute a literal query using a `Statement` object and assign the `ResultSet` to a variable as follows:

```
ResultSet rs = null;
Statement stmt = null;
String sql = "SELECT C1 FROM T1";
Connection con =
    DriverManager.getConnection("jdbc:db2:db2mall");
stmt = con.createStatement();
rs = stmt.executeQuery(query);
```

JDBC Programming

Similarly, we can prepare a SELECT query and obtain a ResultSet using a PreparedStatement object:

```
ResultSet rs = null;
PreparedStatement ps = null;
String sql = "SELECT C1 FROM T1";
Connection con =
   DriverManager.getConnection("jdbc:db2:db2mall");
ps = con.prepareStatement(sql);
rs = stmt.executeQuery();
```

In both examples, we used different forms of the query execution method; however, in each case, a ResultSet object was returned. We process the result set the same way in each case, using the next() method to fetch the next row of data until false is returned, and using getXXX() methods to obtain each column value.

```
while (rs.next()) {
   int col1 = rs.getInt(1);
   // Further process retrieved data
}
rs.close();
```

In this example, we loop through the result set, fetching each column into a local variable within the loop upon each iteration. While we specified the column to fetch by its relative position in the result set, we could have also requested it by name using an overloaded version of each getXXX() method. Later in this chapter, we will show you how to further automate result set processing using ResultSetMetaData objects.

7.2.17 NULL Values

In all of the code we have presented, we assumed that there were no NULL values in the columns retrieved in a ResultSet. Each JDBC type has a default value that is returned if a value is NULL; however, this is not always a reliable mechanism to determine if a value is NULL. Methods that return an object will return Java's null constant, but methods that return primitives will return 0. For example, the getInt() method returns 0 if the value retrieved was NULL, but 0 is certainly a legitimate value for an INTEGER column. For this reason, there is an additional method defined in the ResultSet interface to determine if the last column extracted from the ResultSet was NULL. This method is appropriately named wasNull() and it returns a boolean. There are also setNull() methods in the PreparedStatement interface to allow you to bind NULL values in a query.

7.2.18 Updating Rows in a Result Set

By default, the DB2 JDBC drivers use forward-only read-only cursors. This means that you can only move forward through the result set, and you cannot update or delete any of the rows you retrieve by referencing that cursor. Under this scenario, you would need to create a separate

Statement or PreparedStatement object where you could uniquely specify the row to update or delete using a key. This is less efficient, because DB2 will have to determine which row matches the specified criteria (such as a key). However, this type of strategy may be required at times if you cache an entire result set in a GUI tool. Otherwise, you should use a forward-only updateable cursor such as in the following example:

```
// Queries and cursor name
String sqlSelect = "SELECT C1, C2 FROM T1 FOR UPDATE";
String sqlUpdate = "UPDATE T1 SET C2=? WHERE CURRENT OF ";
String cursorName = null;

// Execute SELECT statement and process result set
Statement stmt = con.createStatement(sqlSelect);
ResultSet rs = stmt.executeQuery();
cursorName = rs.getCursorName();
PreparedStatement ps = con.prepareStatement(sqlUpdate +
cursorName);

while (rs.next()) {
   String c1 = rs.getString(1);
   String c2 = rs.getString(2);

   // Apply business logic on the retrieved row
   if ( businessLogic is true ) {
      String newC2 = "new value";
      ps.setString(1, newC2);
      ps.executeUpdate();
   }
}
rs.close();
ps.close();
stmt.close();
```

Here, we use the getCursorName() method in the ResultSet object to create our second query. In doing so, our code will run more efficiently because DB2 will not have to find the row we want to update; it knows that it is referenced by the current cursor position.

7.2.19 Specifying Result Set Type in JDBC 2.0

JDBC 2.0 overloads the statement creation methods in the Connection interface to specify the result set type and concurrency type you wish to use. Each of these types corresponds to a static integer constant defined in the ResultSet interface. There are two types of concurrency, CONCUR_READ_ONLY and CONCUR_UPDATEABLE, which correspond to whether the query is FOR FETCH ONLY or FOR UPDATE, respectively.

In addition, there are three types of result sets, TYPE_FORWARD_ONLY, TYPE_SCROLL_INSENSITIVE, and TYPE_SCROLL_SENSITIVE. TYPE_FORWARD_

JDBC Programming

ONLY result sets only allow you to scroll forward through them. The other two types are both scrollable, meaning that you can scroll through them backward or forward, either by one record or by a relative number of records. A sensitive result set will show you changes that have been made to the underlying data if you query the same row more than once. A scroll-insensitive result set will not reflect these changes until the query is reexecuted. We describe each concurrency type and result set type supported by DB2 in Table 7-2.

Table 7-2 Supported JDBC 2.0 `ResultSet` Types

`ResultSet` Type	Description
CONCUR_READ_ONLY	The result set is not modifiable using JDBC 2.0 update methods.
TYPE_FORWARD_ONLY	Cursor can only scroll forward through the result set.
TYPE_SCROLL_INSENSITIVE	Cursor is scrollable. Changes made to the result set won't be visible until the query is executed again.

From this table, we can see there are two types of `ResultSet` objects we can create using the DB2 JDBC 2.0 drivers:

- TYPE_FORWARD_ONLY, CONCUR_READ_ONLY.
- TYPE_SCROLL_SENSITIVE, CONCUR_READ_ONLY.

From this, it is important to note that although we have discussed updateable result sets in the previous section, the DB2 JDBC 2.0 drivers do not support the CONCUR_UPDATEABLE parameter. Thus, the `updateXXX()` methods specified in the JDBC 2.0 `ResultSet` interface (used with CONCUR_UPDATEABLE result sets) are not supported. To use updateable result sets, you will have to continue using the technique shown for JDBC 1.22.

7.2.20 Using Scrollable Result Sets

Navigating through a scrollable result set is quite simple, and you only need to know a handful of methods in the `ResultSet` interface. The `previous()` method is analogous to `next()`, in that it moves back one row in the result set, rather than forward. You can also specify a row relative to the current row using the `relative()` method, which takes a positive or negative integer as a parameter.

To move to an absolute position in the result set, use the `absolute()` method, which also takes a positive or negative integer as a parameter. A positive value specifies a position relative to the beginning of the result set, with the first row being 1. A negative value specifies a position relative to the last row in the result set, with –1 being the last row. You can also use the `first()` and `last()` methods, respectively, to move to the beginning or the end of the result set. Both of these methods return a Boolean, which indicates that there were no rows in the result set when the value is `false`.

7.2.21 Calling Stored Procedures

Stored procedures can be called with a Statement, PreparedStatement, or CallableStatement object. If the stored procedure has no parameters, or only input parameters that you are specifying literally, you can use a Statement object. When you wish to use parameter markers and the stored procedure only has input parameters, use a PreparedStatement object. A stored procedure with output parameters is called using a CallableStatement object. Since we have already explained how to use these types of objects, we will focus here on how to use CallableStatement objects.

A CallableStatement object is obtained using a prepareCall() method in the corresponding Connection object. The prepareCall() is issued in exactly the same manner as prepareStatement(). You also bind IN and INOUT parameters for the stored procedure using the setXXX() methods in PreparedStatement. However, for INOUT and OUT parameters, you must make a registerOutParameter() call for each parameter of either of these types. Upon execution of the stored procedure, you use getXXX() methods from the CallableStatement interface, equivalent to the ones you used in the ResultSet interface to retrieve output columns.

One of the main features of stored procedures is their ability to return one or more result sets. If your stored procedure returns a single result set, then to execute your procedure, use the executeQuery() method, which returns a ResultSet object. In the following example, we demonstrate a stored procedure that returns an integer output parameter and a result set.

```
// Prepare and execute a stored procedure call
// for a single resultset stored procedure.
CallableStatement cstmt = con.prepareCall("CALL PROC1(?)");
cstmt.registerOutParameter(1, Types.INTEGER);
ResultSet rs = cstmt.executeQuery();
int output = cstmt.getString(1);
processResults(rs);
```

Here, we obtain the result set and then pass it to another method, processResults(), for handling. If your stored procedure returns zero result sets or more than one result set, then use the execute() method, which returns a Boolean value. If execute() returns true, there are result sets returned. If false is returned, then no result sets were returned. Here is the programming logic to use:

```
if(cstmt.execute()) {
    do {
      ResultSet rs = cstmt.getResultSet();
      processResults(rs);
    } while(cstmt.getMoreResults());
} else {
   int updateCount = cstmt.getUpdateCount();
}
```

Here, we automate the task of determining whether to retrieve result sets or obtain the update count. We also use a loop condition to check whether more result sets are present. Notice that we do not call the `getMoreResults()` method until we have processed our `ResultSet` object. This is because we can only process one `ResultSet` on a stored procedure call at one time. Every time we call `getMoreResults()`, the previous `ResultSet` will be closed, if it has not already been closed.

We note that while `CallableStatement` is a child class of `PreparedStatement`, stored procedure calls are not the same as other dynamically prepared SQL statements. The fundamental difference is that there is no access plan generated by DB2 when calling a stored procedure. However, `CallableStatement` allows you to bind input and output parameters for the stored procedure, conceptually similar to a `PreparedStatement` object. It is important to know this because a stored procedure call will not require the same overhead as other prepared statements if you are concerned about performance. In fact, they may offer significant performance improvements, which we discussed in Chapter 3.

`CallableStatement` methods:

- `void registerOutParameter(int parameterIndex, int jdbc-Type)` — Registers the return type for the corresponding output parameter.
- `boolean wasNull()` — Returns `true` if the most recently retrieved parameter was a NULL value.
- `int getInt(int parameterIndex)` — Standard getter method for output parameters. Other getter methods have similar format.

7.2.22 Batch Execution

DB2 supports JDBC 2.0's performance-improving batch processing feature. When you execute a set of queries against the same DB2 database as a batch, they are all flowed to the DB2 server together, thereby reducing the number of network flows that would be required if they were each executed through separate statement objects. Batch updates are only valid for `UPDATE`, `DELETE`, and `INSERT` statements and for stored procedure calls that have no output parameters nor return any result sets. For example, if a customer has purchased several items and you need to update the inventory of several items in the `product` table of the mall database, you can send all of the updates at once. Here is an example of how to use batch updates:

```
int [] stockReduction = { 10, 20, 30 };
int [] productIds = { 123, 456, 789,};

String sql = "UPDATE product " +
             "SET units_in_stock = units_in_stock - ? " +
             "WHERE product_id = ?";
```

```
PreparedStatement ps = con.prepareStatement(sql);

for(int i=0; i < stockReduction.length; i++) {
   ps.setInt(1, stockReduction[i]);
   ps.setInt(2, productIds[i]);
   ps.addBatch();
}
int [] rowCounts = ps.executeBatch();
```

As you will notice, we use the `addBatch()` method on our `PreparedStatement` to add a statement to a current batch. Thus, the `addBatch()` method understands that if you call `addBatch()` multiple times on the same `PreparedStatement` object, you are actually specifying more than one statement to execute.

In addition, you will notice that the `executeBatch()` method is called to actually run the registered batch queries. This method returns an array of integers, each of which is an update count for the corresponding statement in the batch of queries. Each query in the batch is executed in the order in which it was added.

> **Note**
>
> The `Statement` interface also allows you to add several queries that will execute as a batch. In this case, the `addBatch()` method is overloaded to accept the query as a `String`.

7.2.23 Large Objects

Large Objects (LOBs) such as Binary Large Objects (BLOBs) and Character Large Objects (CLOBs) are handled differently in JDBC 1.22 and JDBC 2.0. In JDBC 1.22, you have several choices about how to bind and retrieve LOB data. We summarize the `getXXX()` methods for LOB data in the following API section. There is a similar `setXXX()` method for each `getXXX()`, which we have not listed (see the Java API documentation for details).

LOB `getXXX()` methods for JDBC 1.22:

- `byte [] getBytes(int columnIndex)` — Returns a byte array containing the value of a BLOB column.
- `String getString(int columnIndex)` — Returns a CLOB column as a Unicode string.
- `InputStream getBinaryStream(int columnIndex)` — Returns a stream to retrieve BLOB data from an output column.
- `InputStream getUnicodeStream(int columnIndex)` — Returns a stream to retrieve CLOB data from an output column. The data is converted from the DB2 server

code page to the DB2 client code page, and then from the DB2 client code page into Unicode.
- `InputStream getAsciiStream(int columnIndex)` — Returns a stream to retrieve CLOB data from an output column. The data is converted from the DB2 server code page to the DB2 client page.

JDBC 2.0 defines interfaces for `Blob` and `Clob` objects, and corresponding getter (`getBlob()` and `getClob()`) and setter (`setBlob()` and `setClob()`) methods for each in `ResultSet` and `PreparedStatement`, respectively. DB2's JDBC 2.0 drivers support the use of these methods and provide implementations of the `Blob` and `Clob` interfaces. You can also use the JDBC 1.22 methods for LOB access with the DB2 JDBC 2.0 drivers. Note that the DB2 V7.1 JDBC drivers do not support BLOB and CLOB data types in stored procedures or UDFs, so you will need to use JDBC 1.22 when implementing these.

7.2.24 Meta Data

Meta data is data that describes other data. There are two types of meta data interfaces, `ResultSetMetaData` and `DatabaseMetaData`. A `Connection` object is used to obtain a corresponding `DatabaseMetaData` object, which you can use to determine the functionality and supported properties about the database to which you are connected. For example, if you connect to a DB2/390 V5.12 database, a DB2 UDB V5.2 database, a DB2 UDB V6.1 database, and a DB2 UDB V7.1 database, each will have slightly different supported properties, such as the maximum number of columns per table. There are over 150 methods in the `DatabaseMetaData` interface that let you query this type of information, and they are fully documented in the JDBC API documentation.

Similarly, a `ResultSetMetaData` object is obtained from a `ResultSet` object. The most popular method used here is the `getColumnCount()`, which returns the total number of columns in the `ResultSet`. Another useful method is `getColumnLabel()`, which returns the name of the specified column. Since most data can be converted to character format and thus retrieved using a `getString()` method from a `Statement` object, using `getColumnCount()` and `getColumnLabel()` is an easy way to write a `for` loop to process any `ResultSet`. There is an example of this in the `processResultSet()` method of the `DB2MetaDataAnalyzer.java` sample included with this book.

This sample calls all of the `DatabaseMetaData` methods from against a JDBC `Connection` object and outputs the result to screen. You can use this sample as an easy way to discover the properties of your DB2 databases, and to assist you in coding your JDBC applications. Since some of the `DatabaseMetaData` methods return a `ResultSet` object, we've written a simple `processResultSet()` method to display any `ResultSet` object. Here is a simplified version of this method:

```
public void processResultSet(ResultSet rs) throws
SQLException
```

```java
{
   ResultSetMetaData rsmd = rs.getMetaData();

   int colCount = rsmd.getColumnCount();

   // Output column labels
   for(int i=1; i < colCount+1; i++)
   {
      System.out.print(rsmd.getColumnLabel(i) + "   ");
   }

   // Scroll through result set and output
   // column values.  No formatting included.
   while(rs.next())
   {
      for(int i=1; i < colCount+1; i++)
      {
         String columnValue = rs.getString(i);
         if(rs.wasNull())
            columnValue = "NULL";
         System.out.print(columnValue + "   ");
      }
      System.out.println();
   }
} // end processResultSet
```

First, we obtain the `ResultSetMetaData` object from the `ResultSet`, then we obtain a column count. We then print out all of the column names and follow up by scrolling through the result set one row at a time. The column count is useful for letting us determine the number of iterations required in the second `for` loop.

> **Note**
>
> The `getTableName()` and `getSchemaName()` methods are not supported by the DB2 JDBC drivers.

7.2.25 Concurrency and Isolation Levels

Achieving the desired concurrency goals in your applications requires considerable planning and thought. You must decide what isolation levels are suitable for your applications and also carefully define your transactions. We discussed both of these points in Chapter 3. In JDBC, the `Connection` interface provides a `setTransactionIsolation()` method, which takes an integer constant defined in the `Connection` interface as an argument.

JDBC Programming

The possible values for this parameter can be referenced using the `static` constants defined in the `Connection` interface; however, it is important to note that the name for a particular isolation level in JDBC does not correspond to the isolation levels specified in DB2. JDBC's isolation levels directly correspond with those defined in ODBC, and we have mapped each of these to the appropriate DB2 isolation level in Table 7-3.

Table 7-3 JDBC to DB2 Isolation Level Mappings

JDBC Transaction Isolation	DB2 Isolation Level
TRANSACTION_READ_COMMITTED	Cursor Stability (default)
TRANSACTION_READ_UNCOMMITTED	Uncommitted Read
TRANSACTION_REPEATABLE_READ	Read Stability
TRANSACTION_SERIALIZABLE	Repeatable Read

7.2.26 Using `DataSource` Objects and `Connection` Pooling

Thus far, we have connected to DB2 using `DriverManager.getConnection()`. The JDBC 2.0 Standard Extension API introduces the `DataSource` interface, which provides an alternative means for connecting to databases. The `DB2DataSource` class implements this interface, and a single `DataSource` object is a factory for connections to a specific DB2 database. As a programmer, you never worry about whether you are using the app driver or the net driver when you use a `DataSource` object. The object itself, based on how you configure its properties, determines this. We summarize the supported `DataSource` properties in the DB2 JDBC 2.0 drivers in Table 7-4. Each property has a corresponding getter and setter method in the `DB2DataSource` class.

Table 7-4 `DB2DataSource` and `DB2ConnectionPoolDataSource` Properties

Property Name	Type	Description
databaseName	String	The name of the DB2 database you will connect to.
description	String	A description of this data source.
password	String	The password to be used for connections to this data source.
portNumber	int	The DB2 Java Daemon port number (net driver).
serverName	String	The DB2 Java Daemon server name (net driver).
user	String	The user account name for connections to this data source.

To obtain a connection to the represented data source, you call a `getConnection()` method, similar to what you called in the `DriverManager` class. However, there are a few important differences.

There is no URL to specify with a `DataSource` object; these details are configured using property setter methods. The `user` and `password` for connection can be set as properties as well. As a result, the `getConnection()` method in `DataSource` has an overloaded form that takes no password. Alternatively, you can use a unique userid and password for each connection by specifying these as parameters to `getConnection()`.

JDBC 2.0 also provides additional `DataSource` interfaces for connection pooling since obtaining a database connection is a costly process. This way, a connection can be pooled when you attempt to close it. The `DB2DataSource` class implements connection pooling using the `DB2ConnectionPoolDataSource` and `DB2PooledConnection` objects, which are based on the `ConnectionPoolDataSource` and `PooledConnection` interfaces in the JDBC 2.0 Standard Extension API. Thus, when you call the `close()` method on the `Connection` object you have received, it doesn't actually close the connection. Here is a simple test you can try:

```
Connection con = null;
DataSource ds = null;

try {
   ds = new DB2DataSource();
   ds.setDatabaseName("DB2MALL");
   con = ds.getConnection();

   // Pause after obtaining connection.
   // Do LIST APPLICATIONS here.
   BufferedReader in = new BufferedReader(
                           new InputStreamReader
                               (System.in));
   in.readLine();

   // This won't actually close the connection
   con.close();

   // Pause again, after the connection has been closed.
   // LIST APPLICATIONS shows that it is still there.
   in.readLine();
} catch (Exception e) { }
```

In this example, we obtain a connection and then close it. Since we only specified the database name in our example, the `DB2DataSource` object knew it should use the app driver to establish the connection. To use the net driver, we would also need to use the `setServerName()` and `setPortNumber()` methods so that the `DB2DataSource` object could construct the equivalent of a valid net driver URL. Note that calling `setPortNumber()` is optional, just like in a net driver URL. If only `setServerName()` is called, then port 6789 will be assumed by default.

Returning to our example, we also created a `BufferedReader` object to prompt you at different stages so that you can issue a LIST APPLICATIONS command from the DB2

Command Line Processor (CLP). If you do this, you will notice that the same connection remains alive after the `close()` method has been called. This is because the connection has been returned to a pool and is not disconnected. This allows the next connection against this database with the same userid and password to reuse the pooled connection, thus saving time and resources. You will notice that pooled connections will provide a large performance gain, especially if your application frequently connects and disconnects.

You can also write your own `DataSource` classes that use DB2's connection pooling classes (`DB2PooledConnection` and `DB2ConnectionPoolDataSource`). In doing so, you can add functionality such as idle timeout and a maximum pool size.

7.2.27 Java Naming and Directory Interface Support

The Java 2 SDK Enterprise Edition includes the `javax.naming` package, which defines the Java Naming and Directory Interface (JNDI). JNDI allows you to create your own directories of `DB2DataSource` and `DB2ConnectionPool` objects within a JNDI Context.

The DB2 JDBC drivers include the `DB2Context` class, which you can use to store `DataSource` objects. When you create an instance of `DB2Context`, you can bind data sources by name. This class is a very basic implementation of the JNDI `Context` API, and it is not intended for production use. However, you may find it useful for development and testing.

When you call the `close()` method in the `DB2Context` object, the names you have registered within the context are stored, along with their corresponding `DataSource` objects, in a file called `.db2.jndi` in the directory specified in the `user.home` Java environment variable. All of your Java applications can access these `DataSource` objects once they are stored, requiring you to only set up their properties once.

7.2.28 JDBC Static SQL

Since the DB2 V7.1 JDBC drivers use the DB2 CLI driver, you can take advantage of CLI's static query execution feature that is new to DB2 V7.1. Accomplishing this task involves modifying your `db2cli.ini file`, and optionally providing a capture file that contains the SQL statements to statically bind. Details of this are in the previous chapter, which focuses on DB2 CLI.

7.3 SQLj Programs

Dynamic SQL provides flexibility and a means to construct universal interfaces with which to develop database applications. One of the drawbacks, however, is that query performance can suffer because of runtime access plan generation. Also, it often takes time to master an API such as JDBC as compared to directly embedding statements into your application. While C/C++ programmers have always had a choice of writing their applications using static or dynamic embedded SQL, or using a dynamic SQL API such as ODBC, this option was not open to Java programmers. The only way for a Java application to execute static SQL was to write static embedded SQL code in C and invoke it using the Java Native Interface (JNI). Obviously, this

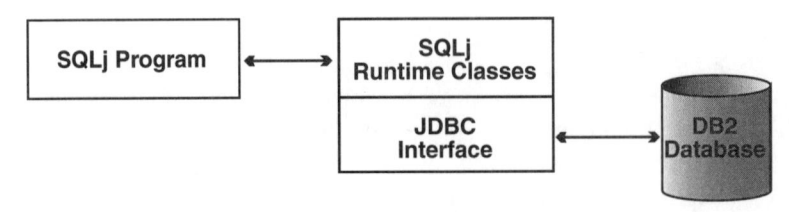

Figure 7-3 SQLj interface with DB2 UDB.

is not a pure Java solution, and the benefits of Java portability are sacrificed when even considering it.

However, DB2 V7.1 provides two solutions for writing static SQL programs in Java. As we have seen in the previous topic, the DB2 CLI driver can be configured to create static queries. Since this requires adding keywords to the db2cli.ini file, this is not the easiest solution to implement as a programmer. With Java, it is better to use SQLj instead. SQLj provides Java programmers with a means to obtain the performance benefits of static query execution. This is achieved by embedding SQL queries into Java applications, similar to DB2's own embedded SQL development specifications.

SQLj is not a replacement for JDBC. In fact, SQLj runtime classes execute their queries using JDBC (see Figure 7-3). So, how does SQLj work then, when it is a layer on top of JDBC itself? To understand this, we must familiarize ourselves with the steps required to compile and run a SQLj program. Analogous with embedded SQL, SQLj programs have source files with the extension .sqlj, which are translated into .java files. During this translation process, the .java file is compiled into corresponding classes by default, and a SQLj serialized profile is also created as a serialized (.ser) file. The serialized file contains all of the SQL statements in the original SQLj source file, each of which is called a profile element. If you view the .java file that was generated, you will also notice that the SQL statements were replaced with calls to the SQLj runtime libraries.

At this point, you can run your SQLj application as dynamic SQL using the generated classes and serialized profile. To go a step further and bind this application statically to a DB2 database, you must use the DB2 Profile Customizer tool. The executable for this tool is called db2profc and it is distributed along with the SQLJ translator in the Application Development Client. The db2profc tool accepts arguments that enable it to connect to the database being accessed in your source file and bind a package on that database using the serialized profile. The package is created with sections corresponding to each SQL query in the serialized profile. The serialized profile is subsequently converted to a format that references the appropriate sections in the DB2 packages. When you run your application now, you will be using static SQL!

But how is this possible when we have said that SQLj uses JDBC, which we know uses CLI? Since CLI has its own packages, how does the application have packages of its own? DB2 solves this problem using a special client-side stored procedure. This implementation may change in the future for performance improvements. We have illustrated this entire process in Figure 7-4. We now describe each of these steps in detail.

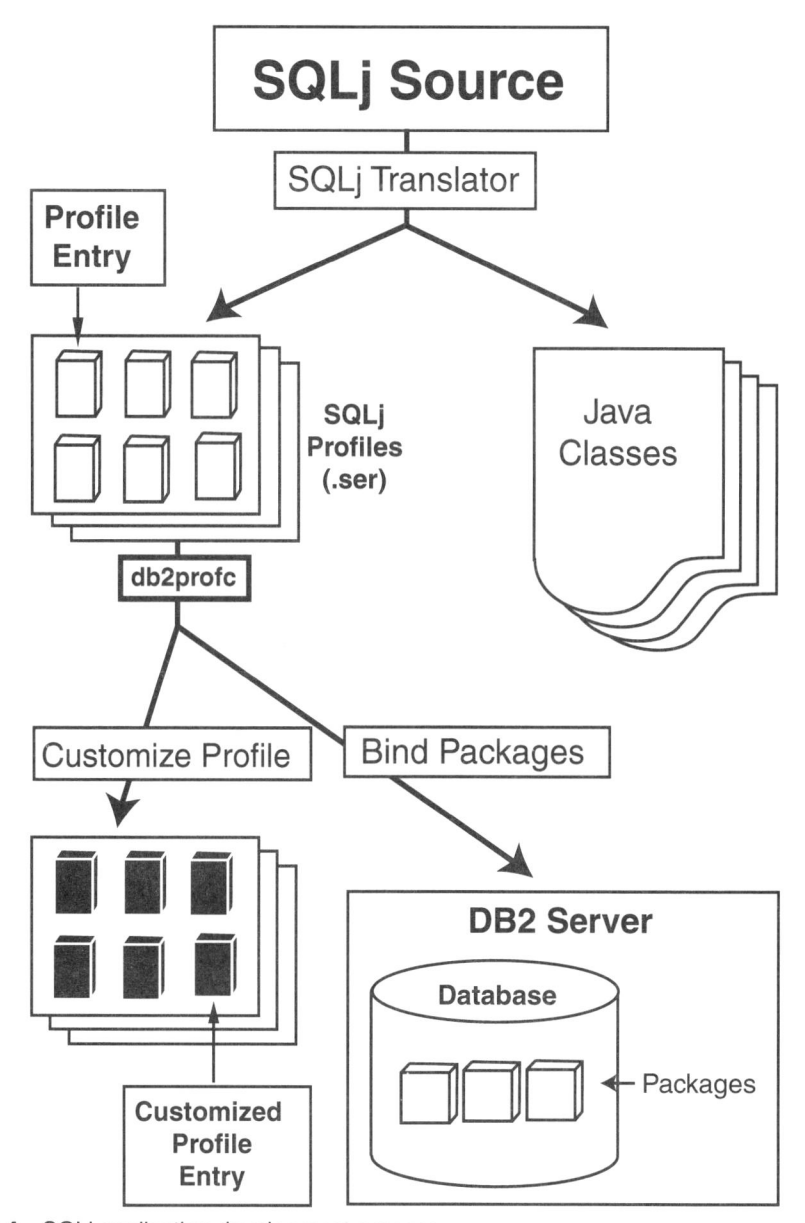

Figure 7-4 SQLj application development process.

7.3.1 Required Packages

In each of your SQLj source files, make sure you include the following import statements.

```
import java.sql.*;
import sqlj.runtime.*;
import sqlj.runtime.ref.*;
```

The `java.sql` packages import the JDBC API that SQLj uses, while the other two packages provide the SQLj runtime classes. These classes are all found in `runtime.zip` in `sqllib/java`.

7.3.2 SQLj Syntax

In your SQLj source file, you should write your Java code as you normally would, with the exception of SQLj-specific code. Each SQLj statement has the following general form:

```
#sql <SQLj syntax>;
```

The variable element here is what we have termed "SQLj syntax." In general, all SQL statements are encased in curly braces {}. For example, code a literal INSERT query as follows:

```
#sql { INSERT INTO T1 VALUES (1, 2) };
```

The syntax for a SELECT statement is a little different. Since most SELECT statements require you to use a cursor to process the result set, the initial SELECT query in SQLj returns a cursor to you in an SQLj object known as an iterator. We will discuss iterators in detail a little later; however, for the moment, simply be aware that the general form of a SELECT query is as follows:

```
#sql myIterator = { SELECT * FROM product };
```

In the above syntax, the iterator is an instance of an `Iterator` class that we declared in our code.

7.3.3 Host Variables

In most cases, you will need to have variable terms in your SQL queries, such as terms in a WHERE clause or the values to UPDATE or INSERT. In this case, we use host variables in our SQL queries, similar to embedded SQL. In fact, host variables are prefaced with a colon (:), just as in embedded SQL applications. Host variables are easier to manipulate in SQLj; however, they do not require a DECLARE section as in embedded SQL. You can use any method parameters, or local or instance variables as host variables. As an example, here is a code fragment where we insert an integer value into a table:

```
public void insertIntoT1( int myInt) {
   #sql { INSERT INTO T1 VALUES(:myInt) };
}
```

Here, we use a method argument as a host variable. Thus, we can call this method with a different argument each time, and thereby insert a different value into the table.

> **Note**
> An array element cannot be used as a host variable.

7.3.4 Result Set Iterators

Unlike JDBC where a result set is returned in a generalized ResultSet object, result sets in SQLj are individually tailored in `Iterator` classes, based on the specific return types or column names. There are two types of `Iterator` classes to accomplish these tasks, positional iterators and named iterators, respectively. In both cases, there are five steps you need to perform:

1. Define the `Iterator` class using a SQLj declaration.
2. Declare a variable of the `Iterator` class.
3. Assign the `Iterator` variable as the return value of a SQLj `SELECT` query.
4. Access each `Iterator` column for each row of data.
5. Close the `Iterator` object by calling the `close()` method of the variable.

Steps 2, 3, and 5 are performed in the same way for both types of iterators, while Steps 1 and 4 differ. In general, you may find that using named iterators is easier and more flexible. We now describe each type of iterator separately so you can become familiar with their use. We also compare each type of iterator in Table 7-5.

Table 7-5 Comparison of SQLj Iterator Types

Positional Iterator	Named Iterator
Iterator column set declaration must match positions of columns in `SELECT` statement column list.	Iterator column list created using names of columns in `SELECT` statement.
Columns must be retrieved in the order specified in the iterator declaration.	Columns can be retrieved in any order.
Two columns in the result set can have the same name.	Two columns in the result set cannot have the same name.
`FETCH INTO` syntax used to retrieve values into host variables.	Methods with the same name as the column are used to retrieve the value of the column in a particular row of the result set.
`endFetch()` call used to determine if end of result set was reached.	`next()` call used to fetch next row of data and indicate if end of result set was reached.

7.3.5 Positional Iterators

When you declare a positional iterator, you specify the return types that the iterator will handle. In addition, in your `SELECT` query itself, you must ensure that you explicitly specify the column names in the order you have specified the return types in your iterator. Let's say we have a table called `MYTABLE`, with the following definition:

```
CREATE TABLE MYTABLE ( C1 CHAR(1), C2 INT, C3 REAL)
```

We have a query we wish to execute against this table, which will return the value for each column in the table. Here is an example of such query:

```
SELECT c2, c1, c3 FROM MYTABLE WHERE c2 > value
```

Notice that we have purposely requested that c2 be the first column returned in our query. Here is the complete code required to execute this query and retrieve the result sets using a positional iterator:

```
public class MyTableQuery {

// A positional iterator to retrieve results for QUERY
#sql private iterator MyTablePosIter(int, String, float);

// Run the following query using the DefaultContext:
// SELECT c2, c1, c3 FROM MYTABLE
// WHERE c2 > greaterThanValue
// Output the the results of this query to System.out.
///////////////////////////////////////////////////////
public void executeQuery(int greaterThanValue )
                          throws SQLException {

// Local instance of MyTablePosIter
MyTablePosIter results;

// Embedded query to be executed.
#sql results={SELECT c2,c1,c3 FROM MYTABLE
            WHERE c2 > :greaterThanValue};

        while(true) {
            // Process result set using local variables
            int c2=0;
            String c1=null;
            float c3=0;
            #sql { FETCH :results INTO :c2, :c1, :c3 };

            // Test if end of result set was retrieved
            // after FETCH
            if(results.endFetch()) break;
```

```
            // Output results
            System.out.println("c1 is: " + c1);
            System.out.println("c2 is: " + c2);
            System.out.println("c3 is: " + c3);
         }
         // Close the iterator
         results.close();
      }
   }
```

Our class, `MyTableQuery`, has a single method, `executeQuery()`, which allows you to specify the value of the condition in the WHERE clause. The first non-Java line of code you likely noticed was the iterator declaration:

```
#sql private iterator MyTablePosIter(int, String, float);
```

As we have already mentioned, a positional iterator only provides the data types for the return values in the SELECT query. The data types are specified in the same order as the positions of the columns specified in the query. We have named this `Iterator` class `MyTablePosIter`, and when we declare an instance of this class, we declare it as follows:

```
MyTablePosIter results;
```

In our example, we used the input parameter for the `executeQuery()` method as the host variable name. We then looped through the result set using a FETCH INTO statement, which populated additional host variables with the contents of the current row of the iterator. After each FETCH INTO operation, it was necessary to call the `endFetch()` function, which returned a Boolean indicating if the most recent FETCH operation was successful. If we do not call this method immediately after the FETCH operation, and choose to access the host variables that were populated in the FETCH, we see the same values as the previous row, since the iterator was not repopulated.

7.3.6 Named Iterators

A named iterator is declared with the names of the columns that will be returned in the query. For example, we can easily modify our previous example to use a named iterator. Our iterator declaration would be as follows:

```
#sql private iterator
   MyTableNamedIter(String c1, int c2, float c3);
```

There are no constraints on the order of the data types in the iterator declaration anymore, since we specify each column in the result set by name. Our `executeQuery()` would then have the following body:

```
    MyTableNamedIter results;
    #sql results= {SELECT c2,c1,c3
                   FROM MYTABLE
                   WHERE c2 > :greaterThanValue};

    // Process result set using local variables
    while(results.next()) {
       System.out.println("c1 is: " + results.c1());
       System.out.println("c2 is: " + results.c2());
       System.out.println("c3 is: " + results.c3());
    }
    // Close the iterator
    results.close();
```

With named iterators, we use the `next()` method, analogous to the same method in the JDBC `ResultSet` interface. When the SQLj source file is translated, the named iterator class is also generated with a method for each named column. These methods serve as getters for that column's value in the currently retrieved row of the result set.

7.3.7 Default `ConnectionContext`

You have probably noticed that none of our examples made mention of a database connection, so you may wonder how the `executeQuery()` method worked. Connections in SQLj are addressed via a connection context defined in the `ConnectionContext` interface of the SQLj runtime libraries. An implementation of a connection context is included in the runtime libraries, known as the `DefaultContext`. The `DefaultContext` class (and all connection contexts in general) contains a static `ConnectionContext` singleton as a property, which itself is known as the `DefaultContext`. The `DefaultContext` class provides static getter and setter methods to access it.

When you execute a query in SQLj, as we have in our first few examples, we are always addressing the `DefaultContext`. In order for this to work, then, we need to establish a connection before calling `executeQuery()`. This is quite easily accomplished using the following line of code:

```
    DefaultContext.setDefaultContext(
      new DefaultContext(
      DriverManager.getConnection("jdbc:db2:sample")));
```

Here, we invoke one of the `DefaultContext` constructors, which takes a JDBC `Connection` as its parameter. The `DefaultContext` class also provides more functionality than simply its static `defaultContext` property. In fact, you can create multiple instances of `DefaultContext` and establish a separate database connection in each. For example, we may have a method called `executeInsert()` that performs a simple INSERT operation. We can provide an argument to this method indicating the `DefaultContext` object to address when performing the INSERT operation, instead of using the `defaultContext` property:

SQLj Programs

```
public void executeInsert(DefaultContext ctx)
throws SQLException {
   if (ctx != null) {
      #sql   [ctx] { INSERT INTO MYTABLE
                     VALUES('Y', 123, 123.2);
   }
}
```

Notice that our SQLj syntax has been slightly modified to specify the variable name of the `ConnectionContext` addressed in the query. To generalize the above method further, we could declare it as follows:

```
public void executeInsert(ConnectionContext ctx);
```

This still allows us to provide a `DefaultContext` object as a parameter, and we can now also provide any other type of `ConnectionContext` as well.

7.3.8 User-Defined `ConnectionContext` Classes

There is a limitation when using multiple instances of the `DefaultContext` class. If you have connections to two different DB2 databases in different instances of `DefaultContext` referenced in the same SQLj source file, all of your queries must be valid using either instance of `DefaultContext`. In other words, the conceptual or exemplar schema must be the same. For example, you may have two connections to the same DB2 database, but each connection accesses objects in a different schema. This is common when you have identical tables defined for different users.

The reason this limitation exists is because only a single serialized profile is generated per context type referenced in a SQLj source file. You can work around this by creating separate source files (and thus, different classes) to handle queries against different conceptual schemas. However, this often does not lead to the best application design.

For this reason, SQLj allows you to define your own `ConnectionContext` classes. You can create multiple instances of each `ConnectionContext` class that you define, and in a SQLj source file, a separate serialized profile will be generated at translation time for each type of `ConnectionContext`. For example, we can declare two different `ConnectionContext` classes as follows:

```
#sql context MyCtx1;
#sql context MyCtx2;
```

Instantiating a class of each type is accomplished using the same type of constructors in `DefaultContext` and `ConnectionContext`. We can then refer to each `Connection-Context` class separately in a method as long as their type is explicitly declared. For example, let's add a second query to the `executeInsert()` method:

```
public executeInsert(MyCtx1 ctx1, MyCtx2 ctx2) {
    if (ctx1 != null) {
       #sql   [ctx1] { INSERT INTO MYTABLE
                       VALUES('Y', 123, 123.2);
    }
    if (ctx2 != null) {
       #sql   [ctx2] { INSERT INTO MYTABLE
                       VALUES('Y', 123, 123.2);
    }
}
```

Notice that in our method arguments, each `ConnectionContext` is distinguished as a different type of class. Thus, when we translate the SQLj source file containing this method, we get two serialized profiles, one per unique `ConnectionContext` class. Notice that this won't hold true if both parameters are `ConnectionContext` objects of the same type. Thus, if both parameters are `MyCtx1` objects, we only get a single serialized file upon translation. As we described at the beginning of this topic, a serialized file is statically bound against a database, thus all of the statements in a serialized file must access valid objects in the database to which you are trying to bind it. The constructors and methods for a user-defined `ConnectionContext` class are implemented from the `ConnectionContext` interface, and extended from the `ConnectionContextImpl` abstract class.

7.3.9 Execution Contexts

Execution contexts are synchronized objects that you can use to get and set additional properties about SQLj statements in your application. You can directly create an object of type `ExecutionContext` using the default class constructor as follows:

```
ExecutionContext eCtx = new ExecutionContext();
```

In addition, every `ConnectionContext` class has a default associated `Execution-Context` class that can be returned using the `getExecutionContext()` method. However, this creates some confusion because any instance of the `ExecutionContext` class can be associated with as many `ConnectionContext` objects as desired. This is because an `ExecutionContext` is associated with a particular statement, not a `Connection-Context`. This is particularly useful when your applications are multithreaded, and you are referencing the same `ConnectionContext` object in different threads. It is better under these circumstances to use separate `ExecutionContext` classes.

You can associate an `ExecutionContext` variable called `eCtx` with the `Default-Context` property using the following syntax:

```
#sql [eCtx] { INSERT INTO MYTABLE VALUES('Y', 123, 123.2) };
```

To associate an `ExecutionContext` with a particular `ConnectionContext`, on the other hand, we precede it with the `ConnectionContext` variable as follows:

```
#sql [ctx, eCtx] { INSERT INTO MYTABLE
                   VALUES('Y', 123, 123.2) };
```

Here, our `ConnectionContext` is referred to as `ctx`, and our `ExecutionContext` is referred to as `eCtx`.

7.3.10 Properties of User-Defined SQLj Classes

As we have discussed, defining an `Iterator` or `ConnectionContext` actually generates code that defines a class in your translated SQLj source. You can see this code if you look at the `.java` file produced after translating a SQLj source file. It is important to note here that each type of class you specify has scope and visibility. You can define your `Iterator` and `ConnectionContext` objects in their own separate files if you choose. In some cases, this may be advantageous and suitable for the design of your application. For example, we could create a SQLj source file called `Ctx1.sqlj` with a single entry:

```
#sql public context Ctx1;
```

With this simple declaration, we can translate this SQLj source file into equivalent Java source. The resulting class will have public visibility. We can also define this class as part of another SQLj source file called `MyClass.sqlj`:

```
#sql context Ctx1;
public class MyClass {
   // Class definition
}
```

Here, we cannot have public visibility since only `MyClass` and its inner classes can have public visibility in a source file called `MyClass.java`. This leads to our final case, where we can define `Iterator` classes as inner classes. `ConnectionContext` classes cannot be defined as inner classes because they contain static variables. If you are using JDK 1.1.x, you can only define an inner class within the class definition, but outside of a method. With the Java 2 SDK, you can define a class within a method.

7.3.11 SQLj Translator

We have previously described that SQLj source files are translated into Java source and compiled into classes using the SQLj translator. During this translation process, we also know that a serialized (`.ser`) file is created per `ConnectionContext` type, and each serialized file has the queries addressed to its corresponding `ConnectionContext`. While the SQLj translator has many options, the simplest way to invoke it is simply:

```
sqlj <source-file>
```

This will generate a `.java` and `.class` file with the same name as the SQLj source filename. Additional `.class` files are generated for inner classes and embedded classes such as iterators and connection contexts. If the source file also contains SQL queries in it, a serialized profile is generated. Thus, for source files that only define an `Iterator` or a `ConnectionContext`, you will not get a serialized file.

7.3.12 DB2 Profile Customizer

When you have translated your SQLj source file, you can execute your SQLj application using dynamic SQL. This may be useful for testing; however, in most cases, you will want to statically bind each of your serialized files to a DB2 database. Each serialized file is named using the following conventions:

ClassName`_SJProfile`*SequenceNumber*`.ser`

Therefore, if our `MyTableQuery` class has two distinct `ConnectionContext` classes in it, each of which performs at least one SQL query, we would get the following two files:

```
MyTableQuery_SJProfile0.ser
MyTableQuery_SJProfile1.ser
```

We bind these files against a DB2 database using the following syntax:

```
db2profc -url:jdbc:db2:DB2MALL -prepoptions="bindfile \
using  mtq.bnd package using mtq" \
MyTableQuery_SJProfile0.ser
db2profc -url:jdbc:db2:DB2MALL -prepoptions="bindfile \
using mtq1.bnd package using mtq1" \
MyTableQuery_SJProfile1.ser
```

In each command, we specify the JDBC URL to connect for binding. We also include two `prepoptions` (precompile options), "`package using`" and "`bindfile using`." The former indicates the name of the package to create on the database, and the latter generates a bindfile. A bindfile is necessary if your SQLj source will be used against multiple databases. You should only run `db2profc` once, and then statically bind the generated bindfiles to additional databases using the `BIND` command as described in Chapter 4.

7.4 Java Stored Procedures

You can write DB2 Java stored procedures in both JDBC and in SQLj, although we recommend the latter for better performance. There are also two ways to pass parameters to stored procedures, which you declare when cataloging your stored procedure with a `CREATE PROCEDURE` statement. The `PARAMETER STYLE DB2GENERAL` requires you to extend a class called `COM.ibm.db2.app.StoredProc` and pass `IN`, `IN/OUT`, and `OUT` arguments in the specified order. One of the drawbacks to this method is that it is more proprietary. It also requires you to instantiate a separate class of the stored procedure with every invocation.

Java Stored Procedures

In DB2 UDB V6.1, we introduced Java stored procedures that use the *SQLJ Routines* standard, and which are cataloged using `PARAMETER STYLE JAVA`. We use this style in all of our examples, since it is the recommended method and provides several advantages:

- All stored procedure methods are `public static`; thus, they do not require a new object to be instantiated each time the stored procedure is invoked.
- `IN/OUT` and `OUT` parameters are passed as single-element arrays, thereby passing them by reference instead of by value to retrieve them again.
- All result sets are returned as an array parameter of JDBC `ResultSet` objects.

Let us consider a stored procedure called `getPurchaseStatistics()` that returns a result set containing information about all of the purchases made between a specific start date and end date. These dates are specified as `IN` parameters to the stored procedure. In addition, the stored procedure returns a single output parameter, with the `product_id` of the most purchased product. This procedure would have the following method signature:

```
public static void getPurchaseStatistics
                (java.sql.Date start,
                 java.sql.Date end,
                 int [] prodID,
                 ResultSet [] rs);
```

We won't worry about the underlying implementation, which could be in either JDBC or SQLj. The main points to consider is how to obtain access to the `Connection` or `ConnectionContext` from the calling program. We should note here that the calling program could be written using any supported DB2 development language and interface. If we are using JDBC, we use the following syntax:

```
Connection con =
DriverManager.getConnection("jdbc:default:connection");
```

Notice that we use a special URL in this case to obtain the connection. Once we have our `Connection` object, we can proceed as we would in any other JDBC application, except for the inherent restrictions of stored procedures.

In SQLj stored procedures, we don't ever need to refer to the `ConnectionContext`. As you may recall, if our SQLj statements do not specify a context, then the `DefaultContext` property is used. In a SQLj stored procedure, the `DefaultContext` property is the context of the calling program.

As we discussed in Chapter 3, in DB2 V7.1, you can COMMIT or ROLLBACK a unit of work within a stored procedure. This only applies to stored procedures that are not called within a distributed unit of work being managed by an XA-compliant transaction manager. Other restrictions and allowances of stored procedures in general apply also to Java stored procedures.

7.4.1 Setting up an Environment for JDBC 2.0 Stored Procedures

DB2 UDB V7.1 supports JDBC 2.0 stored procedures. To run JDBC 2.0 stored procedures, you need to install the Java 2 SDK, JDK 1.2.2 or greater. In addition, you must perform the following configuration steps:

- Set the `DB2_USE_JDK12` profile variable to `true` on your DB2 server, using the `db2set` command (`db2set DB2_USE_JDK12=TRUE`).
- Set your `JDK11_PATH` variable in your database manager configuration to point to the Java 2 SDK installation directory (`db2 UPDATE DBM CFG USING JDK11_PATH c:\jdk1.2.2`).

7.5 Java UDFs

You can write UDFs for DB2 in Java. Again, there are two parameter styles, `DB2GENERAL` and `JAVA`, where the latter follows the *SQLJ Routines* standard. We will focus on the latter again, since it is less proprietary, and generally nicer syntax. All UDFs with this parameter style are static methods that have their input arguments in the method signature, and their output as the return value. For example, let's say we want to delete any leading or trailing spaces in a character column. We can define a function called `TRIM` that does just that as follows:

```
public class JavaUDF {
   public static String trim(String input) {
      return input.trim();
   }
}
```

After we compile this class, we place the `JavaUDF.class` file into the `sqllib/function` directory of the DB2 instance that will use this function, and register the function as follows:

```
create function trim(input varchar(100))
returns varchar(100)
fenced variant no sql no external action
language java parameter style java
external name 'JavaUDF!trim';
```

Once you register your UDF, you can easily test it by calling it with a `VALUES` statement. Try it out. Issue the `VALUES (trim(' 123 '))` statement and verify that the UDF strips the leading and trailing white space.

7.6 Summary

DB2 provides drivers for JDBC and SQLj. DB2 JDBC drivers come in two flavors, the app driver and the net driver. The former uses JNI to invoke DB2 CLI libraries, and the latter uses a

TCP/IP connection to communicate with a DB2 JDBC server. DB2 JDBC drivers also come in to versions, JDBC 1.22 and JDBC 2.0.

JDBC includes `Connection` objects for managing connections, `Statement` objects executing SQL queries, and `ResultSet` objects for manipulating a cursor. In addition, DB2 JDBC 2.0 drivers provide additional support for LOBs, batch updates, scrollable cursors, JTA, and JNDI.

SQLj provides a static SQL alternative to JDBC's dynamic SQL interface. SQLj source files are translated into Java classes, along with a profile that contains the SQL statements within the class module. The serialized profile is then statically bound using the `db2profc` tool. Finally, the SQLj application can run, calling these statically bound packages.

DB2 also provides support for Java stored procedures and UDFs. You can write your Java stored procedures in SQLj and in JDBC. For both stored procedures and UDFs, the *SQLJ Routines* standard can be followed to declare method entry points.

References

DB2 Java Programming Support Web Site:
   http://www-4.ibm.com/software/data/db2/java/

DB2 SQLj Packages Documentation:
   http://www-4.ibm.com/software/data/db2/java/sqljpackages.html

IBM Java Developer Web Site:
   http://www.ibm.com/developer/java/

Official SQLj Web Site:
   http://www.sqlj.org

Official Java Web Site from Sun:
   http://java.sun.com

JDK 1.1.x API Documentation:
   http://java.sun.com/products/jdk/1.1/docs/api/packages.html

Java 2 SDK (JDK 1.3) Standard Edition API Documentation:
   http://java.sun.com/j2se/1.3/docs/api/index.html

Java 2 SDK Enterprise Edition API Documentation:
   http://java.sun.com/j2ee/j2sdkee/techdocs/api/index.html

CHAPTER 8

Net.Data

Net.Data is an application used for generating Web pages with dynamic content. It is bundled with the DB2 UDB Developer's Edition. Net.Data executes within a Web server or application server environment as a Common Gateway Interface (CGI) executable or shared library. It is supported on the Windows NT, OS/2, AIX, Solaris, HP-UX, Sequent, Red Hat Linux, Caldera Linux, OS/390, and OS/400 platforms. It provides a simple, but powerful, alternative to many Web solutions.

The primary use of Net.Data is to access databases and generate Web pages from this data. It retrieves and stores data from local or remote data sources. Net.Data uses a macro scripting language to provide instructions for formatting and processing the data. The data is formatted using Hypertext Markup Language (HTML) or Extensible Markup Language (XML) with style sheets. Users can access resulting HTML or XML pages through a Web browser.

8.1 Objectives

The primary objective of this chapter is to introduce Net.Data. It will discuss the advantages of Net.Data over other Web solutions. It will discuss the structure of the macro language and how to use Net.Data language environments. Finally, it will discuss performance enhancement features that will help reduce the execution time of your Net.Data macros. By the end of this chapter, you should be aware of the following:

- Advantages of Net.Data.
- Structure of the Net.Data macro scripting language.
- Net.Data language environments.
- Methods of increasing performance of Net.Data macros.

8.2 Advantages

An important advantage of Net.Data over other Web solutions is ease of use. The macro scripting language is easy to work with. Net.Data-generated Web pages can be managed by content designers instead of programmers. There are built-in functions for handling common tasks. Net.Data scripts can be easily integrated with other programming or scripting languages such as Java, Perl, or REXX. It works on most platforms, with most Web servers, and has minimal requirements of the Web browser. This allows the application to be used by a wider audience without writing special routines for different browsers and versions.

8.2.1 Easy to Use

Net.Data has built-in functions for handling common tasks. There are string manipulation functions such as concatenation, converting to upper- or lowercase, and finding or replacing a substring. There are math functions such as addition, subtraction, multiplication, division, integer division, and exponents. There are table functions for manipulating and formatting data such as a query result set. There are also miscellaneous functions for tasks such as retrieving system date and time, file manipulation, reading and storing browser cookies, and sending e-mail notifications.

Net.Data interfaces with databases and programming languages using language environments. Several language environments are provided. Net.Data users can write their own language environments for additional functionality. Database language environments include Open Database Connectivity (ODBC) as well as native database APIs for DB2 and Oracle. Programming language environments include system executables and commands, Java applications and applets, Perl, and REXX.

8.2.2 Highly Compatible

Some Web solutions such as JavaScript or Java applets are dependent upon the Web browser for data processing. Some implementations of JavaScript and the Java Virtual Machine (JVM) vary between different browser vendors and versions. This dependency results in different behavior. Programmers may be required to write special handling for each browser and version. These solutions are more difficult to test and maintain. Browser plug-ins are available to help standardize the browser's JVM. However, this is inconvenient for the user to download and install. Many of these dependency problems can be avoided by moving application processing to the Web server machine.

These problems do not exist for server-side applications. Server-side applications do not execute any code on the Web browser. The browser receives the finished HTML or XML document. There are no special requirements of the Web browser. This makes server-side applications highly compatible with most Web browsers. The only requirement is that the browser must be able to interpret the HTML or XML generated. WebSphere and Net.Data are both examples of server-side applications. Net.Data compliments WebSphere by integrating Java code with other programming languages for a complete Web solution.

Macros can generate documents in either HTML or XML. HTML documents may include the use of JavaScript for special tasks such as mouse events and form validation. The HTML tags generated by Net.Data are XHTML compliant. This means that these markup tags can be inserted into an XML document without infringing upon the rules of a well-formed XML document.

8.2.3 Easily Integrated

Net.Data can invoke other applications from inside a macro. It can also execute batch files and shell scripts. Anything sent to standard output will be incorporated into the generated HTML or XML document. Special support is available for certain programming languages by using Net.Data language environments. Net.Data language environments allow the programmer to include code written in other programming languages directly in the macro file. This is referred to as inline code. Net.Data supports language environments for database access, REXX, Perl, Java, system commands, and external executables. Language environments help integrate Net.Data macros with new or existing scripts or Java applications. These Net.Data features facilitate Web enablement of existing data sources and legacy applications.

8.3 Scripting Language

The instructions to generate HTML or XML documents are provided using a scripting language. The scripting language instructions are stored in a file called a macro. A macro is subdivided into sections, referred to as blocks. All macro blocks have the following form:

```
%[block-identifier]{
  block-data
%}
```

block-identifier—Identifies the block type. If it is a function block, it will contain the function name and input and output parameters. If it is a document block, it will contain the document language, HTML or XML, and the document name. For comments, no `block-identifier` is used.

block-data—Contains the comments, language environment statements, and function calls associated with the specified block type.

There are four types of blocks that can be included inside a macro file: comment blocks, define blocks, function blocks, and document blocks. All blocks are optional except for the document block. It is important to order the blocks such that references to functions and variables are made after they are defined.

8.3.1 Comment Blocks

Comment blocks are used to document your Net.Data macros. They can be defined anywhere outside or nested within any other block. Here is an example of a comment block:

```
%{ This is a comment. %}
```

8.3.2 Define Blocks

The define block is used to initialize the values of global variables and settings for a macro. It can contain settings such as database name, login, and password. These values can be referenced anywhere within the macro. Using variables makes it easy to make global changes to your macro without having to change many lines of code. Here is an example of a define block:

```
%DEFINE {
  DATABASE="SAMPLE"
  TITLE="My Net.Data Macro"
%}
```

8.3.3 Function Blocks

Function blocks can be defined anywhere outside of any other block and cannot be nested. Net.Data has two types of function blocks, regular function blocks and macro function blocks. Macro functions are commonly used for code reuse and better logic organization. Regular function blocks are associated with Net.Data language environments. For example, to execute an ODBC query, the macro must contain functions that use the ODBC language environment. Functions can only use one language environment. To use multiple language environments, the macro must contain multiple functions.

8.3.3.1 Macro Function Blocks

```
%MACRO_FUNCTION function-name([usage] parameter, ...) {
  executable-statements
  [report-block]
  ...
  [report-block]
%}
```

8.3.3.2 Function Blocks

```
%FUNCTION(type) function-name([usage] [datatype] parameter,
  ...) [RETURNS(return-var)] {
  executable-statements
  [report-block]
  ...
  [report-block]
  [message-block]
%}
```

type—Identifies a language environment.

function-name—Specifies the name of the function or macro function block.

usage—Specifies whether a parameter is an input (`IN`) parameter, an output (`OUT`) parameter, or both (`INOUT`).

datatype—The data type of the parameter. Some language environments expect data types for the parameters that are passed. For example, the SQL language environment expects them when calling stored procedures.

parameter—The name of a variable with local scope that is replaced with the value of a corresponding argument specified on a function call.

return-var—Specify this parameter, after the `RETURNS` keyword, to identify a special `OUT` parameter. The value of the return variable is assigned in the function block, and its value is returned to the place in the macro from which the function was called.

executable-statements—The set of language statements that is passed to the specified language environment or processed by Net.Data.

report-block—If the output of the function or macro block contains one or more result sets or tables, a report block can be defined for each result set containing processing instructions.

message-block—Defines the error message block, which handles any messages returned by the language environment.

8.3.3.3 Function Calling Syntax

Functions can be called from other functions or document blocks using the syntax shown below. Function calls are identified by preceding the function name with the "@" symbol. Function arguments can contain constants, variables, or other function calls that return an output value. Net.Data functions can be overloaded functions, where multiple functions can be defined with the same name, provided they have a different parameter list. Functions can assign values to output variables or return output in the Web page at the position where the function was called in the macro.

```
@function_name([ argument,... ])
```

function_name—This is the name of the function or macro function to invoke. The function must already be defined in the Net.Data macro, unless it is a built-in function.

argument—This is the name of a variable, quoted string, variable reference, or function call. Arguments on a function call are matched up with the parameters on a function or macro function parameter list.

Example 1: Function call with a text string argument:

@myFunction("abc")

Example 2: Function call with a variable and function call arguments:

@myFunction(myvar, @DTW_rADD("2","3"))

Example 3: Function call with a complex text string argument that contains a variable reference and function call:

@myFunction("abc$(myvar)def@DTW_rADD("2","3")ghi")

Net.Data uses a naming convention for built-in functions. All Net.Data functions begin with "DTW." There are two versions of each function. One version returns the function output to an output variable. The second displays the function output in the Web page at the position where the function was called in the macro. A lowercase "r" after the underscore is used to indicate a function that returns output to the Web page.

8.3.4 Document Blocks

Document blocks are used to define Web pages that can be generated by a macro file. They are the entry points for all macro processing. A macro file must contain at least one document section to be able to execute. Each document block can contain a different set of instructions for generating a document of a specific type.

Net.Data macros commonly contain two document blocks, an input document and an output document. Input documents are used to prompt the user for information or a request. The output document displays the information requested. Although it is possible to put many documents into a single macro, it can slow performance and use more memory if the file size gets too large.

Net.Data supports two types of document sections, HTML documents and XML documents. A macro file can contain both HTML and XML documents. An HTML and XML document inside the same macro file cannot have the same document name.

8.3.4.1 HTML Document Blocks

HTML document blocks automatically generate the document content type header information of an HTML Web page. The opening <HTML> tag is not provided and should be added into the HTML document block. Here is an example of an HTML document block that accepts user input using a form. In this example, the label is called INPUT. The text field, input_data, is passed to another HTML document in the same macro called OUTPUT.

Scripting Language

```
%HTML (INPUT) {
  <HTML><HEAD><TITLE>Input Form</TITLE></HEAD><BODY>
  <FORM METHOD="post" ACTION="OUTPUT">
  <INPUT NAME="input_data" TYPE="text" SIZE="30"><BR>
  <INPUT TYPE="submit" VALUE="Enter">
  </BODY><HTML>
%}
```

8.3.4.2 XML Document Blocks

XML document blocks automatically generate the document content type header information of an XML Web page. However, they do not generate the XML prolog tags, including version and style sheet. These should be added manually into the XML document block. Here is an example of an XML document block that accepts the value from the above INPUT document block sample and displays it to the screen using the ndTable style sheet:

```
%XML (OUTPUT) {
  <?xml version="1.0" encoding="Shift_JIS"?>
  <?xml-stylesheet type="text/xsl" href="ndTable.xsl"?>
  <XMLBlock>
    <RowSet name="Input Data">
      <Row number="1">
        <Column name= "Input">$(input_data)</Column>
      </Row>
    </RowSet>
  </XMLBlock>
%}
```

Net.Data provides three Extensible Style Sheet Language (XSL) files: ndTable.xsl is used for tabular display, ndRecord.xsl is used for record-oriented display, and ndObject.xsl is used for object-oriented display. Additional style sheets may be added or the existing style sheet may be edited for customization.

8.3.4.3 Invoking Net.Data

Net.Data configuration parameters are defined in the Net.Data initialization file, db2www.ini. The initialization file needs to be located in the document root of the Web server. db2www.ini defines the MACRO_PATH used to locate Net.Data macro files. When invoking a Net.Data macro, you must supply a macro name and document label in the Uniform Resource Locator (URL) string. The URL string for calling a Net.Data macro has the following form:

```
http://host-name/cgi-bin/db2www/macro-name/document-label
```

host-name—Identifies the machine host name for the Web server.

macro-name—Identifies the name of the macro file containing the document label. If the macro is in a subdirectory under the path specified by the MACRO_PATH variable, this directory name must be included in the URL string before the macro name.

`document-label`—Identifies which document block within the macro file to execute.

8.4 Language Environments

Language environments are used to access external data sources or include inline functions written in other programming languages. They can be system executables and commands, Java applications and applets, Perl, or REXX. They provide a standard interface between Net.Data and the external data source or internal language processor.

Net.Data provides several language environments. It also provides a mechanism that allows the programmer to add user-written language environments as needed. Language environments are implemented as shared libraries. Since they are not part of the main Net.Data executable, they are sometimes referred to as backend processes. Language environments are defined in the Net.Data initialization file, `db2www.ini`.

Table 8-1 lists predefined language environments and their corresponding reference name. Net.Data indicates that a specific language environment should be used by defining a function that references the language environment name.

Table 8-1 Predefined Language Environments

Language Environment	Description
DTW_ODBC	ODBC data sources.
DTW_SQL	DB2 data sources via native DB2 API calls.
DTW_ORA	Oracle data sources via native Oracle API calls.
DTW_FILE	Flat file data sources.
DTW_WEBREG	Web registry for persistent storage.
HWS_LE	IMS transactions.
DTW_APPLET	Java applets.
DTW_JAVAPPS	Java applications.
DTW_PERL	Perl scripts.
DTW_REXX	REXX scripts.
DTW_SYSTEM	System commands or external applications.

Most language environments have library dependencies on other products. For example, `DTW_REXX` requires the installation of a REXX interpreter. `DTW_SQL` requires that you have DB2 installed. When you are configuring your Web server, it is important to ensure the needed library dependencies are in the Web server environment so they can be loaded by the Net.Data language environment.

> **TIP** UNIX platforms require the installation of an ODBC Driver Manager before using `DTW_ODBC`.

8.4.1 Database Access

Net.Data was designed with the intent to be used as an interface to allow users to access databases from the Internet. Databases can be accessed using ODBC, native DB2 APIs, and native Oracle APIs. There are three main steps for creating a Net.Data macro to be used to access a database: First, you need to configure the macro with the database access information and the desired behavior; second, you need to supply an SQL statement to execute; finally, you need to format the database result set.

8.4.1.1 Configuring Database Access

A macro provides Net.Data with a database name, user ID, and password needed to identify the data source and authenticate the user. These can either be defined inside the macro, or obtained from some other source such as an HTML input form. Additional variables can be modified from the default to further customize the function's behavior. These are shown in Table 8-2.

Table 8-2 Database Access Configuration Variables

Variable	Description
DATABASE	Data source name.
LOGIN	User ID used to connect to the data source.
PASSWORD	Password of the user ID.
TRANSACTION_SCOPE	Data source transaction commit behavior.
SHOWSQL	Displays the SQL statement in the result document.
ALIGN	Used to specify HTML table alignment.
START_ROW_NUM	Starting row position of query result set.
RPT_MAX_ROWS	Limits the number of rows in a result set.
DTW_SET_TOTAL_ROWS	Counts the number of rows in a result set.
DTW_HTML_TABLE	Displays the result set in an HTML table.
DTW_DEFAULT_REPORT	Enables or disables the default report display.

By default, Net.Data will execute all SQL statements in an HTML or XML section before a `COMMIT` or `ROLLBACK` statement is issued. This is called multiple transaction scope. The data source transaction scope behavior can be changed by defining the `TRANSACTION_SCOPE` variable. The `TRANSACTION_SCOPE` variable can be defined as "MULTIPLE" or "SINGLE." A single transaction scope issues a `COMMIT` or `ROLLBACK` after each SQL statement.

`SHOWSQL` is often used as a debugging technique to verify the SQL statement executed by the macro. This variable works in conjunction with an initialization file variable, `DTW_SHOWSQL`. Both must be set to "YES" before the SQL statement will be displayed. Therefore, one could enable `SHOWSQL` for all macros and toggle them on and off by modifying the initialization file variable.

`START_ROW_NUM` and `RPT_MAX_ROWS` are useful for implementing the "Next" and "Previous" buttons for queries that may return multiple-page result sets. Instead of displaying many rows on the same page, the data can be broken down into several smaller pages. This is more visually appealing and easier to navigate. `RPT_MAX_ROWS` will limit the number of rows per page. `START_ROW_NUM` will specify the number of the starting row. This can be calculated by multiplying the page number by the maximum number of rows per page.

8.4.1.2 Creating an SQL Statement

Net.Data executes SQL statements as dynamic SQL. They can include references to variable identifiers. Parameter markers cannot be used. For stored procedures, parameter markers will be handled automatically by declaring input and output parameters. For example:

```
%FUNCTION (DTW_SQL) function_name ([IN datatype arg1, INOUT
datatype arg2, OUT tablename, ...]) {
  CALL stored_procedure [(resultsetname, ...)]
  [report-block]
%}
```

function_name—The name of the Net.Data function that initiates the call to the stored procedure.

stored_procedure—The name of the stored procedure.

datatype—One of the database data types supported by Net.Data. The data types specified in the parameter list must match the data types of the stored procedure. This field is optional for nonstored procedure calls.

tablename—The name of a Net.Data table in which the result set is to be stored (used only when the result set is to be stored in a Net.Data table). If specified, this parameter name must match the associated parameter name for `resultsetname`.

resultsetname—The name that associates a result returned from a stored procedure with a `report-block`, a table name on the function parameter list, or both. The `resultsetname` on a `report-block` must match a result set on the `CALL` statement.

report-block—If the output of the function or macro block contains one or more result sets or tables, a `report-block` can be defined for each result set containing processing instructions. The `report-block` should reference the result set name. For example, `%REPORT(resultsetname) {...%}`.

> **TIP** Net.Data can take advantage of DB2 Extenders by calling stored procedures and User-Defined Functions (UDFs) in SQL statements.

SQL errors and warning messages can be captured and replaced with custom messages and exception handling. By default, these will be written directly on the Web page. This behavior can be overwritten by providing a message block. A message block can be created globally by defining it outside a function block, or locally if defined within a specific function. The locally defined message block will override the globally defined message block if there is overlap. Here is an example of what can be done from a message block:

```
%MESSAGE {
  -204: "Custom message for a SQL0204 error"   : exit
  100: " Custom message for a SQL0100 warning"   :
continue
  -default: {
This is a default error handler for all negative SQL return
codes. The braces allow long messages that span more than
one line. You can use HTML tags, including links and forms,
in this message. %} : exit
%}
```

8.4.1.3 Formatting the Result Set

A result set is formatted by providing a report block definition. If one is not provided, Net.Data will display the data as preformatted text. The default formatting can be changed to display the data in an HTML table. This is enabled by setting `DTW_HTML_TABLE` to "YES." The default report block can be disabled by either providing a report block definition or by setting `DTW_DEFAULT_REPORT` to "NO." If you are calling a stored procedure that returns multiple result sets, you can set `DTW_DEFAULT_REPORT` to "MULTIPLE" to display the default report for each result set. Here is the syntax for defining a report block:

```
%REPORT[(name)] {
  [executable-statements]
  %ROW {
    [executable-statements]
  %}
  [executable-statements]
%}
```

name—This value represents a Net.Data table or result set.

executable-statements—The set of language statements that is passed to the specified language environment or processed by Net.Data. This can include `IF` blocks, variable references, function calls, HTML statements, `include` statements, and `WHILE` blocks.

Providing a report block definition allows a customized display of the query result set. Inside the report or row block, a set of predefined variables is used to reference the values returned from a query. Table 8-3 lists these variables.

Table 8-3 Database Access Reference Variables

Variable	Description
Nn	Column name of column n.
NLIST	Column name list.
NUM_COLUMNS	Number of columns.
ROW_NUM	Current row number.
TOTAL_ROWS	Number of rows in the result set.
V_columnName	Column value of column columnName.
VLIST	Column name list.
Vn	Column value of column n.

8.4.1.4 Sample Database Access Macro

Here is a sample macro that uses the Net.Data DB2 backend, or language environment, to access the sample database. This macro retrieves all the employee numbers for employees who have the first name "Kevin." Notice the syntax of the comment block, DEFINE block, FUNCTION block, and HTML document block. The DEFINE block references the database name and provides a user ID and password. The HTML document, labeled REPORT, calls the function myquery. The function, myquery, accepts FIRSTNME as an input parameter and references the value in the predicate of the SQL statement. The value of EMPNO is referenced by column number using V1. Figure 8-1 shows the result of this macro from a Web browser.

```
%{This is a comment for mymacro.d2w %}

%DEFINE{
  DATABASE="sample"
  LOGIN="userid"
  PASSWORD="password"
%}

%{The DTW_SQL language environment uses the above variables
to establish a database connection %}

%FUNCTION(DTW_SQL) myquery(IN FIRSTNME) {
  select EMPNO from employee where FIRSTNME='$(FIRSTNME)'
  %REPORT {
    %ROW{<P>Employee number is $(V1)</P> %}
  %}
  %MESSAGE {100: "Employee not found": continue %}
%}

%{The function called myquery accepts the string "Kevin" as
an input parameter.  If this string is found more than
```

Language Environments

[Browser screenshot showing "Retrieving employee numbers" with "Employee number is 100000"]

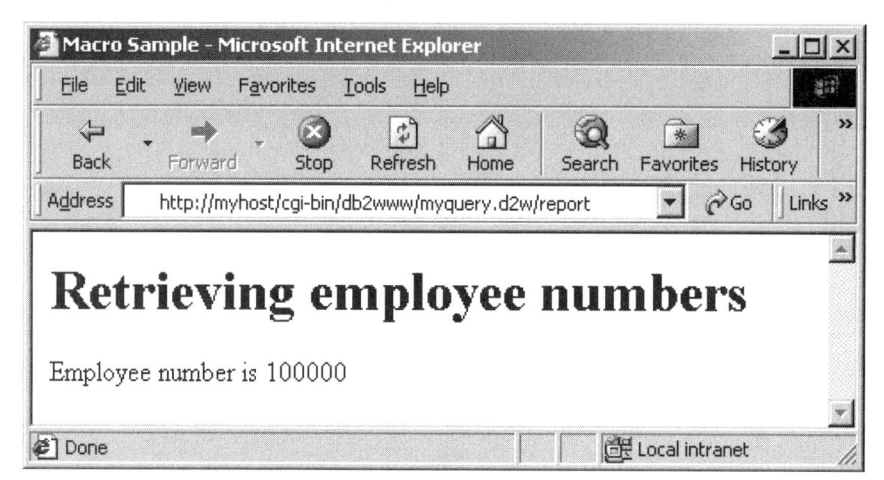

Figure 8-1   Sample Net.Data macro browser output.

```
once, the row block will repeat for each occurrence.  If
this string is not found, you will see the appropriate
message. %}


%HTML(REPORT){
  <HTML><HEAD><TITLE>Macro Sample</TITLE></HEAD><BODY>
  <H1>Retrieving employee numbers</H1>
  @myquery("Kevin")
  </BODY></HTML>
%}

%{This creates a document block called REPORT.  The
document block calls the function myquery with the
parameter "Kevin". %}
```

8.4.2   REXX

Net.Data can execute REXX scripts using two different methods. One method is to execute an external REXX script. The second method is to call a REXX script written directly inside the macro file. This is known as an inline REXX program. The language environment for calling a REXX script is called `DTW_REXX`. Here are some examples showing the difference between an external REXX program and an inline REXX program:

8.4.2.1   External REXX Program

```
% function(DTW_REXX) hello(IN PARAM) {
  %EXEC{ hello.cmd $(PARAM)%}
%}
```

8.4.2.2 Inline REXX Program

```
%function(DTW_REXX) hello(IN PARAM) {
  SAY 'Hello $(PARAM)'
%}
```

In the above sample, REXX will output "Hello," concatenated with the value of the parameter PARAM. For external REXX programs, parameter passing is direct. In the above sample, Net.Data passes REXX the value of PARAM as a command-line argument. For external REXX, ensure that the REXX filename is listed in a path specified for the EXEC_PATH configuration variable in the Net.Data initialization file. Inline REXX can reference a Net.Data parameter indirectly from the variable reference.

8.4.3 Perl

Similar to REXX, Net.Data can execute Perl scripts using two different methods. One method is to execute an external Perl script. The second method is to call an inline Perl script. The language environment for calling a Perl script is DTW_PERL. Here are some examples showing the difference between an external Perl program and an inline Perl program:

8.4.3.1 External Perl Program

```
% function(DTW_PERL) hello(IN PARAM) {
  %EXEC{ hello.pl $(PARAM)%}
%}
```

8.4.3.2 Inline Perl Program

```
%function(DTW_PERL) hello(IN PARAM) {
  open(DTW,"> $ENV{DTWPIPE}");
  print DTW "Hello \" $ENV{PARAM}\"\n";
%}
```

This sample performs the same task as seen previously in the REXX sample. Perl will output "Hello," concatenated with the value of the parameter PARAM. The external Perl program looks similar to calling the REXX script. The parameter passing is direct. In the above sample, Net.Data passes Perl the value of PARAM as a command-line argument. Inline Perl can reference a Net.Data parameter indirectly by referencing the variable from the environment. The output is returned to Net.Data by printing into a data pipe.

8.4.4 Java

Net.Data works with both Java applications and Java applets. Net.Data will execute Java applications created with JDK (Java Development Kit) 1.1 or higher. The Java application language environment requires the use the Net.Data Live Connection Manager. The Live Connection Manager improves performance by maintaining a persistent language environment in a separate process. Each instance of the language environment is called a cliette. Cliettes are put into a

Language Environments   211

sharing pool that can be used when there is a Net.Data macro request. For Java, the Live Connection Manager loads the Java Virtual Machine (JVM), needed to interpret the Java class file, inside the Java application cliette. Java applets are called by using the HTML applet tag.

8.4.4.1 Java Applications

Java applications are invoked using functions defined within the `DTW_JAVAPPS` language environment. Java applications running on the Web server are also known as Java servlets. Here are the steps required to make Net.Data call a Java application from a Net.Data function:

1. Write your Java function.
2. Create a Net.Data cliette for all your Java functions.
3. Start the Live Connection Manager.
4. Run the Net.Data function that invokes the Java language environment.

Net.Data Java cliettes launch the JVM whenever your Java function runs. Cliettes are defined in the Net.Data Live Connection Manager configuration file. Each time you introduce new Java functions, you must recreate the Java cliette. The Live Connection Manager will be discussed in more detail in the topic concerning performance. Once the Live Connection Manager is configured and started, the Java function can be called as follows:

```
%FUNCTION (DTW_JAVAPPS) function_name([arg1, arg2, ...]);
```

`function_name`—The name of the Net.Data function that calls a Java class with the same name.

8.4.4.2 Java Applets

The language environment for Java applets is `DTW_APPLET`. Unlike Java applications, Java applets do not require creating a function defined with its language environment. Net.Data calls an applet by calling the applet class name, preceded by "`DTWA_`". This function will generate HTML using the `<APPLET>` markup tag. Here is the syntax for calling a Java applet from a Net.Data macro:

```
@DTWA_AppletName(parm1, parm2, ..., parmN)
```

`DTWA_`—Identifies the function call to the applet language environment.

`AppletName`—The name of the applet for which tags are generated.

`parm1 to parmN`—Parameters used to generate HTML `PARAM` tags.

The `<APPLET>` tag properties can be modified by defining the properties in the macro `define` block, preceded by the applet name. For example:

```
%define{
  AppletName.codebase = "/netdata-java/"
  AppletName.height = "200"
  AppletName.width = "400"
%}
```

8.5 Performance

Net.Data supports several interfaces for communication with a Web or application server. It will work with most Web servers using the Common Gateway Interface (CGI). Net.Data also supports FastCGI and Web server-specific APIs for selected Web servers.

8.5.0.1 FastCGI

FastCGI improves performance by maintaining a persistent process for executing Net.Data requests. Net.Data supports FastCGI on IBM HTTP Web Server, Apache Web Server 1.2.0 or higher, and Lotus Domino Go Web Server. The URL for calling a Net.Data macro is different when using FastCGI. The "cgi-bin" is replaced with "fcgi-bin". For example:

```
http://host-name/fcgi-bin/db2www/macro-name/document-label
```

> **host-name**—Identifies the machine host name for the Web server.
>
> **macro-name**—Identifies the name of the macro file containing the document.
>
> **document-label**—Identifies the document block within the macro file to execute.

8.5.0.2 API Mode

API mode improves performance by using the Web server's native API calls. Web server-specific API libraries are provided for IBM WebSphere Application Server, Netscape Enterprise Server, and Microsoft Internet Information Server (IIS).

The URL for Web server API mode is different depending on the Web server and platform. For some Web servers, the "cgi-bin" in the URL is replaced with a shared library name. The exact syntax and steps for configuration vary between different Web servers and platforms. Refer to the *Net.Data Administration and Programming Guide* for specific details on configuring API mode on a specific Web server.

8.5.1 Live Connection Manager

The Net.Data Live Connection Manager improves performance by maintaining persistent connections to data sources. It uses a connection pool to keep several connections to the databases active at all times. These connections are called cliettes. Cliettes eliminate the overhead involved with connecting and disconnecting from a database. Cliettes are configured in the Live Connection Manager configuration file. Table 8-4 shows a list of variables needed to configure a cliette pool for database access.

Table 8-4 Live Connection Manager Configuration Variables for Database Access

Variable	Description
MIN_PROCESS	Minimum number of cliettes. This is the number of cliettes that will be created when the Live Connection Manager starts.
MAX_PROCESS	Maximum number of cliettes allowed. If more connections are needed, they will be queued until a cliette becomes available. If additional connections are no longer needed, they will be removed after a period of time, until there is the minimum number of cliettes left.
DATABASE	Data source name.
LOGIN	User ID used to connect to the data source.
PASSWORD	Password of the user ID.

> **Note**
> On Windows NT, the Live Connection Manager is started as an NT service.

8.5.2 Cache Manager

The Cache Manager improves performance by caching the document result of calling a Net.Data macro with a specific set of parameters. If the same macro is called with the same parameters, instead of Net.Data executing the macro, the Cache Manager will recall the resulting document from a previous execution and return this to the Web browser. This is very effective for frequently accessed macros that do not change often.

To enable a macro for use by the Cache Manager, the macro must call the DTW_CACHE_PAGE function. This function calls the Cache Manager to see if the document has been cached. To prevent the document from becoming dated, an expiry date can be set and passed as a function parameter. If the document has not been cached or the cached document has expired, the current result of executing the macro will be cached for future use. Table 8-5 shows a list of variables needed to configure the Net.Data Cache Manager. This table does not include logging and statistical configuration parameters.

8.6 Summary

This chapter introduced the basic concepts of Net.Data. It discussed the advantages of Net.Data Web solutions, the structure of the macro scripting language, language environments, and performance features. The advantages of Net.Data include ease of use, high compatibility with most browsers, and features for easy integration with other Web solutions such as legacy code written in Perl and REXX. The macro scripting language contains three main types of blocks: define blocks, function blocks, and document blocks. Language environments are supplied for database

Table 8-5 Cache Manager Configuration Variables

Variable	Description
`root`	The absolute or relative name of the path and directory where the cache pages are stored.
`caching`	`Yes` indicates that the cache is to be active when the Cache Manager starts.
`fssize`	The maximum space to be used in the filesystem by pages in the current cache; specified in the form of nnB, nnKB, or nnM.
`mem-size`	The maximum amount of memory to be used by all of the pages in this cache; specified in the form of nnB, nnKB, or nnM.
`lifetime`	The maximum length of time a page can be held in the cache; specified in the form of nnS, nnM, or nnH.
`check-expiration`	Specifies whether to mark cache pages as expired and perform lifetime checking. The values can be `yes` or `no`, or they can be in the form of nnS, nnM, or nnH.
`datum-memory-limit`	The maximum amount of space a cached page can occupy within memory; specified in the form of nnB, nnKB, or nnM.
`datum-disk-limit`	The maximum amount of space a cache page can occupy within the file cache; specified in the form of nnB, nnKB, or nnM.

access, REXX, Perl, and Java. Performance can be enhanced using FastCGI and Web server APIs. The Live Connection Manager can help performance by maintaining persistent language environments for Java servlets and database connection pooling. The Cache Manager reduces work by caching frequently accessed Web pages.

References

Net.Data Home Page:
  http://www.software.ibm.com/data/net.data

Net.Data Online Documentation:
  http://www.software.ibm.com/data/net.data/library.html

Net.Data Forum:
  http://netdata.boulder.ibm.com/fcgi-bin/db2www/forum.d2w/main

Net.Data Sample Macros:
  http://www.software.ibm.com/data/net.data/tools/codesamp.html

Net.Data Fixpacks:
  ftp://ftp.software.ibm.com/ps/products/db2/fixes/english-us/net.data/

CHAPTER 9

Perl Programming

Perl is a very popular scripting language that is available for most platforms. Its popularity is especially prevalent on Linux platforms, though it is still popular on most UNIX-based platforms. The Perl scripting language also seems to find widespread use as a CGI (Common Gateway Interface) language for Web servers.

Perl provides a Database Interface, referred to as a DBI. This DBI module provides a standard interface for accessing a vendor's Database Driver (DBD). Using the DBI module to write scripts that access databases, Perl programmers do not need to write vendor-specific code. Rather, if they wish to change a database they want to access, all they need to do is to switch which DBD module is referenced.

The following chapter describes the DBI and uses examples to illustrate access to the DB2 DBD from Perl.

9.1 Objectives

After reading this chapter, you should:

- Understand which components are needed for Perl and DB2 to access a DB2 database.
- Install and configure the components needed for Perl and DB2.
- Have a basic understanding of the program flow required to access DB2 and be able to handle any error conditions that may arise from the process.

9.2 Advantages of Perl

Since Perl is an interpreted language and the Perl DBI module uses dynamic SQL, Perl is an ideal language for quickly creating and revising prototypes of DB2 applications. The Perl DBI module uses an interface that is quite similar to the CLI and JDBC interfaces, which makes it easy for you to port your Perl prototypes to CLI and JDBC.

Most database vendors provide a database driver for the Perl DBI module, which means that you can also use Perl to create applications that access data from many different database servers. For example, you can write a Perl DB2 application that connects to an Oracle database using the DBD::Oracle database driver, fetch data from the Oracle database, and insert the data into a DB2 database using the DBD::DB2 database driver.

Additionally, Perl is a very popular language used for CGI scripts with Web servers. As such, the DBD::DB2 module provides an excellent interface for Web servers to serve information from DB2 databases.

9.3 Setting up the Perl Environment

There are several steps involved with setting up a DB2 UDB Perl environment:

- A DB2 UDB Developer's Edition is needed. The earliest supported version of DB2 UDB at the time of writing is V5.2.
- The database being accessed must be cataloged properly. If the database is remote, a node must also be cataloged.
- DB2 UDB CLI bind files must be bound to the database.
- The CLI environment must be configured using the Client Configuration Assistant (CCA) or edit the `db2cli.ini` file directly. Since the Perl DBD module is built on top of the CLI layer, it is important to remember that settings in the `db2cli.ini` file will affect connections to DB2.
- The Perl environment needs to be installed onto the DB2 client machine. This environment can be found on the Perl Web site: http://www.perl.com
- The Perl DBI needs to be installed and compiled on the client machine. This can be found on the Perl Web site: http://www.perl.com/CPAN-local/modules/by-module/DBI/
- The DB2 UDB Perl DBD needs to be installed and compiled on the client machine. This can be found on the Perl Web site: http://www.perl.com/CPAN-local/modules/by-module/DBD/

9.3.1 DB2 UDB Installation

The *DB2 UDB Quick Beginnings Guide* is a very good reference for installing DB2 UDB, the specifics of which are outside the scope of this book. All that we need to concern ourselves with here is that the appropriate DB2 UDB product be installed so that the Perl DBD module can be compiled.

9.3.2 Database Cataloging

Again, the *DB2 UDB Quick Beginnings Guide* is an excellent reference for cataloging a local or remote database. This can be accomplished by either using the command line prompt with DB2 commands or by using the CCA. The details of which will be left to that manual.

9.3.3 CLI Bind Files

The bind files required for CLI applications will be automatically bound when the first CLI application (including Perl) connects to the database. (An exception to this case is when the first application connects from a Runtime Client. This environment does not include DB2 bind files.) The bind may not be successful if the user does not have BINDADD authority on the database. Therefore, the database administrator may be required to bind the necessary files manually using the DB2 UDB BIND command or the CCA. Each supported DB2 server uses different bind files (see Table 9-1).

Table 9-1 CLI Bind List Files

Bind File	DB2 Server
db2cli.lst	DB2 UDB (OS/2, Windows, UNIX)
ddcsvm.lst	DB2 for VM (SQL/DS)
ddcsvse.lst	DB2 for VSE (SQL/DS)
ddcsmvs.lst	DB2 for OS/390 (MVS/ESA)
ddcs400.lst	DB2 for OS/400

For example, to manually bind the CLI packages from a DB2 UDB command window on Windows NT against a DB2 UDB for AIX database, you would issue the following command after connecting to the database:

```
DB2 BIND @db2cli.lst MESSAGES db2cli.msg GRANT PUBLIC
```

Likewise, if the DB2 database resides on OS/390, you could use the command:

```
DB2 BIND @ddcsmvs.lst BLOCKING ALL SQLERROR CONTINUE
MESSAGES mvsbind.msg GRANT PUBLIC
```

The syntax for the BIND command can be found in the *DB2 UDB Command Reference Guide*.

9.3.4 Configuring CLI

It may be necessary to alter the behavior of deferred prepare. As of DB2 version 5.0, deferred prepare is on by default. This means that a statement is not prepared during a PREPARE statement, but rather deferred until the EXECUTE statement. Since there is no way to alter this behavior from the statement level, it must be altered in the db2cli.ini file.

The `db2cli.ini` file is located in the `sqllib/cfg` directory of the instance owner in UNIX systems, or the `sqllib` directory for OS/2 and Windows operating systems.

An example `db2cli.ini` file is shown below. There are many more options that can be specified in the CLI configuration file. The first line is a comment about the section of the file. Multiple databases may be configured in this file. The second line contains the database alias name in brackets, `[DB2MALL]`. The `DB2MALL` database can still be accessed from a DB2 UDB CLI application without an entry in the `db2cli.ini` file, but if there is no section for the `DB2MALL` database, all of the default values for the parameters will be used. This may not be desirable. The line below the database name alters the behavior of all connections to that data source name. The supported keywords are defined in the *DB2 UDB Call Level Interface Guide and Reference*.

```
; Comment goes here
[DB2MALL]
DEFERREDPREPARE=1
```

The DB2 UDB CCA allows you to configure the CLI environment without editing the `db2cli.ini` file directly. The interface is easy to use and explains each parameter that can be modified.

9.3.5 Installing Perl

At the time of writing, the minimum supported version of Perl for the DBD::DB2 module was 5.004_04. Be sure to check the README file of the DBD::DB2 module for the latest requirements. Perl can be downloaded from the Perl Web site in either its binary form or as source code. If the binary form is not available for your platform, then you will need to compile the source code on your target platform. If you choose the latter option, then you will naturally need a compiler. Be sure to follow all instructions provided by the Perl Web site.

9.3.6 Installing the Perl DBI

Installing the Perl DBI module is fairly straightforward. Be sure to read the README file that comes with the compressed TAR file (make sure that you also refer to the README file for DBD::DB2). The minimum version (at the time of writing) of the DBI module that DB2 requires is 0.93. Once the file downloaded has been extracted to a directory, installation follows the usual Perl practice of:

- `perl Makefile.PL`.
- `make` (`nmake` for Windows with the Microsoft Visual C++ compiler).
- `make test` (`nmake test` for Windows).
- `make install` – only if test passes (`nmake install` for Windows).

9.3.7 Installing the DBD::DB2 Module

The DBD::DB2 driver is currently supported on many platforms. For the latest information, refer to http://www.software.ibm.com/data/db2/perl. The following operating systems and C compilers were supported at the time of writing:

AIX	Operating systems:
	• AIX Version 4.1.4 and later
	Compilers:
	• IBM C for AIX Version 3.1 and later
HP-UX	Operating systems:
	• HP-UX Version 10.10 with Patch Levels: PHCO_6134, PHKL_5837, PHKL_6133, PHKL_6189, PHKL_6273, PHSS_5956
	• HP-UX Version 10.20
	• HP-UX Version 11
	Compilers:
	• HP C/HP-UX Version A.10.32
	• HP C Compiler Version A.11.00.00 (for HP-UX Version 11)
Linux	Operating systems:
	• Linux Redhat Version 5.1 with kernel 2.0.35 and glibc version 2.0.7
	Compilers:
	• gcc version 2.7.2.3 or later
Solaris	Operating systems:
	• Solaris Version 2.5.1
	• Solaris Version 2.6
	Compilers:
	• SPARCompiler C Version 4.2
Windows NT	Operating systems:
	• Microsoft Windows NT version 4 or later
	Compilers:
	• Microsoft Visual C++ Version 5.0 or later

The downloadable database driver from DB2 for Perl is shipped in the form of a compressed TAR file. Once this has been extracted, be sure to read the README file and the CAVEATS file. Installation usually follows the normal Perl practice of:

- `perl Makefile.PL`.
- `make` (`nmake` for Windows with the Microsoft Visual C++ compiler).
- `make test` (`nmake test` for Windows).
- `make install` – only if test passes (`nmake test` for Windows).

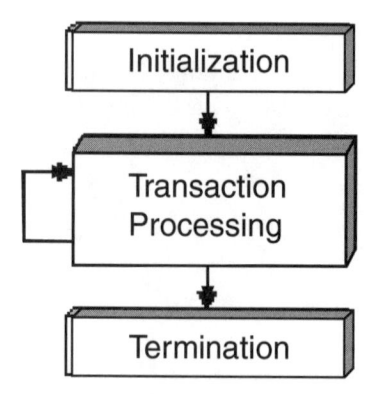

Figure 9-1 Basic program flow.

9.4 Basic Program Flow

The program flow for accessing DB2 and retrieving data from the database is quite similar to that of CLI. There is still an initialization phase, transaction processing phase, and a disconnecting and termination phase. These phases take on a slightly different form than that of CLI, since the DBI methods encapsulate much of the initialization and termination phases for you.

The Perl DBI module supports only dynamic SQL. When you need to execute a statement multiple times, you can improve the performance of your Perl DB2 applications by issuing a `prepare` call to prepare the statement. This method is described below during the transaction phase.

For current information on the restrictions of the version of the DBD::DB2 driver that you install on your workstation, refer to the CAVEATS file in the DBD::DB2 driver package.

9.4.1 Initialization

Within a Perl script, we need to activate the DBI environment before any methods from the module can be used. Once this module has been made available for the script, then the DBD::DB2 module is automatically loaded during the connection method. In fact, many of the initialization steps that are normally required for a CLI application are automatically performed during the connection method, including setting up the environment handle and the connection handle. Looking at the sample excerpt below, we can see that the return value from the connection method is an assigned connection handle.

```perl
#!/usr/bin/perl
use DBI;

my $database='dbi:DB2:db2mall';
my $user='';
my $password='';

my $dbhandle = DBI->connect($database, $user, $password) or
    die "Can't connect to $database: $DBI::errstr";
```

Basic Program Flow

The first line is standard for all Perl scripts and tells the OS (Operating System) that the following script should be interpreted by Perl found in the directory path /usr/bin/perl.

The line:

```
use DBI;
```

is included to enable Perl to load the DBI module.

The DBI module automatically loads the DBD::DB2 driver when you create a database handle using the DBI->connect statement:

```
my $dbhandle = DBI->connect($database, $user, $password)
```

where:

$dbhandle—Represents the database handle returned by the connect statement.

$database—Represents a DB2 alias cataloged in your DB2 database directory. The database name part, "DBI:DB2," tells the connection method that we want to load the database driver for DB2. If Oracle were the backend database then the string would look like "DBI:Oracle."

$userID—Represents the user ID used to connect to the database.

$password—Represents the password for the user ID used to connect to the database.

9.4.2 Transaction Processing

Once a database handle has been created, then we can use that handle to either execute statements immediately (similar to the CLI function SQLExecDirect()) or we can create and prepare a statement handle that will then be executed. This executed statement handle may return a result set that may then be retrieved into the Perl script.

To immediately execute an SQL statement, use the Perl DBI method, do(), provided by the $dbhandle returned from the connect statement. For example:

```
$dbhandle->do("INSERT INTO table1 VALUES (value1)");
```

> **Note**
>
> The do() method cannot be used for SELECT statements. These statements require that a cursor be defined and need to be handled with the prepare() method followed by the execute() method. See the example below.

To first prepare a statement before executing it, use the `prepare()` method provided by the `$dbhandle`. This method will return a statement handle, which can then be executed using the `execute()` method provided by the statement handle:

```perl
my $sthandle = $dbhandle->prepare(
    'INSERT INTO table1 VALUES (value1)');
my $rc = $sthandle->execute();
```

The `execute()` method returns the error code for the execute call.

To enable executing a prepared statement using different input values for specified fields, the Perl DBI module enables you to prepare and execute a statement using parameter markers. To include a parameter marker in an SQL statement, use the question mark (?) character.

The following Perl code creates a statement handle that accepts a parameter marker for the value of the VALUES clause of the INSERT statement. The code then executes the statement twice, using two different values to replace the parameter marker.

```perl
my $sthandle = $dbhandle->prepare(
    'INSERT INTO table1 VALUES (?)'
);

my $rc = $sthandle->execute($value1);

.
.
.

my $rc = $sthandle->execute($value2);
```

A statement handle is required if data from a result fetch is needed by the Perl application. To gain a statement handle, an SQL statement must first be prepared and then executed. The result set may then be retrieved using the `fetchrow()` method of the statement handle. The Perl DBI returns a row as an array, with one value per column. For example, we can prepare the following statement, execute it, and then fetch the results:

```perl
my $sthandle = $dbhandle->prepare(
    'SELECT col1, col2 FROM table1 WHERE col1 = ?');

my $rc = $sthandle->execute($val1);

print "Query will return $sthandle->{NUM_OF_FIELDS} fields.\n\n";
print "$sth->{NAME}->[0]: $sth->{NAME}->[1]\n";

while (($col1, $col2) = $sthandle->fetchrow()) {
    print "$col1: $col2\n";
}
```

9.4.3 Error Handling

To return the SQLSTATE associated with a Perl DBI database handle or statement handle, call the `state` method. For example, to return the SQLSTATE associated with the database handle `$dbhandle`, include the following Perl statement in your application:

```
my $sqlstate = $dbhandle->state;
```

To return the SQLCODE associated with a Perl DBI database handle or statement handle, call the `err` method. To return the message for an SQLCODE associated with a Perl DBI database handle or statement handle, call the `errstr` method. For example, to return the SQLCODE associated with the database handle `$dbhandle`, include the following Perl statement in your application:

```
my $sqlcode = $dbhandle->err;
```

9.4.4 Disconnecting and Termination

The termination phase is really quite simple in Perl. Once finished with a statement handle, all that is required is to call the `finish()` method. Once finished with the database handle, then call the `disconnect()` method. This method will free the database handle and any memory associated with the connection as well as finish any network connection that may have been established with the database. For example:

```
$sthandle->finish();
$dbhandle->disconnect();
```

9.5 Summary

DB2 provides a freely available Database Driver (DBD::DB2) for use with the Perl scripting language. The Perl language provides a Database Interface (DBI) that allows application developers to write generic code for accessing a vendor's database, provided that the vendor supplies its own DBD.

As part of the standard packaging method that Perl requires, vendors must supply a CAVEATS file that details any limitations or special notes about their drivers. Be sure to read this file prior to programming your applications.

All of the Perl files and DBD modules are available from the Perl Web site, http://www.perl.com, but be sure to check DB2's Web site for the latest information at http://www.software.ibm.com/data/db2/perl.

References

The Official Perl Web Site:
  http://www.perl.com

DB2 Perl Developer's Web Site:
  http://www.software.ibm.com/data/db2/perl

CHAPTER 10

DB2 Extenders

DB2 Extenders are used to extend the functionality of SQL when working with different media types. This is accomplished by providing a set of User-Defined Functions (UDFs) and stored procedures for querying and manipulating data of specific media formats. These UDFs and stored procedures can be referenced in SQL statements from user applications.

There are different DB2 Extender products that make up the DB2 Extenders family, including Text Extender, Net Search Extender, Audio, Image, and Video (AIV) Extenders, XML Extender and Spatial Extender. Spatial Extender will not be covered in this chapter. Text Extender is used to provide advanced text search capabilities such as linguistic and fuzzy logic searches. Net Search provides fast, scalable fuzzy logic searches intended for use over the Internet. AIV Extenders provides functions that can be used to identify and manipulate media data with specific properties. The media data can be audio, image, and video. XML Extender enables generation, decomposition, and XPath searches of Extensible Markup Language (XML) documents.

10.1 Objectives

The objective of this chapter is to introduce the DB2 Extender family. It will look at each DB2 Extender product and outline some of its key functionality. By the end of this chapter, you should be familiar with and be able to use the following DB2 Extender products:

- DB2 Text Extender.
- DB2 Net Search Extender.
- DB2 AIV Extenders.
- DB2 XML Extender.

10.2 Text Extender

DB2 Text Extender was designed to perform advanced text searches faster and more efficiently than regular SQL. Before Text Extender, applications would have to use `LIKE` SQL comparisons to find a substring within a text document. This operation was processing intensive since the processing was done at runtime. It was also limited to simple masking characters that cannot find misspelled words or different forms of the same word. (`LIKE` comparisons are incapable of understanding linguistic processing or fuzzy logic.) Text Extender provides a solution to these limitations.

Text Extender improves performance by preprocessing documents and storing the information in indexes. This reduces the cost of the search operation during runtime. The Text Extender indexes created are not stored inside the database. They are stored as files on a local filesystem. The documents can either be stored in a database, or referenced by path and filename on a local filesystem. Documents stored on filesystems can be referenced using the full path name or DB2 data links.

There are different preprocessing techniques used for different types of indexes. Text Extender supports four types of indexes: linguistic indexes, precise indexes, precise normalized indexes, and NGRAM indexes. These indexes are accessed by calling UDFs inside SQL statements or by calling the Text Extender API from an application.

Text Extender is also capable of filtering out the formatting instructions of several popular document formats. This allows documents not stored as simple text to be searched without any file conversion. Additional document formats can be added by creating format conversion user exit applications. Here is a list of supported document formats:

- HTML – Hypertext Markup Language.
- XML – Extensible Markup Language.
- TDS – flat ASCII.
- AMI – AmiPro Architecture Version 4.
- FFT – IBM Final Form Text: Document Content Architecture.
- MSWORD – Microsoft Word, Versions 5.0 and 5.5.
- RFT – IBM Revisable Form Text: Document Content Architecture.
- RTF – Microsoft Rich Text Format (RTF), Version 1.
- WP5 – WordPerfect (OS/2 and Windows), Versions 5.0, 5.1, and 5.2.

Text Extender has two main components, a server component and a client component. The server component is needed to process and search the documents. The client component is used for remote administration and for applications that use Text Extender API function calls. UDFs do not require the installation of the Text Extender client. Figure 10-1 shows the interaction between the client and server components.

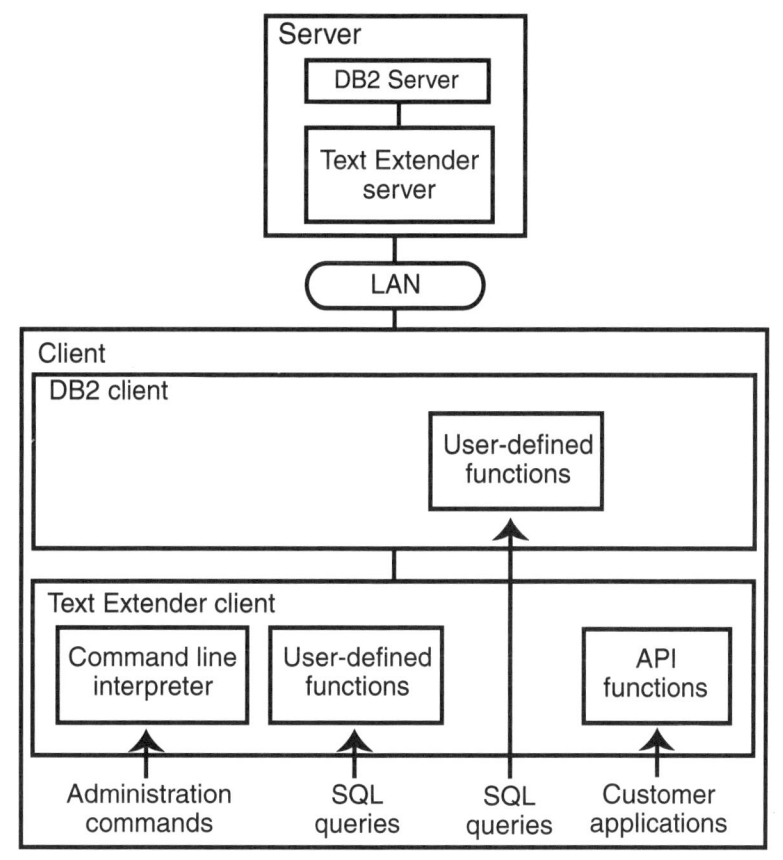

Figure 10-1 Text Extender client server architecture.

The Text Extender server is available on Windows NT, OS/2, AIX, HP-UX, Solaris, and OS/390. Text Extender also supports DB2 Extended Enterprise Edition on NT, AIX, and Solaris. The client component is available on all Windows platforms, OS/2, AIX, HP-UX, and Solaris.

Similar to DB2, Text Extender has its own instance and Command Line Processor (CLP). On Intel platforms, a default instance is created when Text Extender is installed. On UNIX platforms, the instance is created using the `txicrt` command. The Text Extender instance needs to be started before the indexes can be created and searched. This is done using the `txstart` command. The CLP is started by typing `db2tx`. If you are not in the CLP, you can still issue Text Extender commands by preceding the command with `db2tx`.

Before a Text Extender index can be created, the database must be enabled for its use. Enabling a database creates the User-Defined Types (UDTs), UDFs, and administration tables needed for Text Extender to run. The database can be enabled with the following command:

```
db2tx ENABLE DATABASE
```

> **Note**
>
> The `enable database` command requires that the DB2 environment variable `DB2DBDFT` be set to the database being used.

10.2.1 Indexes

Text Extender improves data search performance by preprocessing data before a query is executed. The processed data is stored in indexes external to the database on a local filesystem. After the database is enabled, an index can be created. Planning an index is important to avoid time-consuming mistakes. Planning an index requires the following steps:

1. Checking the format and CCSID of the data.
2. Selecting an index type.
3. Allocating sufficient storage for the indexes.

The first task when creating an index is to check the format and Coded Character Set Identifier (CCSID), or code page, of the data you wish to search. Verify that the document format is a supported document format for Text Extender. Also, some index types are restricted to certain code pages. Depending on the index type used, you may have to verify if the CCSID is supported. Specifying the correct document format and CCSID during index creation is required for proper indexing of the document.

The second task is to choose an index type that best suits your needs. There are four index types available: linguistic, precise, precise normalized, and NGRAM. Finally, enough space must be allocated to store the index. The space required for the index is dependent on the type of index. Precise indexes require about 40% the size of the data being indexed. Linguistic indexes require about 70% the size of the data indexed. NGRAM indexes require 100% the size of the data being indexed. Additional space is required for temporary files used during the reorganization of indexes. As a general rule, there should be at least twice the space required by the original documents allocated.

There are many options that can be specified while enabling a text column. Refer to the *Text Extender Administration Guide* for a complete description of the available options. Any optional parameters not specified during `db2tx enable text column` will receive the default value of the database specified in the Text Extender text configuration file. The current defaults can be checked by using the `db2tx get text configuration` command. Here is the basic syntax for enabling an index:

```
db2tx ENABLE TEXT COLUMN table-name column-name HANDLE
handle-column-name [OPTIONS]
```

> **Troubleshooting**
>
> Enabling or searching a large index may require increasing the DB2 application control heap database configuration parameter (`APP_CTL_HEAP_SZ`).

All index types support a common set of search capabilities, including Boolean searches, proximity searches, thesaurus expansion, abbreviation expansion, and wildcard searches. Boolean searching involve the checking of conjunction, disjunction, and exclusion of search terms. Proximity searches allow queries to identify search terms in the same paragraph or sentence. Thesaurus expansion enables finding words with the same meaning. The user must provide input into a thesaurus file to enable this feature. A sample thesaurus is provided. Abbreviation files allow custom abbreviations to be recognized as nonabbreviated words. For example, IBM would find International Business Machines. Additional search compatibilities are available depending on the index type selected.

10.2.1.1 Linguistic Indexes

Linguistic indexes use dictionary, synonym, and abbreviation-based query expansion. In addition to the common search capabilities, linguistic indexes are also capable of base form reduction, word normalization, phonetic searches, and free text searches. Base form reduction is the process that converts words into their simplest form. For example, *mice* will be reduced to *mouse* and *saw* will be reduced to *see*. Word normalization removes case sensitivity and accent characters if they do not change the meaning of the word. Phonetic searches find words that produce a similar sound. Free text searches are possible through the use of word filters.

Filters are used to identify a list of significant terms. Examples of filters include stop-word filtering and part-of-speech filtering. Stop-word filters remove insignificant words such as "a" and "the." Only significant terms are stored in the index file. During execution of a search, the same filters are applied to the search strings. Only significant terms from the search string are compared to the keywords stored in the index file. Table 10-1 lists processing techniques that are applied to a linguistic index. Figure 10-2 shows an example of stop-word filtering.

Table 10-1 Linguistic Processing Techniques

Processing Type	Description
Word sentence separation	Separates words and sentences.
Dehyphenation	Removes hyphens from hyphenated words.
Normalization	Removes case sensitivity and accents.
Base form reduction (stemming)	Reduces a word to its simplest form. For example, all keywords become singular in the present tense.
Decomposition	Separates compound words.
Stop-word and part-of-speech filtering	Removes small connective words such as "a" and "the."

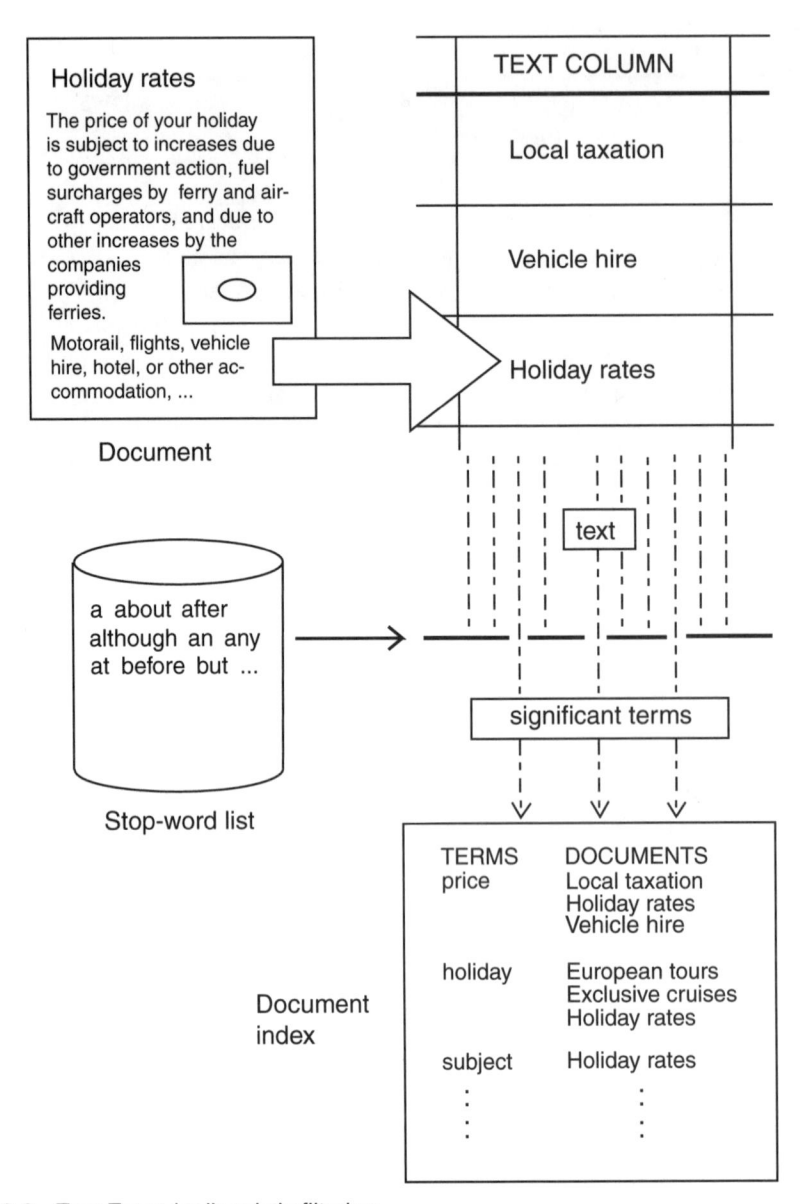

Figure 10-2 Text Extender linguistic filtering.

Here is a sample that enables the sample `DB2MALL` database with a linguistic index. For the `DB2MALL` database, it is useful to enable searching of products by product name. This sample will enable the `product_name` column in the `product` table. The text handle name will be called `product_nameh`.

```
db2tx ENABLE TEXT COLUMN product product_name HANDLE
product_nameh INDEXTYPE linguistic
```

10.2.1.2 Precise Indexes

Unlike a linguistic index, a precise index does not use dictionary query expansion. There is no base form reduction performed on the data. There are two types of precise indexes, precise and precise normalized. Precise indexes are case-sensitive. Precise normalized indexes are case-insensitive. Although case sensitivity and lack of base form reduction can make it more difficult to find a search term, it is useful when too many matches are being returned. If the exact search terms are known, this index type will reduce the number of matches. Table 10-2 lists the filters that are applied to a precise index.

Table 10-2 Precise Filters

Filter Type	Description
Word sentence separation	Separates words and sentences.
Stop-word and part-of-speech filtering	Removes small connective words such as "a" and "the."

10.2.1.3 NGRAM Indexes

An NGRAM index supports fuzzy logic instead of dictionary processing. With fuzzy logic, everything is indexed. No text filtering is used. NGRAM indexes can be used to perform fuzzy searches and precise searches. All searches are case-insensitive. This index type is useful when searching for terms that may be misspelled. The one restriction with fuzzy logic searches is that the first three characters of the search term must match the original word.

NGRAM is limited in the number of supported document formats and code pages. Support for additional document formats and code pages has been added for V7.1. Refer to the *Text Extender Administration Guide* for the complete list of supported document formats and code pages.

10.2.2 Text Extender UDFs

Applications can access Text Extender indexes by referencing UDFs from SQL statements or by calling the Text Extender API. The easiest way to access the Text Extender indexes is by using UDFs. Calling UDFs is convenient because they are referenced inside SQL statements. Therefore, any application that can make SQL statements can take advantage of Text Extender.

The two main functions for performing searches are `db2tx.contains` and `db2tx.search_result`. The `CONTAINS` UDF is easier to use, but is slower on large tables. The `SEARCH_RESULT` function provides faster performance for large tables, but uses a more complicated syntax.

10.2.2.1 CONTAINS Function

The `DB2TX.CONTAINS` UDF has the following syntax. More than one search string can be provided if separated using Boolean logic. The "|" character represents a logical OR. The "&" character represents a logical AND.

```
DB2TX.CONTAINS (text-handle,'"search-text"')=1
```

Here is a sample that shows the `DB2TX.CONTAINS` UDF in an SQL statement. This sample can be executed against the sample `DB2MALL` database. Before this sample can be run, the database and `product_name` column must be enabled. This sample assumes that a column handle called `product_nameh` is created on the `product_name` column.

```
SELECT * FROM mall.product WHERE DB2TX.CONTAINS
(product_nameh,'"books"')=1
```

10.2.2.2 SEARCH_RESULT Function

The `DB2TX.SEARCH_RESULT` UDF has the following syntax. Similar to the `DB2TX.CONTAINS` UDF, more than one search string can be provided if separated using Boolean logic. The schema, table name, and text handle strings need to be in uppercase unless these objects were created as case-sensitive names.

```
DB2TX.SEARCH_RESULT('SCHEMA', 'TABLE', 'TEXTHANDLE','
"search-term"')
```

Here is a sample that replaces the `DB2TX.CONTAINS` UDF from the previous sample and replaces it with the `DB2TX.SEARCH.RESULT` UDF. Unlike the `DB2TX.CONTAINS` UDF, the `DB2TX.SEARCH_RESULT` UDF returns a result set. Therefore, a predicate must be added comparing the handle from the search result to the handle in the original table.

```
SELECT * FROM mall.product t1,
table(DB2TX.SEARCH_RESULT('MALL', 'PRODUCT',
'PRODUCT_NAMEH',' "books"')) t2 WHERE t1.product_nameh =
t2.handle
```

Inequality expressions using Text Extender UDTs require setting the DB2 CURRENT FUNCTION PATH special register to DB2TX. This enables DB2 to locate special inequality functions needed to compare Text Extender data types. Alternatively, these columns can be cast into DB2 data types such as such as CHAR(60) before performing inequality expressions. For example:

```
SELECT * FROM mall.product t1,
table(DB2TX.SEARCH_RESULT('MALL', 'PRODUCT',
'PRODUCT_NAMEH',' "books"')) t2 WHERE CAST(t1.product_nameh
AS CHAR(60))= CAST(t2.handle AS CHAR(60))
```

10.2.3 Text Extender APIs

As an alternative to calling UDFs, applications can also perform searches using Text Extender API function calls. The API functions provide the same search capabilities as UDFs but also allow returning a data stream with the highlighting information for matches. The `DesGetMatches` API function is similar to the `db2tx.contains` UDF. The `DesGetSearchResultTable` API function is similar to the `db2tx.search_result` UDF.

> **Note**
>
> Applications using the Text Extender API must be run locally on the database server or on a machine with the Text Extender client installed.

10.3 Net Search Extender

Net Search Extender is a reduced set of Text Extender functionality, highly optimized for use over the Internet. The benefits of Net Search Extender include improved performance, low overhead, index buffering, and scalability at a very high volume of requests. The trade-off for the performance gain is functionality. Net Search Extender is limited to fuzzy logic indexes. It is currently not available on DB2 Extended Enterprise Edition.

Instance creation and the command interface are similar to Text Extender. On Intel platforms, a default Net Search Extender instance is created. On UNIX platforms, the Net Search Extender instance is created using the `nxicrt` command. The instance is started with the `desfpdem start` command. The Net Search CLP is started by calling `db2nx`.

Additional options are available on the `enable text column` command to assist in optimization. Here is the equivalent syntax needed to enable a text column on the `product` table in the sample `DB2MALL` database. The index name will be `product_nameh`. Please note: We must provide the primary key for the table. In this case, the primary key is `product_id`.

```
db2nx ENABLE TEXT COLUMN product product_name INDEX
product_nameh USING product_id
```

No incremental index update is available for Net Search Extender. If a table with indexed documents is modified and the change needs to be reflected in the index, the whole index needs to be recreated.

10.3.1 Benefits of Net Search Extender

Net Search Extender is highly optimized. In addition, it allows memory caching of selected database tables to avoid the high operational costs associated with file I/O during search result list processing. These tables are called in-memory tables. These tables are read-only and are only updated when the index is updated or refreshed using the `db2nx update index` command. Performance has been increased in the following areas:

- User-defined sorted result list.
- Index creation time.
- Search performance.
- Maximum number of concurrent queries.

10.3.2 Search Capabilities

There is no need to specify the index type during index creation since only one index type is available. Net Search Extender uses a modified fuzzy logic index. This index is able to perform Boolean searches, wildcard searches, section searches, and algorithmic base form reduction for English documents. The section search feature allows you to tag document sections as searchable.

Algorithmic base form reduction is unique to Net Search Extender. Unlike Text Extender base form reduction, algorithmic base form reduction does not use a dictionary. This feature is currently only available for English documents.

10.3.3 Search Functions

Net Search Extender uses a DB2 stored procedure instead of a UDF for performing searches. The main stored procedure is called `desfpssp!textSearch`. Here is the syntax for this stored procedure. Refer to the *Net Search Administration Guide* for a complete description of each stored procedure parameter.

```
desfpssp!textSearch( outTotalDocs, "search-term",
maxHitCount, maxIntermediateHitCount, startRowNum,
maxRowsToReturn, index-name, index-directory, tmp-
directory, sql-statement, data-source, outWordCounts,
outTable)
```

Here is a sample stored procedure call to the Net Search stored procedure for performing a search on the `product` table:

```
CALL desfpssp!textSearch( outTotalDocs, "\"books\"",
"32000", "32000", "0", "50", "PRODUCT_NAMEH", "/home/
db2inst1/indexes", "/home/db2inst1/tmp", "select * from
product", "1", outWordCounts, outTable)
```

10.4 AIV Extenders

Audio, Image, and Video (AIV) Extenders provide extensions to SQL to assist in managing media data. AIV Extenders share a similar client/server model and design to Text Extender. They are available on the same platforms and ship with Text Extender. The additional functionality provided by AIV Extenders is available to applications by referencing UDFs in SQL statements or by coding the applications to call the AIV Extenders APIs. Applications that use AIV Extenders API functions must be run on the database server or on a DB2 client with the AIV Extender client installed. Applications that use the AIV Extender UDFs can run on any DB2 client.

Before AIV Extenders can be used, the database must be enabled. Enabling a database for AIV Extenders creates the UDTs and UDFs needed to execute. Like the other Extender products, AIV Extenders also have an instance and a CLP. The AIV Extenders instance is created with the `dmbicrt` command. The instance is started by typing `dmbstart`. The AIV Extenders CLP is called `db2ext`.

Administrative commands can be entered by starting the AIV CLP or by preceding AIV administration commands with `db2ext`. Here is the syntax for enabling a database and a column for use by AIV Extenders:

```
db2ext ENABLE DATABASE FOR ext-name
db2ext ENABLE COLUMN table-name column-name FOR ext-name
```

ext-name—Can be `db2image`, `db2audio`, or `db2video`.

10.4.1 AIV Extender UDFs

There are many UDFs available to extend SQL functionality for media data. AIV Extenders can be used to display and play video and audio clips. They can also use QBICs for searching for images by content, and for detecting a scene change in a video. Some UDFs are available for more than one media type, and some are available for all three. Table 10-3 lists some of the UDFs that are available and the media types they support.

10.4.1.1 AIV Extender APIs

UDFs are a subset of the available AIV Extender APIs. In addition to displaying and playing video and audio clips, searching for images by content, and detecting a scene change in a video, API functions can also be used to prepare and maintain a database for AIV Extenders. Applications calling AIV Extender API functions must be executed locally on the database searched or on a DB2 client with the AIV Extender client installed.

10.5 XML Extender

XML Extender is a new product recently added to the DB2 Extender family. It was implemented to take advantage of the Extensible Markup Language (XML) used in Business to Business (B2B) applications to relational databases. XML is a subset of Standard Generalized Markup Language (SGML). It is a much larger subset than HTML and capable of defining its own markup tags. The ability to define custom markup tags enables XML documents to mark up text by content type instead of by how the data is formatted. This enables meaningful storage of data in an open standard format.

Table 10-3 AVI Extender UDFs

Function	Description	Media Types
AlignValue	Returns the number of bytes per sample in a WAVE audio, or in the audio track of a video.	Audio and Video
AspectRatio	Returns the aspect ratio of the first track of an MPEG1 and MPEG2 video.	Video
BitsPerSample	Returns the number of bits of data used to represent each sample of WAVE or AIFF audio in an audio, or in the audio track of a video.	Audio and Video
BytesPerSec	Returns the data transfer rate, in average bytes per second, for a WAVE audio.	Audio
Comment	Returns or updates a comment stored with an image, audio, or video.	All
CompressType	Returns the compression format, such as MPEG-1, of a video.	Video
Content	Retrieves or updates the content of an image, audio, or video from a database.	All
DB2Audio	Stores the content of an audio in a database table.	Audio
DB2Image	Stores the content of an image in a database table.	Image
DB2Video	Stores the content of a video in a database table.	Video
Duration	Returns the duration (that is, playing time in seconds) of a WAVE or AIFF audio, or video.	Audio and Video
Filename	Returns the name of the server file that contains the content of an image, audio, or video.	All
FindInstrument	Returns the track number of the first occurrence of a specified instrument in a MIDI audio.	Audio
FindTrackName	Returns the number of a specified named track in a MIDI audio.	Audio
Format	Returns the format of an image, audio, or video.	All
FrameRate	Returns the throughput of a video in frames per second.	Video
GetInstruments	Returns the instrument name of all instruments in a MIDI audio.	Audio
GetTrackNames	Returns the name of all tracks in a MIDI audio.	Audio
Height	Returns the height, in pixels, of an image or video frame.	Image and Video
Importer	Returns the user ID of the person who stored an image, audio, or video in a database table.	All

XML Extender

Table 10-3 AVI Extender UDFs (Continued)

Function	Description	Media Types
`ImportTime`	Returns a timestamp that indicates when an image, audio, or video was stored in a database table.	All
`MaxBytesPerSec`	Returns the maximum throughput of a video in bytes per second.	Video
`NumAudioTracks`	Returns the number of audio tracks in a video or MIDI audio.	Audio and Video
`NumChannels`	Returns the number of recorded audio channels in a WAVE or AIFF audio, or video.	Audio and Video
`NumColors`	Returns the number of colors in an image.	Image
`NumFrames`	Returns the number of frames in a video.	Video
`NumVideoTracks`	Returns the number of video tracks in a video.	Video
`QbScoreFromName`	Returns the score of an image (uses a named query object).	Image
`QbScoreFromStr`	Returns the score of an image (uses a query string).	Image
`QbScoreTBFromName`	Returns a table of scores for an image column (uses a named query object).	Image
`QbScoreTBFromStr`	Returns a table of scores for an image column (uses a query string).	Image
`Replace`	Updates the content of an image, audio, or video stored in a database, and updates its comment.	All
`SamplingRate`	Returns the sampling rate of a WAVE or AIFF audio, or an audio track in a video, in number of samples per second.	Audio and Video
`Size`	Returns the size of an image, audio, or video in bytes.	All
`Thumbnail`	Returns or updates a thumbnail-size version of an image or video frame stored in a database.	Image and Video
`TicksPerQNote`	Returns the clock speed of a recorded MIDI audio, in ticks per quarter note.	Audio
`TicksPerSec`	Returns the clock speed of a recorded MIDI audio, in ticks per second.	Audio
`Updater`	Returns the user ID of the person who last updated an image, audio, or video in a database table.	All
`UpdateTime`	Returns a timestamp that indicates when an image, audio, or video in a database table was last updated.	All
`Width`	Returns the width in pixels of an image or video frame.	Image and Video

XML Extender maps XML documents to and from relational databases. This means that XML documents can be broken down into their elements and inserted into a relational database, or a new XML document can be generated from existing relational database tables. XML Extender also supports validating, storing, retrieving, and searching XML documents stored inside a DB2 database or on a local filesystem. It is currently available on Windows NT, AIX, Solaris, and Linux.

Similar to other products in the DB2 Extender family, XML Extender requires an instance to be created. The XML Extender instance is created with the `xmlicrt` command. XML Extender does not require a server process for the instance to be started. The database must be enabled to use XML Extender. Enabling a database creates the needed UDTs, UDFs, and administration tables. The database can be enabled using two different methods. It can be enabled using the `dxxadm` CLP or the `dxxadmin` Java administration tool. Here is the syntax for enabling an XML Extender database from the `dxxadm` CLP.

```
dxxadm ENABLE_DB database-name [-l userid -p password]
```

> **Note**
>
> The `dxxadmin` Java administration tool requires JDK 1.1.x and Swing 1.1.

10.5.1 Mapping XML to a Relational Database

XML documents can define their own markup language. The grammar for the markup language is defined using a Data Type Definition (DTD) file. There are three object types that can be included in an XML document: elements, attributes, and text. XML Extender provides a DTD for a special XML document called a Data Access Definition (DAD) file. DAD files are used to define how XML documents are mapped to and from a DB2 database. This is called node mapping.

DAD files can use two types of node mapping, SQL node mapping and Remote Database (RDB) node mapping. SQL node mapping provides mapping instructions in the form of an SQL statement. There are special XML Extender rules in the format of the SQL statement that must be followed. Refer to the *XML Extender Administration Guide* for details. SQL node mapping can only be used to compose or create new XML documents from existing data stored in DB2 tables. It cannot break down or decompose an XML document into its elements and insert it into database tables.

RDB node mapping supports both composition and decomposition of XML documents. RDB node mapping uses the Extensible Path (XPath) standard, to identify elements, attributes, and text contained inside an XML document. Each element, attribute, and text object is assigned to a column in a database table. XPath is also used to search XML documents that are not decomposed using XML Columns.

10.5.2 XML Columns

XML Columns are used to store XML documents inside a DB2 column without decomposition. UDFs are provided to perform common tasks. XML Columns support document validation, storage, retrieval, updating, and extraction. Documents are validated using a DTD file. Documents can be stored and retrieved in full or by specified elements and attributes using the XPath standard. Fast searches are available using side tables. Side tables duplicate frequently accessed elements and attributes into DB2 tables indexed with a primary key using RDB node mapping. The XML column must be defined with one of the following data types, depending on the size of the documents:

XMLVarchar—Stores small XML documents with the base type VARCHAR (3000).

XMLCLOB—Stores large XML documents with the base type CLOB(2G).

XMLFile—References an external XML document filename using the base type VARCHAR(512).

UDFs are available for storing, retrieving, updating, and extracting data from XML documents stored in XML Columns. Table 10-4 lists these UDFs.

In general, XML Columns are slower to update and extract values from an XML document than XML Collections. When an update on a single element or attribute is needed on an XML document stored in XML Columns, the entire document is replaced. This is not very efficient. Side tables improve the performance of selecting or extracting elements and attributes, but add extra overhead when inserting or importing XML documents. This is due to the extra cost of maintaining the indexed data stored in a separate table. If performance is a necessity, XML Collections may be more suitable.

Table 10-4 XML Columns UDFs

Function	Description
XMLVarcharFromFile	Import an XML document from a file to an XML VARCHAR.
XMLCLOBFromFile	Import an XML document from a file to an XML CLOB.
XMLFileFromVarchar	Import an XML document from a CLOB format to an XML file.
XMLFileFromCLOB	Import an XML document from a CLOB format into an XML file.
Content	Export an XML document from an XML VARCHAR, XML CLOB, or XML file.
Update	Replace XML document stored in XML Columns by only changing some element or attribute value.
extractInteger	Find an element or attribute within an XML document that only has a single value.
extractIntegers	Find an element or attribute within an XML document that has multiple values.

10.5.3 XML Collections

XML Collections are used for composing and decomposing XML documents to and from relational databases. Composition is useful when there is existing data stored in a relational database that needs to be translated into XML format. Decomposition is useful for improving update performance of frequently modified XML documents where only small parts of the document are updated.

To enable XML Collections, you must provide a DAD file to define the mapping. XML Collections support both SQL node mapping and RDB node mapping. XML Collections use DB2 stored procedures for generating, retrieving, shredding, and inserting XML documents. Table 10-5 lists these stored procedures.

Table 10-5 XML Collections Stored Procedures

Function	Description
db2xml.dxxGenXML	Generate XML documents dynamically by passing a DAD.
db2xml.dxxRetrieveXML	Compose XML documents from enabled XML Collections.
db2xml.dxxShredXML	Decompose XML documents dynamically by passing a DAD.
db2xml.dxxInsertXML	Decompose XML documents into enabled XML Collections.

10.6 Summary

The DB2 Extender family provides a wide assortment of SQL extensions to enhance the functionality of SQL statements. Each DB2 Extenders product provides its own set of User-Defined Types (UDTs), User-Defined Functions (UDFs), and stored procedures that can be used by applications. They also provide individual Command Line Processor (CLP) tools for setting up and maintaining the DB2 Extender products.

In this chapter, we introduced several DB2 Extender products, including Text Extender, Net Search Extender, AIV Extenders, and XML Extender. Text Extender and Net Search Extender enhance SQL text searches. Text Extender has more features, but is not optimized for high-volume Internet searches. AIV Extenders provide functions for displaying and playing video, image, and audio clips. It can also be used for searching for images by content and for video shot detection. XML Extender enables composition, decomposition, update, and retrieval of Extensible Markup Language (XML) documents.

Additional References

DB2 Text Extender Home Page:
  http://www.ibm.com/software/data/db2/extenders/

DB2 Net Search Extender Home Page:
  http://www.ibm.com/software/data/db2/extenders/netsearch/

Summary

DB2 Audio Extenders Home Page:
  http://www.ibm.com/software/data/db2/extenders/audio.htm

DB2 Image Extenders Home Page:
  http://www.ibm.com/software/data/db2/extenders/image.htm

DB2 Video Extenders Home Page:
  http://www.ibm.com/software/data/db2/extenders/video.htm

DB2 XML Extender Home Page:
  http://www.ibm.com/software/data/db2/extenders/xmlext/

APPENDIX A

DB2 UDB Application Development Test Objectives

The Certified Solutions Expert – DB2 UDB V7.1 in Application Development for UNIX, Windows, and OS/2 requires an in-depth knowledge of the difference between programming types (ODBC, CLI, etc.) and when to use them, the difference between embedded dynamic and static SQL, basic and intermediate SQL (Data Manipulation Language, or DML), concepts and usage of binding and prepping, isolation levels, basic database objects and data types (schema, naming conventions), transaction concepts (commit scope, states), and cursor concepts. Furthermore, the Solutions Expert in Application Development should have a basic knowledge of the concepts and features of general errors and diagnostics, advanced SQL (recursive, cube, rollup, Data Definition Language (DDL)), the Explain facility, locking, privileges and authorities, stored procedures, complex database objects (UDTs (User-Defined Types), UDFs (User-Defined Functions), triggers, atomic/nonatomic), database configuration, database management configuration, SQLDA, SQLCA, host variables, parameter markers, connection types, and transaction server.

Here is an in-depth listing of the test objectives for the DB2 UDB Application Development Certification Test:

I. Database Objects

    a. Knowledge of naming conventions of DB2 objects (aliases, views, etc.).
    b. Knowledge of the authorities needed to access data in an application.
    c. Knowledge of complex database objects (temporary tables, summary tables, triggers).

II. Data Manipulation

    a. Ability to query a database across multiple tables.
    b. Knowledge of changing data.
    c. Ability to use DB2 SQL functions.
    d. Ability to use common table expressions.
    e. Knowledge to identify when to use cursors in an SQL program.
    f. Knowledge to identify types of cursors.
    g. Knowledge to identify the scopes of cursors.
    h. Ability to manipulate cursors.
    i. Ability to manage a unit of work (transaction management).
    j. Knowledge of STAR schema table/index design.

III. DB2 Programming Methods

    a. Knowledge to identify the differences between dynamic and static embedded SQL.
    b. Skill in determining when to use CLI/ODBC.
    c. Skill in determining when to use JDBC, SQLj.
    d. Ability to determine when to use SQL routines.

IV. Embedded SQL Programming

    a. Knowledge of identifying steps and output involved in creating an embedded SQL programming application.
    b. Knowledge to identify when host variables are used (`BEGIN-DECLARE`).
    c. Skill in declaring host variables.
    d. Skill in utilizing host variables in queries.
    e. Ability to explain/analyze the content of the SQLCA.
    f. Knowledge of common errors, prep, and `BIND` database programs.
    g. Ability to connect to databases within an embedded SQL programming application.

V. ODBC/CLI Programming

a. Knowledge of different handle types.
b. Knowledge of configuring DB2 ODBC driver.
c. Knowledge of problem determination (diagnostic records).
d. Knowledge of the correct sequence for calling ODBC/CLI functions.
e. Knowledge of various CLI cursor types and when to use them.
f. Ability to connect to databases within an ODBC/CLI programming application.

VI. JAVA Programming

a. Knowledge of various JDBC objects.
b. Knowledge of the difference between SQLj and JDBC.
c. Knowledge of problem determination (JDBC trace, SQL exceptions, JDBC error log).
d. Skill in performing the steps to build SQLj applications.
e. Ability to connect to databases within a Java programming application.

VII. Advanced Programming

a. Utilize dynamic and static SQL within programs.
b. Skill in casting UDTs within a program.
c. Knowledge to identify usage of UDFs.
d. Knowledge to identify when to use stored procedures.
e. Knowledge to identify when to use compound SQL.
f. Knowledge of concurrency considerations within an application.
g. Skill in using Stored Procedure Builder (SPB).
h. Knowledge of programming languages using SPB.
i. Knowledge of Distributed Unit of Work (DUOW).
j. Knowledge of using parameter markers.

APPENDIX B

DB2 UDB Application Development Sample Exam

A sample DB2 UDB Application Development Certification Exam has been provided to assist in preparation. The sample questions have been taken from a pool of questions that were potential candidates for the actual exam. The exam sections are weighted by the anticipated requirements for a DB2 application developer. Sections with higher weight will contain more questions related to that topic. The sample exam can be used as an indicator of the number of questions to expect from each exam task and objective.

B.1 Questions

1. Given that the following message is returned during a precompile: `"QUALIFY.X" is an undefined name`. Which of the following is true for `QUALIFY.X`?

    a. It is defined as a database object.
    b. It is defined as an "undefined" name.
    c. It is not defined as a host variable in the program.
    d. It is not defined as a database object in the database.

2. Given a table created using the statement:

    `CREATE TABLE abc.stuff (i INT)`

    A user called `XYZ` is to be enabled to access data from table `abc.stuff` using an implicit schema. Assuming the necessary privileges have been granted, which of the following statements issued by user `ABC` will provide this result?

    a. `CREATE ALIAS xyz.stuff FOR abc.stuff`
    b. `CREATE VIEW abc.stuff FOR xyz.stuff`
    c. `CREATE ALIAS abc.stuff FOR xyz.stuff`
    d. `CREATE VIEW stuff AS SELECT i FROM abc.stuff`

3. The `FINANCE` application contains static SQL and issues the statements:

    ```
    SELECT name, id FROM prod.employee
    UPDATE prod.dept SET dept=dept+1
    INSERT INTO prod.dept VALUES(:id, :name)
    ```

    Assuming a user can connect to the database, but has no other privileges or authorities, which of the following privileges must be granted to the user so that application `FINANCE` can be run by a user?

        a. `EXECUTE` privilege on `FINANCE`.
        b. `RUN` privilege on tables `employee` and `dept`.
        c. `EXECUTE` privilege on tables `employee` and `dept`.
        d. `CONTROL` privilege on tables `employee` and `dept`.

4. Which of the following privileges is required to successfully execute a DB2 Call Level Interface (CLI) application?

        a. The user must have `EXECUTE` privilege on the application.
        b. The developer must have `EXECUTE` privilege on the application.
        c. The user must have sufficient privileges on referenced tables.
        d. The developer must have sufficient privileges on referenced tables.

5. Assume that the following SQL statements have been successfully issued:

    ```
    CONNECT TO db1 USER user1 USING pw1
    DECLARE GLOBAL TEMPORARY TABLE temp1 (val INTEGER)
    ```

    Which of the following statements will successfully insert a row into the temporary table `temp1`?

        a. `INSERT INTO db1.temp1 VALUES (100)`
        b. `INSERT INTO user1.temp1 VALUES (100)`
        c. `INSERT INTO session.temp1 VALUES (100)`
        d. `INSERT INTO temporary.temp1 VALUES (100)`

Questions   249

6. Given the tables:

```
    employee                              dept
    emp_num    emp_name    dept           dept_id    dept_name
    1          Adams       1              1          Planning
    2          Jones       1              2          Support
    3          Smith       2
    4          Williams    1
```

and the statement:

```
ALTER TABLE employee
  ADD FOREIGN KEY (dept) REFERENCES dept (dept_id)
  ON DELETE CASCADE
```

How many rows will be deleted with the following statement?

```
EXEC SQL DELETE FROM dept WHERE dept_id=1
```

a. 0
b. 1
c. 2
d. 3
e. 4
f. 6

7. Given the tables:

```
    country                                        staff
    id    name       person    cities              id    name
    1     Argentina  1         10                  1     Aaron
    2     Canada     2         20                  2     Adams
    3     Cuba       2         10
    4     Germany    1         0
    5     France     7         5
```

and the code:

```
EXEC SQL DECLARE CURSOR C1 FOR
    SELECT b.name, cities
      country a, staff b
    WHERE a.person=b.id
    ORDER BY 1,2;
EXEC SQL OPEN C1;
EXEC SQL FETCH C1 INTO :name1:n_ni, :city1:c_ni;
EXEC SQL FETCH C1 INTO :name1:n_ni, :city1:c_ni;
EXEC SQL FETCH C1 INTO :name1:n_ni, :city1:c_ni;
```

Which of the following is the value of :city1 after the third FETCH?

    a. 0
    b. 1
    c. 2
    d. 10
    e. 20

8. Given the tables:

```
price                                    sale
item   description   cost   code         sale_id   salefactor
1      camera        10     2            1         2
2      watch         5      1            2         3
3      shirt         20     1
```

and the SQL statement:

```
SELECT a.cost, (a.cost * b.salefactor) AS saleprice
  FROM sale b, price a
  WHERE a.code=b.sale_id
    ORDER BY a.cost
```

Which of the following is the value of saleprice in the second row of the result set returned by the above query?

    a. 10
    b. 15
    c. 20
    d. 30
    e. 40

9. Given the tables:

```
org                                staff
id   name          person          id   name
1    Programming   1               1    Aaron
2    Testing       2               2    Adams
2    Testing       3               3    Jones
```

and the code:

```
stmt="DELETE FROM staff WHERE name='Adams' ";
EXEC SQL EXECUTE IMMEDIATE :stmt;
```

If a referential integrity constraint with the SET NULL option exists between person in org and id in staff, how many rows will be deleted?

    a. 0
    b. 1
    c. 2
    d. 3

10. Which of the following CLI/ODBC functions will return the number of rows affected by an INSERT, UPDATE, or a DELETE statement?

    a. SQLNumRows()
    b. SQLRowCount()
    c. SQLNumParams()
    d. SQLUpdateCount()
    e. SQLNumResultCols()

11. Given the following code from an SQLj source file:

```
Connection con = DriverManager.getConnection(url);
DefaultContext ctx = new DefaultContext(con);
DefaultContext.setDefaultContext(ctx);
```

An UPDATE statement is issued using the ctx context. Which of the following SQLj methods must be used to obtain the number of rows modified by the UPDATE statement?

    a. ctx.rowsUpdated()
    b. ctx.SQLRowCount()
    c. ctx.getUpdateCount()
    d. con.getUpdateCo2unt()

12. In order to bind application variables to an SQL statement or data in the result set, which two of the following CLI/ODBC functions are used?

    a. SQLFetch()
    b. SQLBindCol()
    c. SQLGetData()
    d. SQLBindResult()
    e. SQLBindParameter()

13. Which of the following function types can only be specified in the FROM clause of a SELECT statement?

    a. TABLE function.
    b. COLUMN function.
    c. SCALAR function.
    d. SELECT function.

14. Which of the following is similar to a common table expression?

    a. A temporary view.
    b. A correlated query.
    c. A qualified predicate.
    d. An UPDATE statement.

15. Given the following statement:

    DECLARE cursor1 CURSOR FOR
    SELECT firstname, lastname, street, city FROM citytable

    Which of the following SQL statements will retrieve a row using the defined cursor?

    a. FETCH cursor1 INTO :hvfirst :hvlast :hvstreet :hvcity
    b. SELECT cursor1 INTO :hvfirst :hvlast :hvstreet :hvcity
    c. FETCH cursor1 INTO :hvfirst, :hvlast, :hvstreet, :hvcity
    d. SELECT cursor1 INTO :hvfirst, :hvlast, :hvstreet, :hvcity

16. Given the code:

    EXEC SQL UPDATE t1 SET column1 = :col WHERE CURRENT OF C1;

    Which of the following indicates how the cursor C1 has been defined?

    a. As a normal cursor.
    b. As a WITH HOLD cursor.
    c. As a FETCH ONLY cursor.
    d. As an updateable cursor.

17. Which of the following defines when a cursor is considered a deleteable cursor?

    a. When the DECLARE CURSOR includes a FOR FETCH ONLY clause.
    b. When the DECLARE CURSOR SELECT statement includes an ORDER BY.
    c. When the DECLARE CURSOR SELECT statement includes a HAVING clause.
    d. When the DECLARE CURSOR SELECT statement references one base table.

18. Given the pseudocode:

    ```
    DECLARE CURSOR C1
    DECLARE CURSOR C2
    OPEN C1
    FETCH C1
    OPEN C2
    COMMIT
    FETCH C2
    ```

    Which of the following changes will ensure that FETCH C2 is successful?

    a. BLOCKING ALL during bind.
    b. WITH HOLD on COMMIT statement.
    c. WITH HOLD on DECLARE CURSOR C2.
    d. WITH HOLD on OPEN C2 statement.

19. Which of the following is a characteristic of all cursors in embedded SQL?

    a. Cannot span units of work.
    b. Can be reserved in the database.
    c. Must be unique within a source module.
    d. Must be unique for all applications against a database.

20. A cursor called c2 must be created to fetch rows from table t2, and update column c1 in table t2 for every row fetched. Which of the following cursor definitions will create this type of cursor?

    a. DECLARE c2 CURSOR WITH HOLD FOR SELECT * FROM t2;
    b. DECLARE c2 CURSOR FOR SELECT * FROM t2 FOR UPDATE OF t2;
    c. DECLARE c2 CURSOR FOR SELECT * FROM t2 FOR UPDATE OF c2;
    d. DECLARE c2 CURSOR FOR SELECT * FROM c1 FOR UPDATE OF c1;
    e. DECLARE c2 CURSOR FOR SELECT * FROM t2 FOR UPDATE OF c1;

21. Given a cursor c1 on table t1, for every row fetched from t1, open a cursor c2 on table t2. For every row fetched from t2, update column c1 in table t2 and issue a COMMIT. Which of the following must define cursor c1?

    a. DECLARE c1 CURSOR FOR SELECT * FROM t1;
    b. DECLARE c1 CURSOR WITH HOLD FOR SELECT * FROM t1;
    c. DECLARE c1 CURSOR FOR SELECT * FROM t1 FOR UPDATE OF t2;
    d. DECLARE c1 CURSOR FOR SELECT * FROM t1 FOR UPDATE OF c1;

22. Given a table that has columns defined as follows:

    ```
    SMALLINT_COLUMN SMALLINT NOT NULL
    VARCHAR_COLUMN VARCHAR(20)
    ```

    Which of the following statements is used to retrieve rows from the table if the second column can contain NULL values?

    a. `FETCH * INTO :hv1, :hv2;`
    b. `FETCH CURSOR1 INTO :hv1, :hv2;`
    c. `FETCH * INTO :hv1, :hv2:hv2ind;`
    d. `FETCH CURSOR1 INTO :hv1, :hv2:hv2ind;`

23. Which two of the following are required for the DB2 Optimizer to consider a STAR join?

    a. At least four tables must be joined.
    b. More than one table can be considered to be a fact table.
    c. The fact and dimension tables must contain the same columns.
    d. An (single-column) index on each join column of the fact table.
    e. The fact table must be joined to at least three dimension tables.

24. Which of the following DB2 application development methods/environments must NOT be used when enabling end-users to choose which tables to select data from at application runtime?

    a. CLI.
    b. ODBC.
    c. Net.Data.
    d. Embedded static SQL.
    e. Embedded dynamic SQL.

25. During which of the following are SQL statements optimized when using DB2 CLI?

    a. Precompile.
    b. Bind processing.
    c. Statement preparation.
    d. The closing of each cursor.

26. To access a DB2 database from a workstation that does not have any DB2 code installed, which of the following must be used?

    a. Triggers.
    b. Constraints.
    c. Java applet.
    d. Java stored procedure.

27. Which of the following programming methods does NOT lend itself to accessing DB2 data over the Internet using Web browser-based clients?

    a. Net.Data.
    b. SQLj applets.
    c. JDBC applets.
    d. SQLj applications.

28. Which of the following statements allows an SQL routine to be created?

    a. CREATE VIEW
    b. CREATE ROUTINE
    c. CREATE TRIGGER
    d. CREATE PROCEDURE

29. In order to process an embedded SQL (non-REXX) program, which of the following database components is required?

    a. Binder.
    b. Precompiler.
    c. Control Center.
    d. Visual Explain.

30. Which of the following static SQL statements can contain a host variable?

    a. FETCH
    b. ROLLBACK
    c. DROP INDEX
    d. ALTER TABLE

31. Which of the following SQL statements requires a host variable within the statement?

    a. DELETE
    b. DECLARE
    c. INSERT INTO
    d. SELECT INTO

32. Which of the following data types must be used for a host variable that will be used to retrieve a TIMESTAMP from the database?

    a. A decimal.
    b. An integer numeric.
    c. A character string.
    d. A float (scientific notation).

33. Given the following:
    ```
    EXEC SQL BEGIN DECLARE SECTION;
        char hv_name[20];
    EXEC SQL END DECLARE SECTION;
    ```
    Which of the following examples correctly demonstrates the use of the host variable within an SQL statement?

    a. EXEC SQL name_column INTO :hv<name
    b. EXEC SQL SELECT name_column INTO :hv_name
    c. EXEC SQL SELECT name_column INTO ^:hv_name
    d. EXEC SQL SELECT name_column INTO *:hv_name

34. Which of the following SQLCA elements contains the number of rows affected by the SQL statement?

    a. sqlcabc
    b. sqlcode
    c. sqlerrp
    d. sqlerrd
    e. sqlstate
    f. sqlerrml

Questions 257

35. A package was created by DB2ADMIN and the bind file or DBRM contains only dynamic SQL statements. Also, the package to be created already exists. Which of the following privileges does the user DB2USER require to perform the BIND command on this package?

    a. BINDADD.
    b. DB2ADMIN.
    c. ALTERIN on schema DB2USER.
    d. CREATEIN on schema DB2ADMIN.
    e. IMPLICIT_SCHEMA on schema DB2ADMIN.

36. Which of the following is required when using the REBIND command?

    a. The database.
    b. The bind file.
    c. The application source.
    d. The application executable.

37. Given the following embedded SQL pseudocode:

    ```
    Start Program
      EXEC SQL BEGIN DECLARE SECTION
        USERA       CHARACTER (8)
        USERB       CHARACTER (8)
        PW          CHARACTER (8)
        COLVAL      CHARACTER (16)
      EXEC SQL END DECLARE SECTION

      EXEC SQL INCLUDE SQLCA
      EXEC SQL WHENEVER SQLERROR GOTO ERRCHK

      (program logic)
      (:usera contains the string "usera")
      (:pwa contains a valid password)
      (:userb now contains the string "userb")
      (:pwb contains a valid password)

      EXEC SQL CONNECT TO samplea USER :usera USING :pwa
      EXEC SQL SELECT col1, col2 FROM tablea

      (program logic to retrieve results)

      EXEC SQL COMMIT

      (more program logic)
    ```

```
        EXEC SQL CONNECT TO sampleb USER :userb USING :pwb
        EXEC SQL SELECT col1, col2 FROM tablex
        EXEC SQL DELETE FROM tablea WHERE col1= :colval   //1st
    delete
        EXEC SQL COMMIT

        (more program logic)

        EXEC SQL CONNECT TO samplea
        EXEC SQL DELETE from tablea where col1= :colval   //2nd
    delete
        EXEC SQL COMMIT
        EXEC SQL CONNECT RESET
        ERRCHK

        (check error information in SQLCA)
        (Cleanup)

End Program
```

Which of the following tables will be updated in "samplea" if the second DELETE completes sucessfully?

    a. usera.tablex
    b. userb.tablea
    c. usera.tablea
    d. userb.tablex

38. Which of the following limits the number of concurrent CLI statement handles that can be in use on a given connection?

    a. Unlimited.
    b. Limited to 10 statements.
    c. The number of concurrent connections.
    d. The number of sections in the CLI packages.

39. Which of the following describes where a DSN (Data Source Name) can be registered prior to its use in connecting from a CLI/ODBC application?

    a. In the DCS directory.
    b. In the node directory.
    c. With the DB2 CLI/ODBC driver.
    d. With the ODBC Driver Manager.

Questions

40. For which of the following handle types would you call SQLERROR after SQLExecDirect returns an SQLERROR.

    a. Exception.
    b. Statement.
    c. Connection.
    d. Descriptor.
    e. Environment.

41. Which of the following ODBC/CLI functions must be called before SQLExecDirect() can be successfully executed if the SQL statement contains parameter markers?

    a. SQLColumns()
    b. SQLParamData()
    c. SQLBindParameter()
    d. SQLExtendedPrepare()

42. Given the following table and SQL statement:

    ```
    tablea
    column1
    -------
    R1
    R2
    R3
    R4
    R5
    R6

    SELECT * FROM tablea ORDER BY column1
    ```

    Using a keyset-driven cursor with a rowset size of 3, which of the following rows are returned when the following CLI APIs are issued in the order below:

    ```
    SQLFetchScroll() with the SQL_FETCH_FIRST option
    SQLFetchScroll() with the SQL_FETCH_RELATIVE option,
    offset=1
    SQLFetchScroll() with the SQL_FETCH_ABSOLUTE option,
    offset=3
    ```

    a. R1,R2,R3,R2,R3,R4.
    b. R1,R2,R3,R4,R5,R6.
    c. R1,R2,R3,R2,R3,R4,R3,R4,R5.
    d. R1,R2,R3,R4,R5,R6,R3,R4,R5.

43. Which SQLDriverConnect DriverCompletion option will result in the return code SQL_ERROR if a required field is not supplied in the connection string?

   a. SQL_DRIVER_PROMPT
   b. SQL_DRIVER_NOPROMPT
   c. SQL_DRIVER_COMPLETE
   d. SQL_DRIVER_COMPLETE_REQUIRED

44. Which of the following JDBC objects are queried to determine the indexes defined on a given table?

   a. ResultSet
   b. Statement
   c. Connection
   d. DatabaseMetaData
   e. CallableStatement

45. Which of the following JDBC objects must be queried to determine the SQLSTATE in the event an SQL operation fails?

   a. ResultSet
   b. Statement
   c. Exception
   d. Connection
   e. SQLException

46. Which of the following is a required parameter for running db2profc?

   a. userid
   b. password
   c. prepoptions
   d. profile name

47. Which of the following can be used to specify a userid and password when connecting to a remote database called sample from an SQLj application?

   a. #sql con={CONNECT TO SAMPLE :userid :password}
   b. getConnection("jdbc:db2:sample",userid,password)
   c. getConnection("jdbc:db2:sample/userid:password")
   d. #sql con={CONNECT TO SAMPLE USER :userid USING :password}

48. Which of the following code fragments correctly performs a static SELECT statement of the integer column c1 from table t1? (Assume that the host variable hv has the proper type.)

    a. EXEC SQL SELECT c1 FROM t1 USING cur
       EXEC SQL FETCH cur INTO :hv
       EXEC SQL CLOSE cur

    b. EXEC SQL OPEN cur FOR SELECT c1 FROM t1
       EXEC SQL FETCH cur INTO :hv
       EXEC SQL CLOSE cur

    c. EXEC SQL DECLARE cur CURSOR FOR SELECT c1 FROM t1
       EXEC SQL OPEN cur
       EXEC SQL FETCH cur INTO :hv
       EXEC SQL CLOSE cur

    d. EXEC SQL PREPARE stmt FOR SELECT c1 FROM t1
       EXEC SQL DECLARE cur CURSOR FOR stmt
       EXEC SQL OPEN cur
       EXEC SQL FETCH cur INTO :hv
       EXEC SQL CLOSE cur

49. Which of the following statements uses dynamic SQL?

    a. EXEC SQL DECLARE c1 CURSOR FOR s1
    b. EXEC SQL UPDATE c1 SET name = :name
    c. EXEC SQL SELECT name INTO :name FROM t1
    d. EXEC SQL DECLARE c1 CURSOR FOR SELECT name FROM t1

50. Which of the following is used to convert between a user-defined distinct type and its source type?

    a. CAST function.
    b. COALESCE function.
    c. Built-in SQL function.
    d. User-Defined Function (UDF).

51. Which of the following is NOT a type of UDF?

    a. Table.
    b. Column.
    c. Scalar.
    d. Summary.

52. An application needs to retrieve a large number of rows from a database across the network and compute a single value from the retrieved data. Which of the following methods will reduce the network traffic?

   a. Stored procedure.
   b. Table constraints.
   c. User-Defined Types (UDTs).
   d. Combine all rows into a LOB.

53. Given the code:

    ```
    BEGIN COMPOUND NOT ATOMIC STATIC
      UPDATE country SET cities = :count WHERE CURRENT OF C1;
      INSERT INTO country VALUES (:col1, :col2, :col3);
      INSERT INTO country VALUES (:col4, :col5, :col6);
      INSERT INTO country VALUES (:col7, :col8, :col9);
      INSERT INTO country VALUES (:col10, :col11, :col12);
      COMMIT;
    END COMPOUND
    ```

   If the fifth SQL statement in the block fails, how many rows will be affected in table country?

   a. 0
   b. 1
   c. 2
   d. 3
   e. 4
   f. 5

54. Which of the following indicates when a table CANNOT be locked explicitly?

   a. When using DDL (Data Definition Language).
   b. If it is a catalog table.
   c. If it is from a specific application.
   d. If other users must have access to the table.

55. Application A is bound using Cursor Stability, updates row X, and does NOT issue a COMMIT. Application B reads row X. Which of the following isolation levels must application B be using?

   a. Read Stability.
   b. Repeatable Read.
   c. Cursor Stability.
   d. Uncommitted Read.

Questions

56. Which of the following is NOT available in a Distributed Unit of Work (DUOW)?

    a. IMPORT
    b. UPDATE
    c. INSERT
    d. DELETE
    e. COMMIT

57. Which of the following demonstrates a correct usage of parameter markers?

    a. CALL outsrv(?, ?)
    b. SELECT col1, col2 FROM tab1 WHERE tab1.? = 15
    c. SELECT count(*) FROM foo.tab1 WHERE col1 = '?'
    d. SELECT firstnme FROM employee WHERE lastnme = :?

ANSWERS

1. D	20. E	39. D
2. A	21. B	40. B
3. A	22. D	41. C
4. C	23. D	42. D
5. C	24. D	43. B
6. E	25. C	44. D
7. D	26. C	45. E
8. D	27. D	46. D
9. B	28. D	47. B
10. B	29. B	48. C
11. C	30. A	49. A
12. B and E	31. D	50. A
13. A	32. C	51. D
14. A	33. B	52. A
15. C	34. D	53. E
16. D	35. C	54. B
17. D	36. A	55. D
18. C	37. C	56. A
19. C	38. D	57. A

APPENDIX C

DB2MALL Database

To illustrate the examples and samples in this book, we have created a simple database called DB2MALL.

The plot behind the DB2MALL database is the following:

Consider an actual mall with several stores in it. All the stores are defined in the STORE table. Each store sells products. All the products carried by all the stores are defined in the PRODUCT table. This table has a column called STORE_ID, which associates which store carries which product. Customers, who are saved in a table called CUSTOMER, buy these products. Every time a customer places an order, an entry is inserted into the CUSTOMER_ORDER table. This table holds the general information of the order. Also, an entry is inserted into the CUSTOMER_ORDER_ITEM table, which holds all the items the customer purchased with that specific order. When a store is running out of a certain product, the store places an order with its supplier to receive more of that product. These orders are kept in the STORE_PURCHASE table, and the stores' suppliers are saved in the SUPPLIER table.

Following is a list of all of the tables and columns that can be found in the DB2MALL database.

CREATING THE DB2MALL DATABASE

You can create this database by using the setup program found on the accompanying CD-ROM. The readme file and setup program can be found in the /db2mall subdirectory.

Table C-1   DB2MALL Tables

Table Name	Explanation
PRODUCT	Products that our stores sell.
STORE	Stores within our mall.
CUSTOMER	A repository of all customers who have or are purchasing the mall's products.
CUSTOMER_ORDER_ITEM	A listing of individual items that a customer has ordered.
CUSTOMER_ORDER	Contains the order form for a customer.
SUPPLIER	A listing of suppliers for the products within the mall.
STORE_PURCHASE	To track orders made with the mall's suppliers.
DELIVERY_METHOD	The available delivery methods via which a product is sent to a customer.
PAYMENT_METHOD	The available methods of payment.
ORDER_STATUS	The current status of an order, e.g., "on hold," "complete," "open," etc.
PRODUCT_STATUS	The current status of a product, e.g., "active," "discontinued," etc.

Table C-2   PRODUCT Table

Column Name	Key	Data Type	Explanation
PRODUCT_ID	Primary	INT	Identity column producing a unique ID.
PRODUCT_NAME		VARCHAR(20)	Name of the product.
STORE_ID	Foreign - STORE	SMALLINT	Identifies the store that sells this product.
UNIT_COST		DECIMAL(7,2)	The cost to restock a single unit.
UNIT_PRICE		DECIMAL(7,2)	The MSRP for a single unit.
SALE_PRICE		DECIMAL(7,2)	A temporary sale price.
SUPPLIER_ID	Foreign - SUPPLIER	VARCHAR(10)	Identifies the supplier for this product.
UNITS_IN_STOCK		INT	The number of units on hand.
UNITS_ON_ORDER		INT	The number of units on back order.
STATUS	Foreign - PRODUCT_STATUS	CHAR(1)	Status of the order.
PICTURE		BLOB(102400)	A photograph of the product.

Table C-3 STORE Table

Column Name	Key	Data Type	Explanation
STORE_ID	Primary	SMALLINT	Identity column producing a unique ID.
STORE_NAME		VARCHAR(20)	The name of the store within the mall.

Table C-4 CUSTOMER table

Column Name	Key	Data Type	Explanation
CUSTOMER_ID	Primary	SMALLINT	Identity column producing a unique ID.
CUSTOMER_NAME		VARCHAR(30)	Customer name.
CUSTOMER_PHONE		VARCHAR(12)	Phone number.
ADDR_STREET		VARCHAR(50)	Street address.
ADDR_CITY		VARCHAR(15)	City.
ADDR_STATE		VARCHAR(2)	State or province abbreviation.
ADDR_ZIP		VARCHAR(7)	Zip code or postal code.
ADDR_COUNTRY		VARCHAR(15)	Country.
DATE_ENTERED		DATE	Defaults with current date.

Table C-5 CUSTOMER_ORDER_ITEM Table

Column Name	Key	Data Type	Explanation
ORDER_ID	Foreign - CUSTOMER_ORDER	INT	Cross-references an order made by a customer in the CUSTOMER_ORDER table.
PRODUCT_ID	Foreign - PRODUCT	INT	Cross-references a product from the PRODUCT table.
QUANTIY		SMALLINT	Quantity ordered.
SALE_PRICE		DECIMAL(7,2)	Price of item to the customer.
UNIT_PRICE		DECIMAL(7,2)	Cost of item to the store.
SHIP_METHOD	Foreign - DELIVERY_METHOD	SMALLINT	Cross-references a shipping method from the DELIVERY_METHOD table.
SHIP_CHARGE		DECIMAL(7,2)	The additional charge for shipping.

Table C-6 CUSTOMER_ORDER Table

Column Name	Key	Data Type	Explanation
ORDER_ID	Primary	INT	Identity column producing a unique ID.
CUSTOMER_ID	Foreign - CUSTOMER	INT	Identifies the customer making the order.
ORDER_DATE		DATE	Date that the order was placed.
CREDIT_CARD_TYPE		CHAR(2)	Type of credit card.
CREDIT_CARD_NUMBER		VARCHAR(20)	Credit card number.
CREDIT_CARD_NAME		VARCHAR(10)	Name on credit card.
CC_EXPIRATION_DATE		DATE	Expiration date of credit card.
ORDER_STATUS	Foreign - ORDER_STATUS	CHAR(1)	Whether the order is still pending, filled or cancelled.

Table C-7 SUPPLIER Table

Column Name	Key	Data Type	Explanation
SUPPLIER_ID	Primary	INT	Identity column producing a unique ID.
SUPPLIER_NAME		VARCHAR(30)	The name of the supplier.
SUPPLIER_PHONE		VARCHAR(30)	Phone number.
ADDR_STREET		VARCHAR(50)	Street address.
ADDR_CITY		VARCHAR(20)	City.
ADDR_STATE		VARCHAR(2)	State or province.
ADDR_COUNTRY		VARCHAR(15)	Country.

Table C-8 STORE_PURCHASE Table

Column Name	Key	Data Type	Explanation
ORDER_ID	Primary	INT	Identity column producing a unique ID.
PRODUCT_ID	Foreign - PRODUCT	INT	Cross-references the PRODUCT table for the product on order.
SUPPLIER_ID	Foreign - SUPPLIER	INT	Cross-references the SUPPLIER table for the supplier selling the store the product.
ORDER_DATE		DATE	Date order was made.

Table C-8 STORE_PURCHASE Table (Continued)

Column Name	Key	Data Type	Explanation
QUANTITY		INT	Number of units ordered.
UNIT_COST		DECIMAL(7,2)	Cost of the units on a per unit basis.
STATUS	Foreign ORDER_STATUS	CHAR(1)	Status of the order.

Table C-9 DELIVERY_METHOD Table

Column Name	Key	Data Type	Explanation
DELIVERY_ID	Primary	SMALLINT	Identity column producing a unique ID.
DELIVERY_CHARGE		DECIMAL(7,2)	Cost of delivery method.
DELIVERY_DESCRIPTION		VARCHAR(20)	A brief description of the delivery method, i.e., same day, next day, one week, etc.

Table C-10 PAYMENT_METHOD Table

Column Name	Key	Data Type	Explanation
PAYMENT_METHOD	Primary	SMALLINT	Identity column producing a unique ID.
DESCRIPTION		VARCHAR(20)	A description of this method of payment.

Table C-11 ORDER_STATUS Table

Column Name	Key	Data Type	Explanation
ORDER_STATUS	Primary	CHAR(1)	Identity column producing a unique ID.
DESCRIPTION		VARCHAR(20)	A description of this order status.

Table C-12 PRODUCT_STATUS Table

Column Name	Key	Data Type	Explanation
ORDER_STATUS	Primary	CHAR(1)	Identity column producing a unique ID.
DESCRIPTION		VARCHAR(20)	A description of this order status.

APPENDIX D

Application Troubleshooting

Troubleshooting database applications is our specialty as DB2 service analysts. Problems can occur either because of errors in the application that require debugging, or because there may be a defect in the DB2 code. DB2 releases official fixpacks on a quarterly basis to provide code fixes throughout the product life cycle. In addition, there are interim fixpacks that are released between official fixpacks. Interim fixpacks are not tested as thoroughly, so we only recommend installing them if you have a need for a particular fix that cannot wait until the next official fixpack. All fixpacks are cumulative, meaning that previous fixes are included in the fixpack you are installing.

The FTP site for obtaining both types of fixpacks was listed in the Preface. If you explore this site, you will see that each fixpack directory also has a file called `aparlist.txt`. This file contains a listing of all of the fixes contained in the fixpack. Each fix is referenced with an identifier known as an APAR. You can search for APARs in the DB2 Technical Library, whose site address is also listed in the Preface.

We recommend searching for fixed problems by searching for keywords in the `aparlist.txt` file and using the DB2 Technical Library. You can also call us at DB2 Technical Support if you suspect that a problem is due to a defect. Instructions for applying every fixpack are included in a `readme.txt` file. It is important to note that a fixpack is applicable to problems in the DB2 client runtime code as well as the DB2 server engine, or other components such as GUI tools. For this reason, we suggest regular maintenance on both server and client installations.

The remainder of this chapter will focus on how to do your own troubleshooting, and determine if a problem is likely occurring due to an error in the application, a setup problem, or a defect in DB2.

D.1 Obtaining an SQL Error

If a problem is occurring inside DB2 code, you will generally receive an SQL error or SQL warning when you perform an operation through a DB2 programming interface. SQL errors and warnings have two types of return codes. There is an SQLCODE that is returned, which is a DB2-specific code, with DB2-specific details about the nature of the problem. There is also an industry-standard SQLSTATE, which gives a more general description of the error. We recommend always collecting the SQLCODE for an error. You can then use the *Messages Reference* online book or the CLP (Command Line Processor) to find out details about the error and corrective action. For example, let's say our application is receiving an SQLCODE SQL1032. We can find out what this error means using the following command from the CLP:

```
? SQL1032
```

The description returned advises us that the DB2 server is not active, and that the database manager must be started. We can then take corrective action by restarting the DB2 server with the `db2start` command and determining if someone stopped the server, or if the DB2 server instance crashed.

The DB2 CLI driver also has error codes that may be returned, which can be looked up in the *Messages Reference* online book. Sometimes more serious errors can occur, such as access violations (Windows) or segmentation faults (UNIX). These types of errors should be investigated by the DB2 Service if the fault occurs within a DB2 library.

D.2 Isolating Error Location

It is important to determine where an error is occurring. An error may occur within DB2 client libraries, or it may be returned by a DB2 server instance to the client. As we have discussed in this book, many programming interfaces use the DB2 CLI driver as a common client interface. If the error is returned by the CLI driver, then you can get a better idea about why by taking a DB2 CLI trace. This is described in the tracing section of this appendix.

From the CLI trace, you can determine if the problem occurred because the application used the CLI driver incorrectly. For example, were all of the parameters in a function call correctly specified? Was a step missed? These are steps you should ask yourself when looking at a CLI trace.

If there was an error in how CLI was used by the application (including by any programming interfaces that in turn use CLI), then the error may be occurring at a higher level. Otherwise, the error is occurring within the CLI driver, and the next step is to take a DB2 trace and call the DB2 Service to investigate this issue further.

D.3 Diagnostic Error Files

DB2 records warnings and errors as a normal part of its operation. By default, error logs are placed in the `sqllib\<instance-name>` directory on Windows and OS/2, and in the `<instance-owner>/sqllib/db2dump` directory on UNIX. You can modify the location where errors are logged by setting the `DIAGPATH` variable in the database manager configuration.

D.3.1   db2diag.log

This is the primary diagnostic log for DB2 UDB and should be the first point of reference for the DBA whenever unexpected errors occur. The `DIAGPATH` parameter can be used to alter the location that this file is written to. The default location is `sqllib/db2dump` for UNIX platforms and `sqllib/db2` for Windows platforms. The `DIAGLEVEL` parameter controls exactly how much information is logged in the file.

The `DIAGPATH` parameter is a database manager configuration parameter, so you could change it in the Control Center by right-clicking on the appropriate instance and clicking *Configure*. You could also use the CLP or Command Center:

```
UPDATE DBM CFG USING DIAGPATH <valid pathname for a file>
```

The level of diagnostic information, `DIAGLEVEL`, is also a database manager configuration parameter. The `DIAGLEVEL` parameter can be set to the following values:

0 – No diagnostic data (not recommended).

1 – Severe errors only.

2 – All errors (severe and not severe).

3 – All errors and warnings (default).

4 – All errors, warnings, informational messages, and other internal diagnostic information.

The default `DIAGLEVEL` is usually sufficient for normal DB2 UDB operations. However, during the initial setup of DB2, or when errors are occurring, the `DIAGLEVEL` could be updated to gather as much information as possible:

```
UPDATE DBM CFG USING DIAGLEVEL 4
```

The `db2diag.log` file is used mostly by DBAs, but application programmers may need to look at this log as well, particularly if they are having troubles with their User-Defined Functions (UDFs) or stored procedures. For example, there could be information in here concerning failed DARI (FENCED stored procedures) processes.

D.3.2   db2alert.log

If an error is determined by DB2 to be an alert, then an entry is made in the `db2alert.log` file and to the operating system logs. An alert is an error notification when a *severe* error occurs. Alerts can also trigger SNMP traps.

D.3.3 Dump Files

Sometimes, when a DB2 process or thread fails and signals an error, it will also log extra information in external binary dump files. These files are more or less unreadable and are intended for DB2 Customer Service personnel.

D.3.4 Trap Files

DB2 creates a trap file if an operating system trap/segmentation violation/exception occurs.

D.3.5 jdbcerr.log

A DB2 Java Daemon process will log its errors in this file, located in your `DIAGPATH`, or in the default error-logging directory. This file will indicate successful or failed attempts for the startup of the JDBC net driver. Within this file you can find the keyword, `EINFO=` to some numeric value; unfortunately, many of the error codes that may show up for `EINFO` are not documented. Some of the error codes logged here may actually be TCP/IP protocol errors. Another error code logged here, for example, is error code '2,' which probably indicates that `DB2PATH` is set incorrectly. For the most part, this file is only useful to the DB2 Service.

D.4 Tracing Facilities

DB2 has several tracing facilities that can be used during problem determination. We discuss each of them here.

D.4.1 DB2 Trace (db2trc)

A DB2 trace is a detailed trace about most function calls in the DB2 libraries. It is generally only useful to the DB2 Service since it references specific trace points within the DB2 source code. Running the trace will generally slow down performance because additional code is executed. To reduce performance loss, the trace is written to shared memory by default, which can then be dumped to a file after the trace is completed. The problem with this is that the size of the shared memory buffer must be specified when enabling the trace, so if the trace contents exceed the size of the memory buffer, the buffer contents wrap and information is lost. There is an option to trace directly to file, but this can be painfully slow and is not generally recommended.

Tracing against DB2 UDB can be started with the **db2trc** command. The following is the suggested sequence for tracing:

`db2trc on -l 8000000`	This command is run from the command line and starts the tracing facility. The '-l 8000000' option specifies the use of an 8M buffer of memory, and that the last 8M of traces should be kept in the event that tracing wraps. '-i' can be used instead to specify that the initial 8M of tracing be kept. Type 'db2trc ?' for a complete list of options.

Tracing Facilities   275

`Reproduce the problem`	Since tracing usually occurs within a limited buffer space, you want to try to keep the reproduction of the problem as small as possible so that the buffer does not wrap. Also, be aware that `db2trc` traces all DB2 activity for the instance that started it. So if you are tracing a server, try to keep unnecessary activity against the database to a minimum.
`db2trc dmp <db2trc.dmp>`	Once the error has been reproduced, the buffer can be dumped to a file.
`db2trc off`	This turns the tracing facility off and frees the memory buffer that was used.
`db2trc fmt <db2trc.dmp> <db2trc.fmt>`	The dump file is a binary file. To read it we need to format it. This will create a text-viewable file that lists function calls made through DB2 in chronological order. It will also show pieces of data that are passed through various functions, including the SQLCA.
`db2trc flw <db2trc.dmp> db2trc.flw`	This is another text-viewable file that flows the function calls by process and thread. This file will only show return values from each function.

For more information on tracing in DB2, refer to the *DB2 Troubleshooting Guide*.

D.4.2 CLI Trace

To trace a CLI application, all that is required is that you switch tracing on and specify a file for the trace output. Since ODBC, Java, and OLE DB eventually use the CLI code base, these applications can be traced in this manner as well, although doing so will not show the high-level commands that were used to call the lower-layer CLI. You can use the Client Configuration Assistant (CCA) to turn the necessary switches on to start tracing. Select an ODBC data source in the CCA window and click *Properties*. This will bring up the *Database properties* window. Click the *Setting* button in the *CLI/ODBC* field, and then click the *Advanced* button in the *CLI/ODBC setting* window. You will see the *CLI/ODBC Advanced settings* window.

The interface gives you tips on each parameter. You can switch on tracing, specify a filename to write to, or name a directory to which multiple files will be written (one for each thread; this is usually preferred). Table D-1 lists the various options that are available. You can also specify these options by directly editing the `db2cli.ini` file found in the `sqllib` directory on Windows and `sqllib/cfg` on UNIX. For example, you could add the following lines:

```
[COMMON]
Trace=1
TraceFlush=1
TraceComm=1
TracePidTid=1
TraceTimestamp=1
TraceFileName=C:\trace\trace.txt
```

Table D-1 CLI Trace Keywords

Keyword	Description
TRACE	1 or 0 – Turns CLI tracing on or off.
TRACEFLUSH	1 or 0 – Performs a file flush after each function call. If your application is crashing, it is recommended to turn this option on.
TRACECOMM	1 or 0 – If this is turned on, network flows will be added to the trace file.
TRACEPIDTID	1 or 0 – If on, then include process and thread information.
TRACETIMESTAMP	1 or 0 – If this is on, then include a timestamp for each function call.
TRACEFILENAME TRACEPATHNAME	Only one of TRACEFILENAME or TRACEPATHNAME may be specified. The first requires a complete path definition to the name of a file to write to. The second requires the complete path to an existing directory to write to. The latter's files will be given names in the form of pid.tid.

The files produced during CLI tracing are ASCII text files and are reasonably straightforward to read, especially if you have an understanding of ODBC/CLI calls. The trace will even show error messages that the application has not retrieved. This tracing facility can be very useful for debugging ODBC/CLI applications.

Sample output from a CLI trace is shown below. It shows a failed connection to the database server.

```
[ Process: 1164, Thread: 1072 ]
[ Date & Time:              07-29-2000 19:38:30.000025 ]
[ Product:                  QDB2/NT 7.1.0 ]
[ Level Identifier:         02010105 ]
[ CLI Driver Version:       07.01.0000 ]
[ Informational Tokens:     "DB2 v7.1.0","n000428","" ]


SQLAllocEnv( phEnv=&0012fde8 )
    ---> Time elapsed - +6.026574E+000 seconds

SQLAllocEnv( phEnv=0:1 )
    <--- SQL_SUCCESS   Time elapsed - +5.490000E-004 seconds

SQLAllocConnect( hEnv=0:1, phDbc=&0012fdec )
    ---> Time elapsed - +8.159000E-003 seconds

SQLAllocConnect( phDbc=0:1 )
    <--- SQL_SUCCESS   Time elapsed - +2.780000E-004 seconds
```

Tracing Facilities 277

```
SQLSetConnectOption( hDbc=0:1, fOption=SQL_ATTR_AUTOCOMMIT,
vParam=0 )
    ---> Time elapsed - +9.426000E-003 seconds

SQLSetConnectOption( )
    <--- SQL_SUCCESS   Time elapsed - +8.900000E-005
seconds

SQLConnect( hDbc=0:1, szDSN="sample", cbDSN=-3, szUID="",
cbUID=-3, szAuthStr="", cbAuthStr=-3 )
    ---> Time elapsed - +4.500000E-005 seconds

SQLConnect( )
    <--- SQL_ERROR   Time elapsed - +1.083020E-001 seconds

SQLFreeConnect( hDbc=0:1 )
    ---> Time elapsed - +3.635000E-003 seconds
( Unretrieved error message="SQL1032N  No start database
manager command was issued.  SQLSTATE=57019

" )


SQLFreeConnect( )
    <--- SQL_SUCCESS   Time elapsed - +2.805100E-002
seconds

SQLFreeEnv( hEnv=0:1 )
    ---> Time elapsed - +3.569000E-003 seconds

SQLFreeEnv( )
<--- SQL_SUCCESS   Time elapsed - +2.746300E-002 seconds
```

Note
Tracing a CLI/ODBC application will slow down performance considerably. Also, a large amount of data is written to the output trace file and may use up a large amount of disk space. Do not forget to turn it off!

D.4.3 JDBC Trace

Adding keywords to the db2cli.ini file enables a JDBC trace. It can be used for Java programs that use the DB2 app driver. JDBC tracing is generally used concurrently with CLI tracing, to see how JDBC calls are translated into corresponding CLI calls. To enable JDBC tracing, add the following lines to the COMMON section of the `db2cli.ini` file on the client machine where the Java program is running:

```
[COMMON]
JDBCTrace=1
JDBCTraceFlush=1
JDBCTracePathName=<path>
```

The path specified must be an existing path. It is important to ensure that the user that is running the Java program has write access to the path specified. The files created will include the Process ID (PID) of the application that was running, with a separate file for each Java thread. You must restart your application for tracing to take effect. After you have edited the `db2cli.ini` file as above, you can turn off JDBC tracing by changing the `JDBCTrace` keyword value to 0.

INDEX

A

access plan 15, 16, 34, 58, 91–92
accessing databases from the Internet. *See* Net.Data
AD (Application Development) Client 3, 4
Administration Client 3, 4
Administrative API (Application Programming Interface). *See* API (Application Programming Interface)
ADO (ActiveX Data Objects) 23
advanced programming, test objectives for 245
AIV (Audio, Image, and Video) Extender
    APIs 235
    Description of 234–235
    UDFs 235, 236–237
alias, database 6
ALTER command 9
ambiguous cursor 67
API (Application Programming Interface)
    AIV Extender 235
    application migration considerations for 111
    back-level supported 112
    context management 20, 111, 113–114
    definition of 20
    function names 106–110
    Net.Data and 212
    Text Extender 233
applet (or net) driver 159–160
application (or app) driver 160
Application Development (AD) Client 3, 4
Application Development Certification Exam
    objectives of 244–245
    sample 247–264
application migration, considerations for API 111
auto-commit mode 128
avoiding lock timeouts 42–43

B

back-level supported API 112
batch execution in JDBC 175–176
Binary Large Objects (BLOBs) 176–177. *See also* Java
bind files 120, 217
BINDFILE 60–61
binding applications (for embedded SQL) 62–66
binding parameters 134. *See also* SQL (Structured Query Language): statements
BLOBs (Binary Large Objects) 176–177. *See also* Java
blocking, record 67–68
bookmark 139–145

279

C

CACHE 35
Cache Manager 213, 214
CallableStatement object 174–175
calling stored procedures in JDBC 174–175
CATALOG 5–6, 8
catalog functions in CLI 132–133
CCA (Client Configuration Assistant) 66
CGI (Common Gateway Interface) 212
Character Large Objects (CLOBs) 176–177. *See also* Java
CLI (Call Level Interface)
    advantages of 116–119
    bind files 120, 217
    catalog functions 132–133
    configuring 121
    cursors in 131–132
    DB2 installation and 119
    definition of 23
    developing applications in 23
    diagnostics and error processing in 129–131
    disconnection and termination of 125
    function return codes 129
    initializing 123–124
    ODBC and 116, 117
    programming, test objectives for 245
    trace 275–277
    transaction processing 125–128
    See also ODBC (Open Database Connectivity)
client components 3, 4
Client Configuration Assistant (CCA) 66
cliettes 210–211, 212–213
CLOBs (Character Large Objects) 176–177. *See also* Java
CLOSE 17
CLP (Command Line Processor) 5, 18, 20, 66–67
column-wise array insert 135–136. *See also* parameters
column-wise binding 146–149
Command Center 5, 18
Command Line Processor (CLP) 5, 18, 20, 66–67
command object 150. *See also* OLE DB (Object Linking and Embedding Database)
comment block 200
COMMIT 11, 17, 18
common table expression 31–32
compiled 92
compound SQL 32–33
concurrency problems 43
concurrent access to a database 113
CONNECT 14
CONNECT RESET 18
connecting to a database
    DriverManager and 163
    general syntax for 14–15
    host variables and 72–74
    JDBC and 163, 179–181
    Net.Data and 205–209
    ODBC and 121–122
    SQL statement for 70–71
    SQLj and 188–189
connection handle 124
connection object in JDBC 164–165, 177
ConnectionContext 188–190, 191
consistency token 62. *See also* timestamp
Context Management API 20, 111, 113–114
CREATE 8
CREATE DISTINCT TYPE 31
CREATE SUMMARY TABLE 29
CREATE TABLE 9
CREATE TRIGGER 37
CURRENT REFRESH AGE 30
CURRENT SCHEMA 11
cursor
    CLI and 131–132, 138–146
    introduction to 16–17
    SQL and 33–34
    static embedded SQL and 83–89

Index

D

Data Control Language (DCL) 12
Data Definition Language (DDL) 12
Data Manipulation Language (DML) 12–13.
    See also DELETE; INSERT; SELECT;
    UPDATE
data manipulation, test objectives for 244
data source object 150. *See also* OLE DB (Object
    Linking and Embedding Database)
data type
    Java programming and 162–163
    tables and 9
database alias 6
database configuration parameter, updating 7
database directory 5
Database Interface (DBI) 24
database manager, configuring 6–7
database object
    creating 8
    deleting 9
    naming 9
    schemas and 11
    test objectives for 244
    See also cursor; index; package; schema
DataSource 179–181
DB2
    client 3
    commands, entering, in 5
    product packages 2
    programming methods, test objectives for 244
    trace 274–275
DB2 Extenders 25, 225. *See also* AIV (Audio,
    Image, and Video) Extender; Net Search
    Extender; Text Extender; XML Extender
DB2 SPB
    creating a project with 49
    creating Java stored procedures with 49–54
    creating SQL stored procedures with 53–54
    definition of 48
    development environment interface 49
    executing from 54
    launching 49

    parameters and 52–54
    supported procedure types 48–49
db2alert.log 273–274
db2diag.log 273
DB2INSTANCE 7, 8
DB2MALL 265–270
DB2set 7
DBI (Database Interface) 24
DCL (Data Control Language) 12
DDL (Data Definition Language) 12
Decision Support Systems (DSS) 1. *See also*
    OLAP (Online Application Processing)
    applications
DECLARE 16, 69
deferred binding 58, 59, 62, 90
deferred prepare 35, 94, 217–218
define block 200
DELETE 14
descriptor handle 124
disconnecting
    CLI and 125
    instructions for 18
Distributed Unit of Work (DUOW) 44, 45, 71–72
distribution statistics 34
DML (Data Manipulation Language) 12–13.
    See also DELETE; INSERT; SELECT;
    UPDATE
document block 202–204
driver
    applet (or net) 159–160
    application (or app) 160
    JDBC and 156–161
DriverManager 163
DROP 9
DSS (Decision Support Systems) 1. *See also*
    OLAP (Online Analytical Processing)
    applications
dump files 274
DUOW (Distributed Unit of Work) 44, 45, 71–72
dynamic embedded SQL
    definition of 21
    phases of 93–94
    reasons for using 22

static versus 90, 100–103
types of statements 95–96
dynamically bound statement 55
DYNAMICRULES 63–64

E

EE (Enterprise Edition) 2, 4
EEE (Enterprise Extended Edition) 2, 4
embedded SQL
    authorization considerations and 62–66
    binding applications and 62–66
    connecting from an application and 72–74
    creating packages and 58–62
    cursors and 83–89
    driver-based solutions and 22–24
    error handling and 74–78
    host languages and 20–21
    overview of 58
    precompile file extensions and 60
    programming, test objectives for 244
    searched updates/deletes in 89
    static 21, 68–70
    static versus dynamic 90–91, 100–103
Enterprise Edition (EE) 2, 4
Enterprise Extended Edition (EEE) 2, 4
enumerator object 150. *See also* OLE DB (Object Linking and Embedding Database)
environment handle 124
environment settings 7
error files, diagnostic 272–274
error management (troubleshooting) 271–278. *See also* errors, handling
error object 150. *See also* OLE DB (Object Linking and Embedding Database)
errors, handling
    CLI and 129–131
    embedded SQL and 74–78
    JDBC and 167
    Net.Data and 207
    Perl and 223
    SQL and 272
    See also error management (troubleshooting)

EXECUTE 16, 93
executing statements in JDBC 168–169

F

FETCH 16–17, 94
function block 200–202
function names in API 106–110
function return codes in CLI 129

G

g option 7
GET DBM CFG 6

H

handle 123–124. *See also* CLI (Call Level Interface): initializing
host languages supported 20
host variables 68–70

I

i option 7
identity column 35
index 10–11, 39
indicator variables 78–80
input host variables 69
INSERT 13, 14
IPC (Inter-Process Communication) 8
isolation level 42, 178–179
iterators 185–188, 191

J

Java
    developing applications in 24
    Net.Data and 210–212
    programming, test objectives for 245
    stored procedures 6–47, 49–54, 192–194. *See also* DB2 SPB
    UDFs 194
    See also JDBC (Java Database Connectivity); SQLj

Index

JDBC (Java Database Connectivity)
    batch execution in 175–176
    CallableStatement object and 174–175
    calling stored procedures in 174–175
    concurrency goals in 178
    connecting to a database in 163, 179–181
    connection object and 164–165, 177
    data types supported in 162–163
    DataSource and 179–181
    definition of 24, 155
    development prerequisites for 158–159
    driver, applet (or net) 159–160
    driver, application (or app) 160
    driver, registering 161–162
    DriverManager 163
    drivers for 156–161
    error checking and 167
    executing statements in 168–169
    interface, introduction to 163
    introduction to 156–158
    isolation levels and 178–179
    Large Objects (LOBs) and 176–177
    meta data and 177–178
    prepared statements 169–170
    result set, retrieving, in 170–171
    result set, specifying type, in 172–173
    result set, updating rows of, in 171–172
    result set, using scrollable, in 173
    resultset object and 166–167, 170–173
    setting up an environment for stored procedures in 194
    SQLException and 167–168
    statement object and 165–166
    static SQL 181
    trace 277–278
jdbcerr.log 274
JNDI (Java Naming and Directory Interface) 181

L

language environments 204–212
Large Objects (LOBs) 176–177
linguistic indexes 229–231. *See also* Text Extender
LIST 6
Live Connection Manager 210–211, 212–213
local client
    definition of 3
    versus remote client 8
lock 12, 40, 41–44, 89
lock timeouts, avoiding 42–43

M

macros 199–204, 205–209
manual-commit mode 128
media functionality 25
message blocking 207
meta data 177–178
modifying data 13–14

N

Net Search Extender 233–234. *See also* DB2 Extenders
Net.Data
    accessing databases with 205–209
    advantages of 198–199
    API mode and 212
    blocks and 199–204
    built-in functions of 198
    Cache Manager and 213, 214
    CGI and 212
    cliettes and 210–211, 212–213
    comment block and 200
    communicating with server using 212
    define block and 200
    document block and 202–204
    error handling 207
    function block and 200–202
    introduction to 25, 197
    invoking 203–204
    Java and 210–212

language environments and 204–212

Live Connection Manager and 210–211, 212–213

macros and 199–204, 205–209

message blocking and 207

Perl and 210

result set and 207

REXX and 209–210

scripting language and 199–204

SQL and 206–209

NGRAM indexes 231. *See also* Text Extender

node directory

adding entries to (cataloguing instances) 5–6

cataloguing databases in 6

definition of 5

listing nodes in 6

O

ODBC (Open Database Connectivity)

accessing a database via 121–122

CLI versus 116, 117

definition of 23

developing applications 23. *See also* CLI (Call Level Interface)

programming, test objectives for 245

OLAP (Online Analytical Processing) applications 1, 39

OLE DB (Object Linking and Embedding Database)

automation 150–152

description of 23, 149–150

driver, installing 152

OLTP (Online Transaction Processing) applications 1, 39

Online Analytical Processing (OLAP) applications 1, 39

Online Transaction Processing (OLTP) applications 1, 39

output host variables 69

output SQLDA 98–100

P

package

bound statements and 54–55

creating, in embedded SQL 58–62

definition of 12, 58

timestamps and 64–66

package cache 55, 94–95

parameter marker 34, 95–96

parameters

arrays of 134–138

binding 134

DB2 SPB and 52–54

setting 7

updating 7

PE (Personal Edition) 2, 4

performance, investigating problems with 16. *See also* concurrency problems; error management (troubleshooting); errors, handling

Perl

advantages of 215–216

CLI bind files and 217

CLI configuring and 217–218

disconnecting and termination in 223

environment, setting up 216

error handling in 223

initializing 220–221

installing 218–219

introduction to 24, 215

Net.Data and 210

transaction processing in 221–222

Personal Edition (PE) 2, 4

precise indexes 231. *See also* Text Extender

precompile file extensions 60

precompiler 21

PREP 21

PREPARE 15, 55, 92, 98–100

prepared statements 169–170

product packages 2

profile registry 7

Index

programming interfaces. *See* ADO (ActiveX Data Objects); API (Application Programming Interface); CLI (Call Level Interface); DB2 Extenders; embedded SQL; JDBC (Java Database Connectivity); Net.Data; ODBC (Open Database Connectivity); OLE DB (Object Linking and Embedding Database); Perl; SQLj

Q

querying
    data 13
    tables 28–29

R

record blocking 67–68
refresh 29–30
REFRESH DEFERRED 30
REFRESH IMMEDIATE 29
REFRESH TABLE 29
registering JDBC driver 161–162
remote client
    configuring for 3
    versus local client 8
resource conflicts, reducing. *See* concurrency problems; lock; transaction (unit of work)
result set
    JDBC and 170–173
    Net.Data and 207
    SQLj and 185
ResultSet object 166–167, 170–173
REXX 68, 209–210
ROLLBACK 11, 17, 18
rowset 139–145
rowset object 150. *See also* OLE DB (Object Linking and Embedding Database)
row-wise array insert 135, 136. *See also* parameters
row-wise binding 147–149
RUNSTATS 9, 15
Runtime Client 3, 4

S

Satellite Edition (SE) 2
schema 11
scripting language 199–204
SE (Satellite Edition) 2
section 58
SELECT 13, 16, 57, 80, 184
session object 150. *See also* OLE DB (Object Linking and Embedding Database)
setting parameters 7
special registers 81
SQL (Structured Query Language)
    Assistant 52
    compound 32–33
    definition of 1, 12–13
    dynamic 15, 18, 21–22, 34, 56
    embedded. *See* embedded SQL
    error handling in 272
    media and 25
    Net.Data and 206–209
    statements 125–128, 133–138. *See also* CLI
    static 15, 18, 21, 34, 56
    stored procedure and 46–48, 53–54
SQLCA (SQL Communications Area) 74–78, 129
SQLCODE 74, 78
SQLDA
    data structure 96–97
    header information 97
    output 98–100
    See also SQLVAR
SQLException 167–168
SQLj
    connecting to a database in 188–189
    ConnectionContext and 188–190, 191
    definition of 24
    executing, using dynamic SQL 192
    execution contexts and 190–191
    illustration of application development process 183
    introduction to 181–182
    iterators, classes of, and 185, 191

iterators, named, and 187–188
iterators, positional, and 186–187
profile customizer and 192
required packages for 184
result set and 185
SELECT statements in 184
syntax 184
translator 191–192
variables and 184–185
SQLJ (command) 21
SQLSTATE 78
SQLVAR
    definition of 96
    elements 97–98
    See also SQLDA
STAR schema 39–40
statement handle 124, 125
statement life cycle 15
statement object 165–166
static embedded SQL 21, 68–70
static SQL 15, 18, 21, 34, 56
statically bound statement 54
statically prepared 90
statistics 9. *See also* distribution statistics
stored procedure
    benefits of 44–46
    cache 46
    calling, in JDBC 174–175
    executing 54
    Java 46–47, 49–54, 192–194
    limitations of 46
    SQL and 46–48, 53–54
    writing 44, 47
stored procedure builder. *See* DB2 SPB
Structured Query Language (SQL). *See* dynamic embedded SQL; embedded SQL; SQL (Structured Query Language)
summary table 29–31
system catalog tables 28–29

T

table 9
TCP/IP loopback 8
test. *See* Application Development Certification Exam
testing remote applications 8
Text Extender
    APIs 233
    client server architecture 227
    creating indexes with 228
    description of 226–228
    linguistic indexes and 229–231
    NGRAM indexes and 231
    precise indexes and 231
    supported document formats for 226
    UDFs 231–232
    See also DB2 Extenders
timestamp 64–66. *See also* consistency token
tracing facilities 274–278
transaction (unit of work) 11, 17, 40–41. *See also* DUOW (Distributed Unit of Work)
transaction object 150. *See also* OLE DB (Object Linking and Embedding Database)
transaction processing
    CLI and 125–128
    Perl and 221–222
transition table 37
transition variable 37
trap files 274
trigger 36–38
troubleshooting 271–278. *See also* errors, handling

U

UDFs (User-Defined Functions)
    AIV Extender 235, 236–237
    definition of 25, 38
    for consolidating code 28, 38
    Java 194
    Text Extender 231–232
    XML Extender 239
UDTs (User-Defined Types) 9, 31–32
unit of work (transaction). *See* transaction

UPDATE 14
UPDATE DBM CFG 7
User-Defined Functions (UDFs). *See* UDFs (User-Defined Functions)
User-Defined Types (UDTs) 9, 31–32

V

VALUES 13–14, 81–82

W

WE (Workgroup Edition) 2, 4
web solutions. *See* Net.Data
WHERE 13, 14
WITH 31–32
WITH HOLD 33, 42

WITHOUT HOLD 33
wizard
    Java stored procedure creation 52–53
    SQL stored procedure creation 53–54
Workgroup Edition (WE) 2, 4

X

XML Extender
    collections 240
    columns 239
    description of 235, 238
    mapping, to a relational database 238
    UDFs 239
    See also DB2 Extenders

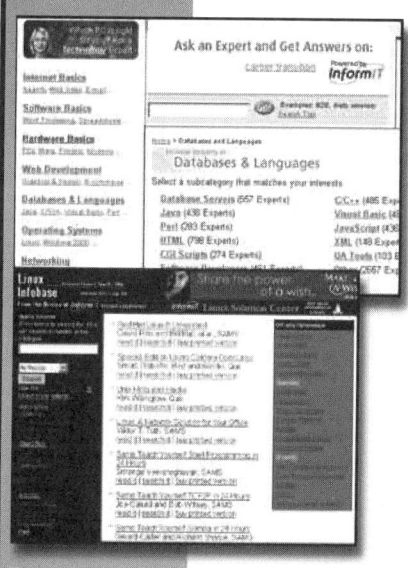

PRENTICE HALL

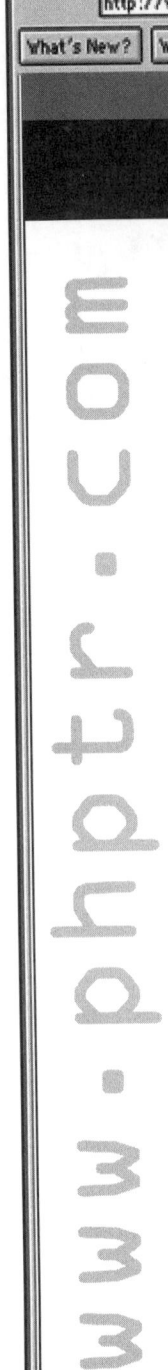

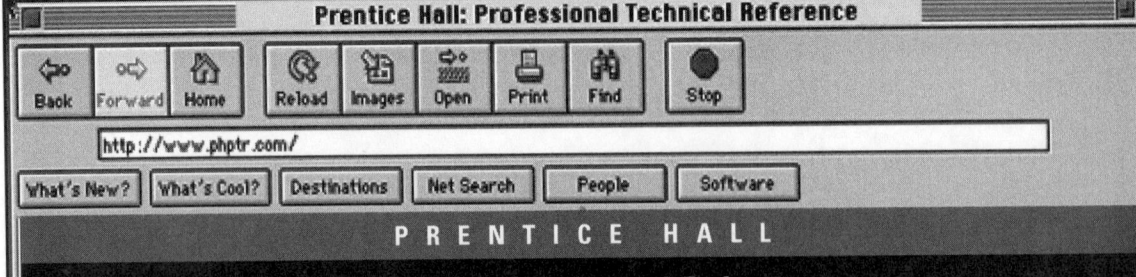

Professional Technical Reference
Tomorrow's Solutions for Today's Professionals.

Keep Up-to-Date with
PH PTR Online!

We strive to stay on the cutting-edge of what's happening in professional computer science and engineering. Here's a bit of what you'll find when you stop by **www.phptr.com**:

@ **Special interest areas** offering our latest books, book series, software, features of the month, related links and other useful information to help you get the job done.

☞ **Deals, deals, deals!** Come to our promotions section for the latest bargains offered to you exclusively from our retailers.

$ **Need to find a bookstore?** Chances are, there's a bookseller near you that carries a broad selection of PTR titles. Locate a Magnet bookstore near you at www.phptr.com.

! **What's New at PH PTR?** We don't just publish books for the professional community, we're a part of it. Check out our convention schedule, join an author chat, get the latest reviews and press releases on topics of interest to you.

✉ **Subscribe Today!** **Join PH PTR's monthly email newsletter!**

Want to be kept up-to-date on your area of interest? Choose a targeted category on our website, and we'll keep you informed of the latest PH PTR products, author events, reviews and conferences in your interest area.

Visit our mailroom to subscribe today! **http://www.phptr.com/mail_lists**

International License Agreement for Evaluation of Programs

Part 1 - General Terms

PLEASE READ THIS AGREEMENT CAREFULLY BEFORE USING THE PROGRAM. IBM WILL LICENSE THE PROGRAM TO YOU ONLY IF YOU FIRST ACCEPT THE TERMS OF THIS AGREEMENT. BY USING THE PROGRAM YOU AGREE TO THESE TERMS. IF YOU DO NOT AGREE TO THE TERMS OF THIS AGREEMENT, PROMPTLY RETURN THE UNUSED PROGRAM TO IBM.

The Program is owned by International Business Machines Corporation or one of its subsidiaries (IBM) or an IBM supplier, and is copyrighted and licensed, not sold.

The term "Program" means the original program and all whole or partial copies of it. A Program consists of machine-readable instructions, its components, data, audio-visual content (such as images, text, recordings, or pictures), and related licensed materials.

This Agreement includes Part 1 - General Terms and Part 2 - Country-unique Terms and is the complete agreement regarding the use of this Program, and replaces any prior oral or written communications between you and IBM. The terms of Part 2 may replace or modify those of Part 1.

1. License

Use of the Program

IBM grants you a nonexclusive, nontransferable license to use the Program.

You may 1) use the Program only for internal evaluation, testing or demonstration purposes, on a trial or "try-and-buy" basis and 2) make and install a reasonable number of copies of the Program in support of such use, unless IBM identifies a specific number of copies in the documentation accompanying the Program. The terms of this license apply to each copy you make. You will reproduce the copyright notice and any other legends of ownership on each copy, or partial copy, of the Program.

THE PROGRAM MAY CONTAIN A DISABLING DEVICE THAT WILL PREVENT IT FROM BEING USED UPON EXPIRATION OF THIS LICENSE. YOU WILL NOT TAMPER WITH THIS DISABLING DEVICE OR THE PROGRAM. YOU SHOULD TAKE PRECAUTIONS TO AVOID ANY LOSS OF DATA THAT MIGHT RESULT WHEN THE PROGRAM CAN NO LONGER BE USED.

You will 1) maintain a record of all copies of the Program and 2) ensure that anyone who uses the Program does so only for your authorized use and in compliance with the terms of this Agreement.

You may not 1) use, copy, modify or distribute the Program except as provided in this Agreement; 2) reverse assemble, reverse compile, or otherwise translate the Program except as specifically permitted by law without the possibility of contractual waiver; or 3) sublicense, rent, or lease the Program.

This license begins with your first use of the Program and ends 1) as of the duration or date specified in the documentation accompanying the Program or 2) when the Program automatically disables itself. Unless IBM specifies in the documentation accompanying the Program that you may retain the Program (in which case, an additional charge may apply), you will destroy the Program and all copies made of it within ten days of when this license ends.

2. No Warranty

SUBJECT TO ANY STATUTORY WARRANTIES WHICH CANNOT BE EXCLUDED, IBM MAKES NO WARRANTIES OR CONDITIONS EITHER EXPRESS OR IMPLIED, INCLUDING WITHOUT LIMITATION, THE WARRANTY OF NON-INFRINGEMENT AND THE IMPLIED WARRANTIES OF MERCHANTABILITY AND FITNESS FOR A PARTICULAR PURPOSE, REGARDING THE PROGRAM OR TECHNICAL SUPPORT, IF ANY. IBM MAKES NO WARRANTY REGARDING THE CAPABILITY OF THE PROGRAM TO CORRECTLY PROCESS, PROVIDE AND/OR RECEIVE DATE DATA WITHIN AND BETWEEN THE 20TH AND 21ST CENTURIES.

This exclusion also applies to any of IBM's subcontractors, suppliers or program developers (collectively called "Suppliers").

Manufacturers, suppliers, or publishers of non-IBM Programs may provide their own warranties.

3. Limitation of Liability

NEITHER IBM NOR ITS SUPPLIERS ARE LIABLE FOR ANY DIRECT OR INDIRECT DAMAGES, INCLUDING WITHOUT LIMITATION, LOST PROFITS, LOST SAVINGS, OR ANY INCIDENTAL, SPECIAL, OR OTHER ECONOMIC CONSEQUENTIAL DAMAGES, EVEN IF IBM IS INFORMED OF THEIR POSSIBILITY. SOME JURISDICTIONS DO NOT ALLOW THE EXCLUSION OR LIMITATION OF INCIDENTAL OR CONSEQUENTIAL DAMAGES, SO THE ABOVE EXCLUSION OR LIMITATION MAY NOT APPLY TO YOU.

4. General

Nothing in this Agreement affects any statutory rights of consumers that cannot be waived or limited by contract.

IBM may terminate your license if you fail to comply with the terms of this Agreement. If IBM does so, you must immediately destroy the Program and all copies you made of it.

You may not export the Program.

Neither you nor IBM will bring a legal action under this Agreement more than two years after the cause of action arose unless otherwise provided by local law without the possibility of contractual waiver or limitation.

Neither you nor IBM is responsible for failure to fulfill any obligations due to causes beyond its control.

There is no additional charge for use of the Program for the duration of this license.

IBM does not provide program services or technical support, unless IBM specifies otherwise.

The laws of the country in which you acquire the Program govern this Agreement, except 1) in Australia, the laws of the State or Territory in which the transaction is performed govern this Agreement; 2) in Albania, Armenia, Belarus, Bosnia/Herzegovina, Bulgaria, Croatia, Czech Republic, Georgia, Hungary, Kazakhstan, Kirghizia, Former Yugoslav Republic of Macedonia (FYROM), Moldova, Poland, Romania, Russia, Slovak Republic, Slovenia, Ukraine, and Federal Republic of Yugoslavia, the laws of Austria govern this Agreement; 3) in the United Kingdom, all disputes relating to this Agreement will be governed by English Law and will be submitted to the exclusive jurisdiction of the English courts; 4) in Canada, the laws in the Province of Ontario govern this Agreement; and 5) in the United States and Puerto Rico, and People's Republic of China, the laws of the State of New York govern this Agreement.

Part 2 - Country-unique Terms

AUSTRALIA:

No Warranty (Section 2):

The following paragraph is added to this Section:

Although IBM specifies that there are no warranties, you may have certain rights under the Trade Practices Act 1974 or other legislation and are only limited to the extent permitted by the applicable legislation.

Limitation of Liability (Section 3):

The following paragraph is added to this Section:

Where IBM is in breach of a condition or warranty implied by the Trade Practices Act 1974, IBM's liability is limited to the repair or replacement of the goods, or the supply of equivalent goods. Where that condition or warranty relates to right to sell, quiet possession or clear title, or the goods are of a kind ordinarily acquired for personal, domestic or household use or consumption, then none of the limitations in this paragraph apply.

GERMANY:

No Warranty (Section 2):

The following paragraphs are added to this Section:

The minimum warranty period for Programs is six months.

In case a Program is delivered without Specifications, we will only warrant that the Program information correctly describes the Program and that the Program can be used according to the Program information. You have to check the usability according to the Program information within the "money-back guaranty" period.

Limitation of Liability (Section 3):

The following paragraph is added to this Section:

The limitations and exclusions specified in the Agreement will not apply to damages caused by IBM with fraud or gross negligence, and for express warranty.

INDIA:

General (Section 4):

The following replaces the fourth paragraph of this Section:

If no suit or other legal action is brought, within two years after the cause of action arose, in respect of any claim that either party may have against the other, the rights of the concerned party in respect of such claim will be forfeited and the other party will stand released from its obligations in respect of such claim.

IRELAND:

No Warranty (Section 2):

The following paragraph is added to this Section:

Except as expressly provided in these terms and conditions, all statutory conditions, including all warranties implied, but without prejudice to the generality of the foregoing, all warranties implied by the Sale of Goods Act 1893 or the Sale of Goods and Supply of Services Act 1980 are hereby excluded.

ITALY:

Limitation of Liability (Section 3):

This Section is replaced by the following:

Unless otherwise provided by mandatory law, IBM is not liable for any damages which might arise.

NEW ZEALAND:

No Warranty (Section 2):

The following paragraph is added to this Section:

Although IBM specifies that there are no warranties, you may have certain rights under the Consumer Guarantees Act 1993 or other legislation which cannot be excluded or limited. The Consumer Guarantees Act 1993 will not apply in respect of any goods or services which IBM provides, if you require the goods and services for the purposes of a business as defined in that Act.

Limitation of Liability (Section 3):

The following paragraph is added to this Section:

Where Programs are not acquired for the purposes of a business as defined in the Consumer Guarantees Act 1993, the limitations in this Section are subject to the limitations in that Act.

UNITED KINGDOM:

Limitation of Liability (Section 3):

The following paragraph is added to this Section at the end of the first paragraph:

The limitation of liability will not apply to any breach of IBM's obligations implied by Section 12 of the Sales of Goods Act 1979 or Section 2 of the Supply of Goods and Services Act 1982.

Z125-5543-01 (10/97)

LICENSE INFORMATION

The Program listed below is licensed under the following terms and conditions in addition to those of the International License Agreement for Evaluation of Programs.

Program Name: IBM(r) DB2(r) Universal Database(tm) Personal Edition, Version 7.1, Evaluation Version

Specified Operating Environment

The Program Specifications and Specified Operating Environment information may be found in documentation accompanying the Program.

Evaluation Period

The license begins on the date you first use the Program and ends after 365 days.

U.S. Government Users Restricted Rights

U.S. Government Users Restricted Rights - Use, duplication, or disclosure restricted by the GSA ADP Schedule Contract with the IBM Corporation.

About the CD-ROM

The accompanying CD-ROM contains trial DB2 software and additional development tools. Please refer to the readme.txt file on the CD-ROM for details on each product. Included on the CD are the following software packages:

*DB2 UDB V7.1 Enterprise Edition Try-and-Buy Version

*DB2 UDB V7.1 Text Extender

*DB2 UDB V7.1 Net-Search Extender

*DB2 UDB V7.1 Audio, Image, and Visual Extenders

*DB2 UDB V7.1 XML Extender

*DB2 Pearl DBI Driver, DBD::DB2 Version 0.73

*DB2 OLE DB Driver

*Net.Data V7.1

The CD also includes chapter-specific samples and exercises located in the \Book directory.

For installation instructions and system requirements for each product, refer to the setup.exe file in the product's directory.

Technical Support

Prentice Hall does not offer technical support for any of the programs on this CD-ROM. However, if there is a problem with the CD or it is damaged, you may obtain a replacement copy by sending an email describing the problem to: disc_exchange@prenhall.com